LAW AND IDENTITY IN ISRAEL

What makes Israeli law Israeli? Why is the word "Jewish" almost entirely absent from Israeli legislation? How did Israel succeed in eluding a futile and dangerous debate over identity, and construct a progressive, independent, original, and sophisticated legal system? *Law and Identity in Israel* attempts to answer these questions by looking at the complex bond between Zionism and the Jewish culture. Forging an original and "authentic" Israeli law that would be an expression and encapsulation of Israeli-Jewish identity has been the goal of many Jewish and Zionist jurists as well as public leaders for the past century. This book chronicles and analyzes these efforts, and in the process tackles the complex meaning of Judaism in modern times as a religion, a culture, and a nationality. Nir Kedar examines the challenges and difficulties of expressing Judaism in, or transplanting it into, the laws of the state of Israel.

NIR KEDAR is a professor of law and history at Bar Ilan University and the Vice President for Academic Affairs of Sapir College in Israel. His main fields of interest are modern legal history, legal and political theory, and comparative law. He has published five books and numerous articles, including *Mamlakhtiyut: David Ben-Gurion's Civic Thought* (Hebrew) (2009), which won the 2009 Shapiro Prize for Best Book on Israel.

Cambridge Studies in Law and Judaism

Series Editor – Mark Goldfeder

The law and religion movement is a growing field dedicated to studying the religious dimensions of law, the legal dimensions of religion, and the interaction of legal and religious ideas, institutions, norms and practices. *Cambridge Studies in Law and Judaism* cultivates scholarship on Jewish topics in law and religion including translations, historical accounts of the foundations of the Jewish legal system, and innovative comparative studies. Its mission is to break new ground in studying what Jewish law has, can, and should offer to public, private, penal, and procedural law and legal theory.

Books in the Series

Nir Kedar, *Law and Identity in Israel: A Century of Debate*
Yehezkel Margalit, *The Jewish Family: Between Family Law and Contract Law*

Law and Identity in Israel

A CENTURY OF DEBATE

NIR KEDAR
Bar-Ilan University

Translated by Haim Watzman

CAMBRIDGE
UNIVERSITY PRESS

CAMBRIDGE
UNIVERSITY PRESS

University Printing House, Cambridge CB2 8BS, United Kingdom

One Liberty Plaza, 20th Floor, New York, NY 10006, USA

477 Williamstown Road, Port Melbourne, VIC 3207, Australia

314–321, 3rd Floor, Plot 3, Splendor Forum, Jasola District Centre, New Delhi – 110025, India

79 Anson Road, #06–04/06, Singapore 079906

Cambridge University Press is part of the University of Cambridge.

It furthers the University's mission by disseminating knowledge in the pursuit of education, learning, and research at the highest international levels of excellence.

www.cambridge.org
Information on this title: www.cambridge.org/9781108484350
DOI: 10.1017/9781108670227

First published 2019

Printed in the United Kingdom by TJ International Ltd. Padstow Cornwall

A catalogue record for this publication is available from the British Library.

ISBN 978-1-108-48435-0 Hardback

To Nadav and Shira

Contents

Introduction

Law as an Expression of Jewish Culture

Law is society's supreme system of norms. As such, it seeks to express that society's values, ways of life, and culture. It is intuitively obvious to us that the content and form of the law differs from place to place and from one era to another. But what is it that, for example, makes Israeli law Israeli and French law French? Is it the specific content of the law? Is it the particular form of legal norms and institutions? That is, is there an Israeli template of norms and cultural assumptions that necessarily molds the particular legal content of Israeli society? Or is it Israeli law simply because it is created and used by free and sovereign Israelis, who shape their laws in accordance with their culture and needs?

This question preoccupied many in the Zionist movement and the Yishuv, the Jewish community in Palestine prior to the establishment of the state of Israel, from the beginning of the twentieth century onward. It was clear to them that the rebirth of the Jewish people in their ancestral land needed to be accompanied by a revitalization of the ancient Jewish legal tradition, adapted and transformed as needed to make it into the living law of a modern, self-governing polity. For the same reason, the question of what makes Israeli law Israeli has continued to be a subject of argument in Israeli society from the founding of the state to this day. For example, in the constitutional debate just following independence, it was decided not to draft a written constitution, largely because of the fear that it would spark a culture war over the question of Israeli identity. Likewise, the polemic of the last twenty years over Israel's so-called constitutional revolution has centered on the question of Israel's definition of itself as a Jewish and democratic state. Arguments over the Israeli character of Israeli law have also been at the center of legislative discussions and the debates over the legal sources that ought to be used by Israeli courts.[1]

This book is about that debate. I will discuss a number of questions that are central to it: What is independent Israeli law? Is it possible to fashion law that is of specifically Israeli content or character? Conversely, could Israeli law ever be "un-Israeli"? I will consider a number of attempts that have been made, since the Zionist movement was established, to shape a modern legal system for the Jewish state rooted in the nation's language, history, and culture. Specifically, its advocates envisioned molding traditional Jewish law to the requirements of a modern state with a secular government and legal system. Following the debates over the proper form the Israeli legal system ought to take, I will examine the risks inherent in the efforts to create a legal system of a fundamentally Israeli nature.

While law is a distinct field, the story of Israeli law is in fact the story of Zionism itself. The issues that have troubled Israeli jurists are the same ones the Zionist movement grappled with from its inception – the question of Jewish and Israeli identity and culture. And the answers to those questions have grown out of those the Zionist movement and Israeli society have found to more general issues. Zionist history is the larger context in which Israeli law has developed, the framework that has granted it meaning. It also forms the background that enables us to understand the story of the specifically Israeli character of Israeli law.

Throughout Zionist history, the central issue in this regard has been the content of the law. While questions of the language, form, and source of authority have been debated, most of those involved believed that Israeli law needs to have specific and identifiable Israeli *content*. But what should that special Israeli content be? That question is very difficult to answer, for two reasons. First, it is difficult to define a national culture and hard to express this culture in legal norms. Second, the law is not the proper arena for cultural debate and for elucidating questions of identity.

A people's national culture can certainly be described with reference to unique folkloristic elements, the language spoken by its members, and sometimes also their religion. The people may observe particular customs; its history can be recounted; perhaps a certain "national character" can be spoken of. Yet it is very difficult to generalize from language, religion, folklore, customs, history, and national character to arrive at a clearly defined national culture. Thus, while it is intuitively easy for us, in our imaginations, to tell a

[1] Clause 1 of the Foundations of Law Act of 1980 requires Israeli judges to refer to "the principles of freedom, justice, equity and peace of Hebrew Law and Israel's heritage."

French person from a German one and see that both are different from an Indian, when we think deeply about it we find that it is very difficult to formulate precisely what French, German, or Indian culture actually is. It is even harder to translate this national culture into general and abstract legal norms, that is, norms that apply uniformly to a broad public. The sociologist and expert of nationalism Anthony Smith referred to it as "the most perplexing feature of investigation into ethnic and national phenomena: the curiously simultaneous solidity and insubstantiality of ethnic communities and nations." Nations, and even ethnic communities, Smith notes, "so easily recognizable from a distance, seem to dissolve before our eyes the closer we come and the more we attempt to pin them down."[2]

Thus, while it is clear that the law is dependent on culture and history, it is difficult to say clearly what "national law" might mean. Every national culture obviously has legal norms that ground some of its religious or cultural customs and parts of its folklore. But that is not enough to constitute a national legal system. For example, most Israelis presumably would not think that the existence of a few laws such as the Pig-Raising Prohibition Law of 1962, the Passover Law of 1986, or even the Law of Return of 1950 are sufficient to make the country's legal system specifically Jewish or Israeli.[3] Such a view, shared by many Israelis, is the substrate for the ongoing debate that this book covers.

No human society is free of concern about identity and culture. As the American anthropologist Clifford Geertz noted in his *The Interpretation of Cultures*, "man is an animal suspended in webs of significance he himself has spun."[4] But in Israeli society, the question of the Israeli nature of the law touches a raw nerve of angst about identity and culture that Jews have been wrestling with for the last 250 years. Zionism was born out of the profound changes brought on by the processes of secularization and modernization that swept through Europe and its Jewish communities in the modern age. For the Jews, these changes produced tensions between long-held traditions and the values and mores of modern and secular life. Zionism emerged out of modern Jews' problems of culture and identity. Zionism's ultimate aim was "cultural" as well: enabling the Jews to live full and free Jewish lives. But the means to achieve that end were political – the establishment of a Jewish nation-state in the Land of Israel, in which Jews would constitute a majority. The Zionists

2 Smith, *Ethnic Origins*, 2.

3 The Passover Law, formally named the Festival of Matzot (Prohibition of Leaven) Law, 1986, prohibits the public display of leavened food (such as bread) during the Jewish holiday of Passover. The Law of Return allows Jews the right to immigrate to Israel and gain Israeli citizenship.

4 Geertz, "Thick Description," 5.

believed that nationality would bridge disputes over identity and culture and the conflicts they engendered by fashioning a common national identity to which Jews of all kinds could subscribe, and that a sovereign state would guarantee the long-term survival of a free Jewish culture. They drew this conclusion from what they saw in Europe of the nineteenth and early twentieth centuries. Even in countries where Jews had won emancipation and civil equality, the Zionists argued, there was no way of guaranteeing the perpetuation of a productive Jewish culture. They would face depletion and assimilation in such places. Jews living in lands where they did not enjoy equal rights would face constant physical and cultural danger. The Zionist solution was thus based on defining the Jews as a nation and seeking to manifest this nationhood in an independent state, or at the very least some lower level of sovereignty that could enable the perpetuation of Jewish physical and cultural life freely and over many generations.

This highlights two principal problems in the Zionist movement's attitude toward the question of Jewish identity and culture in the modern age, problems that plague Israeli law to this day. The first is that of defining Judaism and Jewish nationality in and of themselves. Zionism's strongest selling point was not the nature of the solution it offered to the oppressed Jewish masses of Europe in the form of an independent Jewish state in the Land of Israel. Much more important was the national story that it offered to those Jews. It told the Jews that they were a nation with a common historical past, culture, and destiny, and that by virtue of this they were entitled to self-determination. Zionism was first of all a narrative, a structure that gave modern Jews meaning, helping them overcome cultural differences and doubts about their identities. It offered collective-national solutions that would provide for autonomous Jewish life.[5] As the Jewish national movement, Zionism had to address, at least in a basic way, the questions of identity and culture that so exercised nineteenth- and twentieth-century Jews: What is the nature of Judaism? What is its connection to religion and tradition? How should modern Jewish nationalism be fashioned? How can the destructive and revolutionary forces inherent in Zionism be reconciled with the need and desire to preserve continuity between Zionism and the Judaism of the past? How can the gaps

[5] Zionism was not the only national solution on offer. In fact, most Jews preferred other national solutions – cultural autonomy for Jews in Europe, a Jewish territory elsewhere than in Palestine, or schemes for enabling Jewish cultural life of a collective national nature within the multicultural milieu of the United States (or the West as a whole). But Zionism was the national framework for thinking about all these national solutions, in the sense that Zionism "invented" modern Jewish nationalism. See Smith, "Zionism and Diaspora"; Stanislawski, *Zionism*. I discuss this issue at length in Chapter 9.

between religion and modern secularism be bridged? Can Judaism serve as a model for fashioning the civil society of a Jewish state?

The second problem was a second-order issue regarding the proper place of the cultural debate in Zionist thought, discourse, and action. It was a meta-cultural matter, a political-institutional issue regarding the culture itself, growing out of the fact that Zionism not only proposed to see the Jews as a nation but also demanded that nation's right to self-determination and sovereignty in a nation-state. Given the passion and turbulence characteristic of debates over Jewish identity and culture, this inevitably raised the question of whether such culture wars were advantageous or detrimental to the realization of Zionism's goal, the establishment of a Jewish national home. The fear that infighting over culture put the national project at risk was expressed as early as the 1880s in a famous exchange between a prominent Jewish enlightenment poet in Russia and a leader of the proto-Zionist Hovevei Zion movement. It remained the subject of profound Zionist political disputes up until World War I.

The Zionist movement thus found itself between a cultural rock and a hard place. On the one hand, it was the *Jewish* national movement. Its principal source of power and the fuel that fired its practical action was its definition of the Jewish people as a national collective and its success in largely bridging gaps of culture, identity, and religion. On the other hand, the debate over these issues, while contained within Zionism, remained heated and threatened the movement's ability to unite different groups of Jews for the purpose of achieving its goal of establishing an independent Jewish state. Zionist history, and within it the history of the Zionist and Israeli legal system, has thus swung between the desire and need to address questions of modern Jewish identity in a profound way and the need to stifle, or at least mute, these very same debates so that they would not become hindrances to the building of the Israeli state and society and thus frustrate the goal of establishing a free Jewish life.

The meta-cultural problem also has another aspect, the danger of cultural coercion. Differences of opinion over identity, culture, and religion have a tendency to be strident and intolerant. Every side forcefully defends its values, symbols, and culture, and more often than not tries to impose them on the opposing parties to the debate. Modern history has shown that a lack of religious-cultural tolerance is a common feature of conservative (and certainly religious) groups in any society. They fear change and thus fortify themselves within cultural ghettoes and seek to enforce a cultural status quo ante. But it is also evident among revolutionary secular-modernist groups, which seek to augment political change with cultural change that is often rigid and brutally enforced. The violence and terror of the French, Russian, and Chinese revolutions are extreme examples of attempts to impose a new modern culture on those societies. Similar cultural coercion, involving varying levels of violence, can also be found in the Islamic world. In Kamalist Turkey, Iran under the Shah, and the Arab world, a secular and modern culture was imposed on a broad population. Many intellectuals have cooperated with cultural violence, of both the conservative and the revolutionary modernist kind. They have justified it, served as its mouthpieces, and have played an active role in the culturally coercive project of one or another camp. As a general rule, they have turned a blind eye to acts of coercion and violence and even to terror and the harshest atrocities.[6] The law has also lent a hand in these countries. Laws have forbidden the use of new or old cultural systems and legal systems have tried to impose either past or new standards by force.

Cultural coercion was an imminent peril to the Zionist movement and the state of Israel. Since the end of the nineteenth century, intellectuals of all camps have insisted that the Zionist revolution ought to be first and foremost a cultural revolution. They have demanded that the practical achievement of Zionist political goals be preceded by cultural reeducation. Practical Zionism, they declared, had to be accomplished in tandem with cultural projects. The arguments among writers, rabbis, and thinkers were tempestuous and fanatical. In practice, it was the Zionist political leadership that kept the flames down. Of course, these leaders of the Yishuv and Israel viewed Zionism as a total revolution that encompassed not just politics but also economics and culture. They sincerely subscribed to the enlightenment idea that an exemplary society can be created on the basis of a worthy model. Nevertheless, with the exception of local projects of cultural and religious coercion (especially among the immigrants who arrived in Israel from the Islamic world in the country's early years), the Zionist movement was able to carry out a profound secular and modernist revolution without engaging in cultural warfare or violent compulsion. It succeeded in creating an open, dynamic, democratic, and, in the final analysis, pluralist society.[7] As Nissim Calderon has put it, Israelis became "pluralists despite themselves."[8] This was a pluralism less motivated by a coherent liberal or multicultural worldview and more a product of sharing a country with a socially, ideologically, and religiously diverse population that, facing mortal danger from enemies outside its borders and major economic and social challenges from within, had to find a way to

6 See Lila, *Reckless Mind*.
7 Rozin, *Rise of the Individual*; Rozin, *Home for All Jews*.
8 This is Hebrew title of Calderon's *Multiculturalism versus Pluralism*.

live together. But whatever the origins of Israeli pluralism, the Zionist movement and Israeli society conducted themselves in the end with relative moderation on the cultural front.

Zionism succeeded in establishing a sovereign democratic state and in building an open and vibrant civil society. Moreover, it was able to implant in Jews (even among most of its opponents) the view that they constitute a modern nation. In the end, Zionism managed to navigate the cultural labyrinth. It became a source of identity for millions of Jews and put in place a common modern Jewish culture while at the same time preventing cultural clashes from descending into violence and intimidation. Nevertheless, even after 140 years of Zionism, cultural tensions are still clear and present and threaten Israel's ability to face its internal and external challenges.

Israeli law prominently displays the Zionist movement's ambiguity about culture on two counts. As the principal normative system of Israeli society, it seeks to treat (in both senses of the word) modern Jewish doubts about the nature of Jewish identity and to articulate a new national culture that seeks to bridge over those doubts, as well as over the differences between different Jewish groups (and, in Israel, between Jews and non-Jews).[9] Yet the law is a quite problematic place to treat cultural problems. As already noted, it is very difficult to translate the national character, culture, customs, and values into "national law." The attempt to define national culture and translate it into legal norms is all the more difficult in the Jewish nation, which has undergone major transformations in lifestyle, ways of thinking, and culture, and which sought to found, for the first time in its history, a state based on modern values. The demand that Israeli law give expression to "Israeli culture" assumes that the different worldviews and values of Israelis – Jews and non Jews, religious and secular – form an identifiable Israeli culture that can be expressed in legal norms. The French, Columbians, and Thais have similar problems with making their legal systems express their cultures. But the fact that other countries have the same problem is no consolation to those Israelis who continue to demand that Israeli law manifest Jewish-Hebrew identity and culture.

Therefore, it is plausible to claim that it is not the content of the law that makes a legal system a national one. On the contrary, we distinguish between, say, Belgian and Dutch law not through distinguishing their specific provisions but simply because, in a formal sense, each code is the law of a different country. It is much like the quip popularized by the linguist and Yiddishist

[9] Likhovski, *Law and Identity*; Mautner, *Law and Culture of Israel*.

Max Weinreich: "A language is a dialect with an army and a navy." Along the same lines, national law is a formal system of norms with an army.[10]

The difficulty in ascertaining the Israeli nature of Israeli law has another source as well, connected to the nature of law as a social institution. I call this the problem of decision. As the society's principal normative system, the law's major (but not sole) purpose is to establish social order and resolve conflicts. These objectives require the law to decide: it must resolve a given dispute or provide legal norms that guide behavior. Legal institutions are the main societal institutions charged with the task of deciding cases in which rival values clash. The law is a system whose social role is to translate (or convert) disputes about culture, values, and interests into "legal" disputes that can be decided, with relative clarity, on the basis of established procedure and well-defined rules of the game.[11] Herein lies the danger of bringing the polemic over identity and culture into the legal realm. Law, by its definition and social role, would then have to reach a decision about these issues and put an end to the conflict. The legal system is simply not sensitive enough to address cultural disputes.

The discourse of identity needs to be distinguished from its legal manifestations. The former, in its true form, is primarily a perpetual private dialogue that takes place on an ongoing basis within each individual. On the one side are tradition and the world of values into which a person was born, to which he or she is connected and obligated (like it or not); on the other are the cultures and values the person encounters over the course of his or her life, as well as the needs, difficulties, and possibilities life presents. It takes place between the closed past and the open future; between the familiar and the foreign, new, and mutable; between the need for certainty and stability and the no less potent longing for change and growth. Of course, the discourse of identity is also a social process. It is an ongoing dialogue between individuals and groups, a constant, perpetual interpretation of the traditions, values, and culture of individuals and communities, carried out in the presence of other cultures and worldviews.[12]

Law is not the proper arena for such a dialogue. It cannot delve deeply into such individual and collective ambiguities about identity, nor can it express the complexity of human identity and culture. It cannot conduct an open,

[10] Weinreich, "YIVO and the Problems," 13. Chapter 10 deals with this issue at length.

[11] That is why we speak of the "legal system" and "legal institutions" but not of systems or institutions governing morals, religion, or mores (while there are religious institutions, they have an entirely different function than the institutionalized legal system).

[12] See Giddens, *Modernity and Self-Identity*; Goldberg and Krausz, *Jewish Identity*.

continuing intercultural dialogue about the complex and changing identities. At most, we can ask the law to recognize every person's need to belong to an identity group bearing a certain tradition and culture (even if these are dynamic and shifting). The law can be expected to be considerate of the sentiments and needs emerging from this affiliation and to recognize rights that they imply (e.g., the right to speak a language or educate one's children in accordance with one's values). But even in these cases, the law must smooth out uncertainties about identity and culture and place the disputes that emerge from them in a Procrustean bed of procedures and legal rules so that they can be decided in a practical way.

This explains the behavior of Israeli courts when called on to rule on the "Who is a Jew?" question. According to Israeli law, every citizen is registered in the civil registry as belonging to a certain faith community. In the "Who is a Jew?" cases the court was asked to order the civil registrar to register a certain person as a Jew, according to that person's declaration. When judges have failed to find a way to dismiss such cases on procedural grounds, they have avoided discussing the substance of the issue (the definition of "Jewish"). They understood that the question touches on the very foundations of Jewish identity for most Israelis (as well as for Jews outside the country), and there is no way to prove or decide which definition is correct. Instead, judges have examined only a small segment of the dispute – the question of whether the Ministry of the Interior's registrar has discretion to decide to register (or refuse to register) a given person as a Jew.[13] The question of a state official's powers is one that can be litigated and subject to a final binary decision – it is either legal or not. In the same spirit, Israeli Chief Justice Aharon Barak opened his judgment on the Bar Ilan Street case by stating that the court would discuss only the question of governmental power:

> [T]he issue at bar involves the scope of the Central Traffic Authority's discretion to direct its local counterpart in regulating traffic on Bar-Ilan Street, so that the street will be closed to traffic during certain hours during

[13] See HCJ *Rufeisen v. The Minister of Interior Affairs* [1962] IsrSC 16 2428. The case involved Oswald Rufeisen (also known as Brother Daniel), a Polish-born Jew who survived the Second World War, during which he converted to Catholicism and became a friar of the Discalced Carmelite Order. On immigrating to Israel, he sought citizenship under the Israeli Law of Return, but was refused by the Israeli Interior Ministry. And see HCJ 58/68 *Shalit v. The Minister of Interior Affairs* [1970] IsrSC 23(2) 477. In this case, an Israeli Jew married to a Protestant woman filed suit asking the court to order the Ministry of the Interior's population registrar to register their children as Jewish. The ministry had refused to do so, on the grounds that, according to Jewish law, a Jew is a person born to a Jewish mother or who has converted to Judaism.

> the Sabbath.... Our concern is not with the relationship between the secular and the religious in Israel; nor is it with the relationship between religion and state in this country. Nor is our concern the character of Jerusalem. We are simply concerned with Bar-Ilan Street, in its literal sense, and with the Central Traffic Authority's powers and the scope of its discretion.[14]

When suits regarding questions of identity and culture cannot be translated into binary questions of authority, the courts generally dismiss the suits before hearing them on the grounds that the questions are not justiciable. By this they mean that the law as a social tool, or the court as an institution, is not appropriate for deciding the question. That is what the Jerusalem District Court did in 2008 when it turned down a petition in which a group of Israelis asked that the court order the Interior Ministry to record on their identity cards that their nationality (i.e., ethnic affiliation, as opposed to citizenship) was "Israeli" rather than "Jewish." The court declared that the demand is not justiciable:

> The statement that there is an *Israeli nationality* has far-reaching consequences for the identity of the State of Israel.... From a *normative* point of view, the issue may be analyzed with legal tools, but it is *not justiciable* from an *institutional* point of view [i.e., the court is not the appropriate institution to make that decision]. The main character of the subject is meta-legal: public, ideological, social, historical, and political. The Court's opinions in these matters is not privileged over other opinions. The legal aspect of the subject is ancillary to the main point.[15]

Even though the law expresses society's values and culture, the people involved in the law cannot allow themselves to spend a lot of time pondering cultural issues. They must in the end decide for one side or the other on the question before them. This is true of legislators, political leaders, and state officials, and of course also of judges and attorneys offering their clients legal advice. It is, of course, necessary to provide reasons for a legal decision, reasons

[14] HCJ 5016/96 *Horev v. Minister of Transport* [1997] IsrSC 51(4) 1; [1997] IsrLR 149. The English translation is taken from the Israeli Judicial Authority website: http://elyon1.court.gov.il/files_eng/96/160/050/A01/96050160.a01.htm.

[15] HP 07/6092 (Jerusalem) *Ornan v. The Minister of Interior Affairs* [2008]. The Supreme Court ruled on appeal that the issue is also institutionally justiciable. Nevertheless, the Supreme Court too avoided reaching a substantive cultural decision on the question. It rejected the appeal on the evidential-procedural ground that the appellants had not proven that there is a distinct Israeli nationality (but did not explain how such a claim might be proved), and as such their demand to be recognized as members of the Israeli rather than Jewish nation was redundant. CA 8573/08 *Ornan v. Minister of the Interior* [2013].

based on the society's conceptions of justice, values, and culture. But a sober view makes it clear that, in practice, legal institutions primarily make decisions. They explain their decisions only sketchily, if at all, and take up values and culture only on the symbolic margins of the legal debate, in exceptional formal debates in parliament and in a small number of court rulings issued by the highest bench. Even parliaments, which represent the public at large and give voice to its opinions, must allot most of their time to fleshing out policy initiatives, drafting bills, and enacting legislation, and to oversight, appointments, and other responsibilities assigned by the law to parliament. Discussions of values take place only under special circumstances. That explains why modern societies tend to decry legislators who devote much of their energy to ideological declarations and to submitting bills designed to make statements but which have little chance of passing.

The decision-making imperative is even more pronounced in other legal institutions. Litigants obviously expect the judge who hears their case to make a decision consistent with their society's cultural norms and to offer reasons for deciding as she does. But all sides to a court case know that the principal purpose of litigation is to resolve the dispute at hand. A minority of the world's legal systems permit judges to issue lengthy accounts of the values behind their decisions, but even in these systems only a small percentage of judgments are actually accompanied by such detailed opinions, generally those issued by the country's supreme or constitutional court. The judges are also aware that most of the public (and sometimes even most litigants) do not read these opinions and are interested only in the bottom line, the judgment. This makes it even more difficult for courts to rule on questions of political or cultural controversy. Deputy Chief Justice Moshe Landau put it this way in his opinion in the *Dawikat* (Elon Moreh) case:

> I see myself here as obligated to rule according to law on every issue properly brought before the court. [This duty] is an imposition, given that I know full well that the public at large will pay no attention to my legal reasoning, only to the final decision, and the court's proper status as standing above partisan or public dispute is likely to be damaged. But there is nothing to be done; this is our job and our duty as judges.[16]

Thus, even though the law is society's principle normative system, legal institutions are not the principal ones in which value and cultural issues are elucidated. Rather, they translate the debate over culture and values into

[16] HCJ 390/79 *Dawikat v. The Government of Israel*, IsrSC 34(1)1.

binding legal norms and put them into action, implement them, and interpret them. Obviously, culture and values are present in the work of all actors in the legal system – legislators, judges, officials, and police personnel all live in their societies and are influenced in all their actions by culture and their society's traditions, beliefs, values, and fashions. Legal norms also clearly not only express culture but shape it. That being the case, jurists play a central role in creating and disseminating cultural symbols.[17] But, in general, legal institutions do not directly and explicitly elucidate cultural identity; they lack the tools for doing so, and if they were to try it would impinge on their ability to perform their principal social roles. That is why the institutions of the Zionist movement, the Yishuv, and the state of Israel decided, very early on, that their role was to make decisions, not to conduct cultural debates.

In the Zionist movement and state of Israel, the need to make decisions took precedence also because they faced changing, uncertain, and dangerous circumstances. Disputes over identity and culture do not fade away in any society, and Israeli society has continued to wrestle with them. But the leaders of the Zionist movement and the country's leaders and jurists simply did not have the leisure to ponder identity and the question of how to translate Jewish national culture into Israeli law. Identity needed to be shaped, but at the same time a state had to be built as a difficult war was being fought. Hundreds of thousands of Jews needed to be brought into the country and their basic needs had to be provided for at a time of severely strained and even depleted resources. Israelis have thus been doubly careful not to descend into a culture war. In politics, the best way to avoid a culture war was to establish a consensus democracy based on a web of flexible coalition agreements notable for their avoidance of clear decisions between mutually exclusive alternatives and for their attempts to exploit and stress the common denominator between rival political groups while preserving their ideological distinctiveness. So acted Zionists in the Diaspora, where they often cooperated with anti-Zionist Jewish groups; so acted the Zionist movement; and so Israeli politics are conducted to this day. In the legal realm, the way to avert *kulturkampf* has been to pursue a policy of muting or distancing cultural divisions threatening the national-state bonds that tie Israelis together.

In view of this Zionist policy, we come back to our original question: What is Israeli about Israeli law? This book seeks to answer that question in three parts. Parts I and II recount attempts to imbue Israeli law with a specifically Israeli character by incorporating Jewish content into it. Part III discusses

[17] See Geertz, "Local Knowledge."

other ways Israeli jurists have found to express Israeli law's independence and special nature.

Part I offers a chronological survey of repeated attempts to base the law of the Yishuv and the state of Israel on specifically Jewish content. Chapter 1 considers the accounts of law offered by early Zionist utopian works and clarifies the distinction between the cultural and the meta-cultural debate in Zionism. Chapter 2 recounts the failure of the Yishuv's autonomous system of arbitration, the Hebrew Peace Courts. Chapter 3 tells of the rise and fall of the Hebrew Law Society, which sought to base the law of the Jewish state on secularized and modern Jewish content. Chapter 4 analyzed abortive attempts to create a national Jewish system of law at the founding of the state. Chapter 5 shows that the fear of cultural war was a central factor in the Knesset's decision not to promulgate a written constitution during the first years of independence. Finally, Chapter 6 addresses Israeli legislative policy. These chapters together show that all these attempts were doomed from the outset. Their historical account demonstrates that the Yishuv and Israeli legal system have adhered to a meta-cultural decision to avoid a cultural war in the legal realm at all costs.

Part II, consisting of Chapters 7 and 8, addresses a period beginning in the 1980s. At this time the Israeli political and legal elite drew back from their policy of avoiding issues of culture and identity and once more sought to base Israeli law on Jewish content. In light of previous failures, the Knesset did not seek this time to insert norms from Jewish law in its legislation. Rather, it proclaimed Jewish values as guiding legislation, court rulings, and the operation of Israeli law. The Knesset passed legislation stating that the values of "Israel's heritage" should be the residuary law, that is, the general law to which judges should turn when they find no answer to the question before them in law or precedent. Furthermore, the actions of all state institutes were required to be consistent with the values of Israel as a "Jewish and democratic state." Chapter 7 describes the return of identity discourse to Israeli law by means of including the expressions "Israel's heritage" and "Jewish and democratic state" in Knesset legislation, and by the enactment of Basic Law: Israel – The Nation-State of the Jewish People. It describes the legislative process and the courts' disregard for the new expressions of identity inserted into the law. Chapter 8 provides the broader context of reinserting the identity discourse into Israeli law. It notes the rise of identity and cultural discourse throughout the world, Israel included, and then recounts the fiery polemic that broke out in Israel at the end of the twentieth century and the central role the law played in this debate. The chapter also briefly considers the dangers presented by the legalized polemic of identity and culture.

Part III, comprising Chapters 9 and 10, surveys other ways in which the Zionist movement and Israeli legal system have expressed Jewish-Israeli identity in the law. In light of my claim that the history of Israeli law is a specific case of Zionist history, Chapter 9 examines Zionism's complex relationship with the question of culture. Chapter 10 offers a similar discussion of the complex interaction between Israel law and Jewish heritage. I address the Zionist-Israeli resolve to ensure its political and legal independence, that is, an independent Israeli legal system that is not subordinate to foreign law and which legislates for itself in accordance with Israeli society's needs, interests, and values. I also consider the attention the Israeli legal system gives to symbols of national independence. This includes both what might be called general symbols, such as the Hebrew language, and specifically legal symbols, such as the effort to promulgate a constitution and civil code. Finally, I show that the Zionist movement and Israel have adopted a modern cultural option centered on muting cultural debates while adopting common cultural symbols that arouse no dissension – the Hebrew language, devotion to the Land of Israel, evocation of Jewish history, and a long list of consensual symbols, values, and concepts with roots in Jewish heritage. I show that Israeli law cannot *not* be Jewish and Israeli, and that Israeli law and culture are today *lieux de mémoire* of primary importance in the preservation of Jewish heritage. They are, in fact, the most important guarantee of the future of Jewish culture in Israel and the world.

PART I

Seeking to Fashion National Law

1

Law and Culture in Early Zionist Literature

That law would be central when Zionism considered the issue of Jewish culture was clear from the movement's inception at the end of the nineteenth century. In fact, debate over the substance of the laws that would govern a future Jewish state was subsumed under larger meta-cultural polemic. At this early juncture, the movement had yet to establish legal institutions, and the debate over a future legal system had yet to begin. The issue was, however, intimated in a genre that aroused fervent discussion among Zionist intellectuals – utopian literature. Zionist thinkers and leaders from all currents composed works of the imagination portraying life in the future Jewish state in Palestine.[1] While few of these works addressed the law in a direct way, their brief references to the topic evinced profound cultural, and especially meta-cultural, differences that augured future debates.

Those differences are evident when two contrasting examples of such utopias are placed side by side. One is Elhanan Leib Lewinsky's *A Journey to the Land of Israel in Year 800 of the Sixth Millennium (2040)*, published in 1892. Lewinsky was a member of the circle of secularized Zionist Jewish intellectuals of the Hovevei Zion movement who were active in Odessa during this period. The most prominent of them was Asher Hirsch Ginzberg, who wrote under the pseudonym Ahad Ha'am. The second is *Altneuland (The Old New Land)*, published in 1902 by the founder of the World Zionist Organization, Theodor Herzl. The picture of the future state painted by Lewinsky is clearly influenced by the cultural Zionism (known at the time as "spiritual Zionism") taught by Ahad Ha'am, for whom Zionism was a national cultural enterprise aimed at renewing Judaism. According to this view, Zionist political aims were to be put off until the Jewish people

[1] Eliav-Feldon, "First Jewish Utopias."

underwent a fundamental cultural transformation that would prepare the nation for the future. Ahad Ha'am sought to accomplish this through large-scale educational and cultural projects, aimed principally at preserving Jewish cultural heritage while adapting it to the modern world, for the most part through secularization.

Accordingly, the society Lewinsky depicts is not religious, but its law is based on a secularized version of traditional Jewish law. Lewinsky noted in his utopia that, in the Jewish state, "the prevailing law will be the laws of the Hebrews." So, for example, he mentions a poster on a notice board in Jaffa that declares: "The District Court in Jaffa will notify the heirs of the late Palti ben Laish that they are to come to inherit their estate in the area of Be'er Binyamin, which is returning to them in the Jubilee Year."[2] Similarly, the Moses and Aaron Book Store stocks, in addition to nonfiction and scholarly works, encyclopedias and literature, *Hoshen Mishpat*, a classic compendium of Jewish religious law, "in four parts, with all the commentaries, on silk paper."[3] Personal and labor laws were based on "the Torah of Moses, in accordance with the glosses of the sages … [which] stands against all of Europe's new laws on labor matters. According to these laws, there is no labor question and no property question in the Land of Israel, because there are no workers and no bosses, all are workers and all are bosses."[4]

Altneuland, like Herzl's earlier *The Jewish State*, depicts a state governed by the rule of law. A parliamentary democracy, it has a well-developed system of private law. It grants universal citizenship and respects human rights.[5] In fact, the civil and economic order that Herzl portrays is much like Lewinsky's. For both of them, the Jewish state is a welfare state based on the rule of law. The difference is not in the substance of the arrangements but in the fact that Lewinsky speaks of a country whose laws and culture derive from a secularized Jewish tradition, whereas Herzl in large part refrains from speaking of the Jewish state's law and culture as explicitly Jewish. Herzl prefers to stress that the Jewish state operates in accordance with the rule of law and modern civil procedure. It has a market economy based on the freedom of property ownership and contract, but its government also regulates the economy and society. Unlike Lewinsky, Herzl does not get into the details of legal norms or their cultural or legal source.

[2] Lewinsky, *Journey to*, 22. The title of Lewinsky's book refers to the year 5800 in the Jewish calendar (2039–2040 in the Gregorian calendar).

[3] Lewinsky, *Journey to*, 26.

[4] Lewinsky, *Journey to*, 35.

[5] Herzl, *Old New Land*, 139; Herzl, *Jewish State*, 136–152.

Even during his lifetime, Herzl's position was seen as that of an assimilated Western Jew turning his back on Jewish tradition, including the new secular Hebrew culture that had emerged in Eastern Europe during the period of the Haskalah (Jewish enlightenment). In a venomous review of *Altneuland*, Ahad Ha'am censured Herzl's omission of a Jewish-Hebrew cultural dimension to his program. The society Herzl described, he charged, was one that mimicked Western Europe in a monkey-see-monkey-do manner. At the end of his essay, Ahad Ha'am wrote sarcastically that the plan of action presented in *Altneuland* would do very well for the national revival of the Nigerians.[6] The critique set off a stormy debate between supporters of Ahad Ha'am and those of Herzl.[7] Often depicted as a cultural debate between Eastern European intellectual Jewish modernists (the so-called Maskilim) and Central and Western European assimilationists, to a certain extent that was true. According to this common wisdom, the Jewish "cultural problem" was central for the former, who believed that Zionism ought to be primarily a movement for the renewal of Jewish culture. The Jewish state's main role, in this view, was to lead this cultural renaissance. In contrast, the Jews of Western Europe felt less cultural tension, because many of them had been able to integrate into general society. They were thus not only less concerned about the character of modern Jewish culture, but also believed that the adoption of universal liberal or social-democratic views was incumbent on the Zionist movement. As they saw it, such egalitarian and inclusive political approaches were progressive, and would allow different concepts of Jewish culture to flourish at the same time. Some later scholars have claimed that the Zionist movement decided in favor of the Western cultural and legal model, and against both the religious camp and the Maskilim, who viewed Judaism as a culture.[8] In contrast, others have maintained that this dichotomous template, which opposes cultural Zionism to political Zionism, is overstated, and that most jurists held cultural-national views, in varying degrees, while at the same time advocating the adoption of Western principles, such as the rule of law and other norms that have their source in modern Western law.[9]

My position is close to the latter, but I take one step further and argue that the dispute was not so much cultural as meta-cultural. By that I mean that the differences were about the very question of whether there ought to be a debate about culture. Herzl's position, I will show, expresses a fundamental and

6 Ahad Ha'am, "Old New Land," 319.

7 On the debate, see Goldstein, "Altneuland"; Laskov, "Altneuland."

8 Mautner, *Law and the Culture of Israel*, 14–21.

9 Likhovski, *Law and Identity*, 155–156.

consistent Zionist decision in favor of the establishment of institutions to carry out a plan of action.

Herzl's Zionist movement, it should be kept in mind, was born out of a belief that no Jewish culture could long survive if the Jews did not assert their claim to be a nation with a right to self-determination. For that reason, from its earliest days, Zionism put all its strength and efforts into creating a Jewish polity and building a civil society. Despite the internal tensions between religious and secular Zionists, and between advocates of the practical work of Zionist immigration and settlement and those who gave preference to political-diplomatic efforts, all were united against the cultural Zionists' insistence on setting practical Zionist action aside so as to first conduct an internal Jewish cultural discourse that would boldly face up to the issues of the secularization and modernization of Jewish society, and the ways to fashion a new Jewish culture.[10]

So, for example, in the 1880s, more than a decade before Herzl founded the World Zionist Organization, Moshe Leib Lilienblum and other leaders of the Hovevei Zion movement rejected the demands of Judah Leib Gordon, one of the most prominent voices among the Russian-Jewish Maskilim. Gordon insisted that energies should be focused on overhauling the Jewish religion and Russian-Jewish society. He called for a culture war against traditional Jewish forces in Europe. In contrast, Lilienblum declared that the cultural battle over the character and definition of Judaism should be put off to the indefinite future, so as not to interfere with the incipient and still fragile movement to establish settlements in Palestine.[11] It was against this demand by the leaders of Hovevei Zion to muzzle the internal Jewish cultural discourse that Ahad Ha'am came out so passionately when he declared, in 1888, "This is not the way!" Furthermore, he was pessimistic about Zionism's prospects for large-scale settlement in Palestine. The conditions in that country, and the sorry state of Eastern European Jewish society, were such that, as he saw it, at most only a small Jewish entity with limited sovereignty could be established in Palestine, one that would not and could not serve as a magnet or refuge for Europe's millions of oppressed Jews. It could, however, serve as a cultural beacon for their identity as Jews and assist them in their daily effort to

[10] Sokolow, *To Our Teachers*; Borokhov, "Our Platform"; Lilienblum, "If Not Now"; Lilienblum, "On the Vicissitudes"; Don Yehiyeh, "Ideology and Politics" (discussing the opposition of religious Zionist and its leader Rabbi Yitzchak Yaacov Reines to cultural Zionism); Luz, *Parallels Meet*, 137–158; Holtzman, "Born Culture," 29–30.

[11] On the Gordon–Lilienblum debate, see Lilienblum, *Letters of Moshe*; Luz, *Parallels Meet*, 39–41. On Lilienblum's opposition to Ahad Ha'am, see Lilienblum, "Between the Imaginary"; "A Temple"; "To the Keepers."

wrestle with the tension between their desire to preserve their Jewish culture and their desire to assimilate into the modern world. He thus wanted to begin the Jewish revolution from the inside, by fashioning a modern Jewish culture that would preserve the ancient spiritual characteristics of Judaism, that "national I" and "spirit of the people" that beat within it, while adapting these, especially via secularization, to the modern world. Only such a society, Ahad Ha'am believed, could provide a spiritual foundation and motivating force for realizing Zionism's goals.[12]

The demand to address questions of identity and culture was sincere, growing as it did out of painful and very real quandaries faced by modern European Jews. Those were especially acute in Eastern Europe. That region's Jews did not have the option that their brethren in the West did, of assimilating as individuals into the local culture. As such, the cultural question was a burning public problem. The cultural debate raged in Eastern and Central Europe, in the small community that Jews from these areas built in Palestine, and of course in Hovevei Zion and Herzl's Zionist movement. Hundreds of articles about it appeared in the Hebrew-language daily press and periodicals around the turn of the century. Books and pamphlets also addressed it, most of them published in connection with Zionist Congresses or other important convocations, such as the conventions of Russian Zionists in Warsaw (1898), Minsk (1902), and Helsingfors (Helsinki, 1906).[13] The "cultural polemic," as it later came to be called, served as the framework for discussions of a number of matters relating to Jewish culture and identity – the debate between religious and non-religious Jews, between conservative Haredi (ultra-Orthodox) Jews and progressive religious Jews with secular educations, and between secularists holding different positions about Jewish culture. One group of secularists believed in a rigid "religious" approach to culture. Ahad Ha'am was the most notable member of this group, which maintained that at the basis of the manifestations of culture lay a Jewish "nature" or "spirit." These secularists sought to preserve the core of Jewish culture by updating and secularizing it and adapting it to the modern world. Another group of secularists believed in an extreme, even revolutionary, dynamic approach to culture. This group, whose most prominent spokesman was Micha Josef Berdyczewski, and with which Nachman Syrkin was also identified, viewed Zionism as a total

[12] Ahad Ha'am, "At the Crossroads," and especially "This Is Not the Path," "The Jewish State," and "The Spiritual Revival."

[13] Holtzman, "Born Culture," 25. The Helsingfors conference convened after the early Zionist cultural controversy had abated. But the questions of culture and "the work of the present" continued to roil the Zionist movement, and Russian Zionists in particular, as a result of the winds of change that swept through Czarist Russia after the failed 1905 revolution.

Jewish revolution. Its membered maintained that adherence to traditions of the past would be detrimental to the creation of a new Jewish culture, modern and vital, that grappled boldly with the challenges of the modern world. A third group, that of Hovevei Zion and Eliezer Ben-Yehuda, did not come down firmly on either side of the debate over the nature of Jewish culture and identity. They maintained that Jewish culture was simply "what Jews do," and focused on the objective national cultural characteristics that connect all Jews, such as the Hebrew language and the yearning for the Land of Israel.

Each of these positions had, of course, variations and sub-variations, and many of the participants in the discourse expressed a mixture of different ideas. The poet Hayim Nahman Bialik, for example, clearly took the more rigid cultural position, but had no compunctions about declaring that "all that is being created in Palestine by Jews . . . is also a part of Judaism."[14] Every Zionist writer and intellectual took part in the debate. As the cultural polemics heated up, they all realized that the meta-cultural question had to be answered: Was the argument over culture the principal problem that needed to preoccupy Europe's Jews, and the Zionist movement in particular, or should Zionism focus on taking concrete action to settle in Palestine and build Jewish communities there?

The emergence of the Zionist movement further fanned the flames of the cultural debate, granting it a framework and new dimensions. Following the establishment of the World Zionist Organization in 1897, a meta-cultural debate ensued between the advocates of the centrality of culture and the supporters of diplomatic action, immigration, and settlement. The issue was taken up on the floor of Zionist congresses and in the Zionist press.[15] The demand to give priority to the spiritual and cultural came not only from critical intellectuals who did not join the Zionist Organization, such as Ahad Ha'am and Berdyczewski, but also from many delegates to the congresses, who viewed culture as one of the principal issues that needed to be debated. Keeping faith with the Russian Haskalah tradition of Judah Leib Gordon, their principal demand was that the Zionist movement devote itself not only to the "work of the future," meaning the efforts to establish a Jewish national home in Palestine, but also to the "work of the present" (*Gegenwartsarbeit*), meaning the full range of problems faced by Diaspora Jewish communities,

[14] Bialik, "The Question"; Luz, *Parallels Meet*, 137–202.

[15] Lilienblum was well aware that his debate with Gordon paralleled the cultural controversy in the Zionist Organization. See Lilienblum, "Peace Thoughts."

in particular education and culture.[16] While people made enthusiastic speeches on culture at Zionist Congresses and other gatherings, they had trouble agreeing on a definition of culture, and they were unable to translate their flowery rhetoric into practical action. For example, the Second Zionist Congress resolved to set up bodies devoted to promoting the Hebrew language and Jewish culture, and appointed committees charged with carrying out the decision. It also produced directives on the subject. But nothing was done in the period before the next Congress. No funds were provided, and no practical action was taken. For all intents and purposes, the decisions were set aside. An essayist and translator, Reuven Brainin, complained after the Second Zionist Congress, with no little justice, that "Our best Zionists and members of Hovevei Zion, our authors and thinkers, speak morning and night about Hebrew culture, but none of them have offered a proper explanation of that pair of words, on which our little world stands."[17]

At the Fifth Zionist Congress, held in 1901, the loudest voices in the cultural debate came from the Democratic Faction, composed largely of young intellectuals from Eastern Europe who had studied at German universities.[18] The faction had thirty-seven members, from among the eighty delegates from Russia; the ones whose names are most familiar today were Chaim Weizmann, Martin Buber, and Leo Motzkin. The faction protested the undemocratic procedures of the Zionist Organization under Herzl's leadership. In particular, its members claimed that Herzl was deliberately keeping the Zionist movement from taking up the question of Jewish culture, despite its fraught significance for the world's largest concentration of Jews, those of Eastern Europe. They claimed that the culture question was not nearly as vague and as controversial as Lilienblum, Herzl, and the movement's other leaders feared. Later, in its working program for 1902, the faction defined Jewish culture: "the products of the Hebrew spirit in the past and present as they are an integral part of human culture as a whole."[19] But the members of the Democratic Faction were unable to explain what this meant, or derive any concrete action from it. Nevertheless, the issue was debated passionately at the Fifth Zionist Congress in 1901, which reiterated its commitment to cultural activity. Yet, once again, no funds were allotted, no body to address the issue

[16] On the cultural debate, see Luz, *Parallels Meet*, 137–158; Holtzman, "Born Culture"; Almog, *Zionism and History*, 84–176.

[17] Brainin, "Second Zionist." And see also Holtzman, "Born Culture," 25–29.

[18] On the Democratic Faction, see Klausner, *Opposition to Herzl*; Luz, *Parallels Meet*, 138–140, 149–157.

[19] Motzkin, "Program and Organization." According to Holtzman ("Born Culture," 298, note 40), it was Israel Klausner who formulated this working program.

was established, and for all intents and purposes nothing was done.[20] The Congress's preference for political and economic action was clear in its decision to found the Jewish National Fund (JNF, Keren Kayemet in Hebrew), an organization charged with purchasing and settling land in Palestine, which stood in sharp contrast to the vague decisions regarding the promotion of culture and national education. The former decision was carried out, and the JNF became one of the most important and influential Zionist institutions. Only years later were the plans to establish a Hebrew University and national cultural and literary institutions actually carried out.

In other words, at the end of the nineteenth century the majority of the Zionist leadership had already utterly rejected the cultural Zionist position. The first to reject it were Hovevei Zion, followed by Herzl and his loyalists, the members of the early labor movement, and the leaders of the religious Zionists. True, Herzl was compelled to accept the demands of the Russian Zionists that the cultural question be addressed by the Zionist Congresses. But at the Third Congress, in 1899, he confessed that he did not understand what the argument was about. Furthermore, when delegates spoke on the issue, he made a show of leaving his place on the dais.[21] After Herzl's death, as well, the cultural position was rejected by the practical Zionists, led by Chaim Weizmann, the labor movement, and the Revisionists. The Zionist movement as a whole viewed cultural Zionism as a useless and even dangerous tendency. It was useless because culture alone could not save Judaism from its predicament of assimilation and depletion, and certainly could not save the Jews from their many troubles. There could be no future for Jewish culture without a sovereign political entity that would make it possible for that culture to flourish, and without a civically aware public committed to strengthening that entity. What was the point of interminably arguing cultural questions when there were no institutional, social, and political guarantees of the existence of such a culture?

Furthermore, the Zionist mainstream consistently viewed the insistence on plumbing matters of the spirit, education, and the shaping of a modern Jewish culture as a real threat. The majority maintained that the culturalists were mistaken in their belief that all that was good and beautiful in traditional Judaism could be preserved while at the same time fashioning a new, enlightened, and modern Judaism that could be inculcated in the Jewish masses.

[20] Luz, *Parallels Meet*, 152–153, 188–190; Holtzman, "Born Culture," 30.

[21] Herzl was compelled, at the Fifth Zionist Congress of 1901, to offer a half-hearted statement that he supported the cultural effort (Luz, *Parallels Meet*, 149–150), but it seems to have been a tactical political move.

In fact, the project was a bumpy road with no clear contours. From the dawn of the Haskalah, Jews had argued over what defined Jewish culture, which parts of traditional Judaism ought to be preserved and which abandoned, and what the Jewish attitude toward foreign cultures ought to be. Zionism's leaders knew that the cultural debate would demand precious resources, threaten the unity of the Zionist movement, and thus be detrimental to its ability to carry out the weighty tasks it faced. It could even deteriorate into a culture war. Lilienblum summed it up after the Third Zionist Congress in 1899:

> If the good of our people is precious to you, if you are true Zionists, advocate Zion alone.... We have not yet gained purchase on Palestine and have not established our governance there, so we have no need for ministries of higher education and matters of the spirit. Much work lies ahead of us, much for many decades and thousands of people – do not destroy our unity, let no person demand of his compatriot what he will not give up under any circumstances. Unite around one goal: practical action; in matters of the spirit let each person do as he sees fit. I say: remove the sign of envy and animosity from the sanctuary of action of the Zionists.[22]

It was not an unfounded fear. The cultural polemic of the turn of the century was the principal cause of the formation of distinct Zionist parties. It gave birth not only to the Democratic Faction but also to Mizrahi, which aimed to be an organized religious force within the Zionist movement that would oppose demands to debate issues of culture and the attitude toward religion. In the end, it also prompted the labor movement to organize itself as a separate bloc within the Zionist Organization.

Even though the goal of Zionism was, in the final analysis, to ensure the survival of the Jews, and even though the Zionist movement defined itself as the national movement of the Jewish people, it opposed, from its earliest days, substantive decisions about the nature of Judaism, and in particular formal attempts, including legal ones, to define Judaism, the Jewish people, and Jewish (later Israeli) culture.[23] The movement did not, of course, entirely disregard Jewish wishes regarding identity and culture, for the simple reason that no national movement and no nation-state can entirely ignore that issue. Indeed, the movement firmly rejected the Uganda plan and other territorial options for a Jewish state, understanding that the aspiration to shape an exemplary Jewish national society could not be realized if it were detached from Zion symbolically and practically. In keeping with this, the Zionist

[22] Lilienblum, "Symbol of Jealousy."
[23] See Tsurumi, "Neither Angels."

movement explicitly recognized, on a number of occasions, that it needed to engage in cultural and educational activity as well, especially with regard to the Hebrew language and establishing a Hebrew university. Such were the decisions favoring action in the cultural sphere that were passed (if unenthusiastically) by the Congresses of 1898 and 1901, and a firmer decision passed by the Tenth Zionist Congress in 1911, as well as that passed by the Third Convention of Russian Zionists, held in Helsingfors, in 1906. It was at that Congress that the Zionist movement explicitly accepted the need to act also to answer the needs of Diaspora communities.[24] But, for the large part, the movement always preferred practical action and the effort to establish a state and an independent civil society to the risky discussion of culture and the nature of Judaism. In those few cases in which the leaders of the Congress were given no choice but to address the issue, the debate ended with general and vague declarations, but no operative decisions or allotment of funds.[25] The Zionist conventional wisdom was that the culture of the Jewish state would be Jewish in any case, since most of its citizens would be Jews, and because the state framework would express and support the culture of the Jewish majority.[26]

Herzl's and Lewinsky's different opinions aligned with the two sides of the meta-cultural question. Their two books present, of course, two different cultural worlds, East versus West, but the difference between their utopias, like the fundamental difference between Ahad Ha'am and Herzl, indicates that there was not just a profound cultural disagreement between them, but even more so a meta-cultural dispute about whether the cultural debate (or, in fact, culture war) should take a central place in Zionist discourse and action. Herzl did not delve deep into the substance of culture and law in the Jewish state, because he was primarily interested in achieving the goal of an independent state and the shaping of its government and its legal system. From his acquaintance with the different parts of European Jewry, the Eastern Europeans in particular, he knew that the cultural debate was furious and difficult and could not easily be resolved, and that focusing on it was liable to place at risk the achievement of Zionism's political goal. That being the case, he chose to remain silent about culture. He evinced this approach to culture as early as 1895, when he wrote in his diary that a fight could break out because of a

[24] But, even then, many in the Zionist leadership stressed that their principal concern was poverty and discrimination against Jews, rather than the cultural and identity issues faced by the Jews of modern Europe.

[25] Luz, *Parallels Meet*, 152–153.

[26] Compare to 1937 Ze'ev Jabotinsky's speech to the Royal Commission that took up the partition of Palestine into Jewish and Arab states. Jabotinsky, *Works*, vol. 5, 224.

"debate over words." And, he wrote, "people argue with each other because they use different words for the same matter ... [whereas I] make the greatest concessions with words. I do not trade blows over words. I don't have time for that."[27]

The significance of this "silence" was, ostensibly, the adoption of the Western political-social model, but in that regard Herzl was no different from any other Zionist in the world. All the Zionists (and most Jews) warmly welcomed the Western concepts of a state, the rule of law, and universal citizenship. They believed in scientific progress and some form of a regulated free market economy; they also enthusiastically adopted many aspects of modern popular culture.[28] The Maskilim and advocates of cultural Zionism never rejected these Western modes of thinking and behavior, but simply sought to use them as a framework or foundation and to integrate modern Jewish content into them, or at least to grant them a Jewish "character" (the nature of which they disputed). So, for example, they wanted their nation-state (a concept invented in the West) to express their Jewish culture; they wanted the future Jewish state to have an independent legal system that embodied the Western concept of the rule of law. But, at the same time, they wanted the law to serve as an expression of their Jewish identity. This is an important point, and needs to be emphasized: there was never a "Jewish" camp that entirely rejected Western culture. All the participants in the debate were proud Jews who accepted modernity and the values of Western culture, which they sought to integrate with their traditions.

Fundamentally, the real debate between Herzl, on the one hand, and Ahad Ha'am and Lewinsky, on the other, was not one of culture and identity, distinguishing "Judaism" (which Ahad Ha'am and Lewinsky claimed to support) from "democracy" (which Herzl ostensibly placed before Judaism). It was a *meta-cultural* debate. The question was whether it was in fact proper for the Jewish national movement to postpone the debate over culture for later, while first working on creating the framework (state, law, society, economy), or whether it needed to set aside the Zionist project itself while it first took up the issue of culture; even if doing so threatened to create dissension over semantics. Herzl's disregard of the question of the Jewish content of the law testifies to the thinking and action of the Zionist movement that he founded. The first priority was establishing Zionist institutions (including a legal

27 Herzl, *The Diaries*, vol. 128, June 20, 1895.

28 On the modernization process of nineteenth-century East European Jews, see Meir, *Kiev*; Nathans, *Beyond the Pale*; Zipperstein, *The Jews*. And see also Moss, "At Home"; Miron, "Modernization, Assimilation," and the many sources mentioned there.

system), prior to considering their cultural content. That remained the line taken by the Zionist movement until at least the 1980s. It could be seen in the response to those members of the First Knesset who demanded that the Mandate laws the country had adopted be replaced with original Israeli legislation. The first Israeli minister of justice, Pinchas Rosen, rejected the demand, using language echoing that of Herzl: "We must respect the laws of the state, whether they are laws that came us from the time of the Mandate or laws that we legislated ourselves; otherwise chaos will reign in the country."[29]

From the great polemic between Herzl, Nordau, Ahad Ha'am, Lewinsky, and their contemporaries emerged the fundamental Zionist meta-cultural decision to silence the cultural debate. Zionist thinkers and leaders of the first generation did not address the issue of the law directly. They did not establish legal institutions, did not draft legal norms, and did not consider in depth the question of the character and content of the law. Their heirs, in contrast, were called on to deal with the law as the Jewish community in Palestine grew, and as a result of political developments in the world and in Palestine. Zionist settlers in Palestine needed laws and a legal system, and this gave rise to cultural debates in the legal arena. This, too, almost immediately set off a meta-cultural polemic about whether the legal system and norms ought to address cultural disputes in depth or, rather, to circumvent them, at least until society, and its legal system, stabilized.

[29] Bondy, *Feliks*, 435. In conversation with me, Haim Cohn, who served as attorney general throughout the 1950s, told me that, at every opportunity, Justice Minister Rosen stressed the need for legal certainty (*Rechtssicherheit*).

2

The Hebrew Peace Courts

The Yishuv Judicial System That Failed

The first time that the Jews of the Zionist Yishuv had to address cultural tensions in the legal field, and thus also needed to make a decision on the meta-cultural issue, came with the Hebrew Peace Courts, an autonomous arbitration system established in 1909.[1] The conventional wisdom, for which there is no evidence, was that the institution took its name from the Bible's book of Zechariah (8:16): "Render judgment of truth and peace within your gates." As its name implies, the Hebrew Peace Courts were meant to make peace among members of the Jewish community in Palestine by resolving disputes among parties who did not want to resort to the Ottoman court system, which they considered debased and corrupt, or to the judicial systems operated by foreign consulates in Palestine.[2] It was inspired by the new winds blowing through the Yishuv, which also led to the establishment of Degania, the first Jewish communal farming settlement, and Ahuzat Bayit, the Jaffa neighborhood that would later become the nucleus of the city of Tel Aviv.

The Hebrew Peace Courts could be termed a "popular" system, inasmuch as its judges were not professional jurists but rather well-known public figures appointed by the World Zionist Organization's Palestine Office and the boards of neighborhoods and *moshavot*, the Jewish farming colonies founded during the previous three decades.[3] Proceedings were not conducted

[1] On the Hebrew Peace Courts, see Shamir, *Colonies of Law*; Dickstein, *A History*; Hacohen, "Hebrew Law"; Kidron, *Between Nationality*.

[2] Under the terms of international treaties called the Turkish Capitulations, foreign nationals in Palestine were exempted from civil litigation in Ottoman courts, and had the right to bring their cases before the consul of the country whose citizenship they held. As the Yishuv expanded in size and complexity, invoking this privilege grew ever less effective for new Jewish immigrants.

[3] The Palestine Office, established in 1908, was the World Zionist Organization's executive arm in the country and coordinated Zionist activity there. In practice, its primary role was

according to formal legal procedures; rather, they took the form of brief hearings in which the judges rendered decisions on the basis of common sense and their construal of general principles of justice. The Palestine Office allotted a room to the first of the courts and funded the salary of its first court secretary, the writer Shmuel Yosef Agnon. At first, most hearings were held there, but the judges took a horse-drawn carriage to more distant *moshavot* when a case had to be heard at one of them.[4] After World War I, the system expanded and Hebrew Peace Courts were established in several locations, as was a supreme court in Tel Aviv.[5] Even then, most of the judges did not have formal legal educations, and the procedures, restricted to local civil suits, were brief – an hour or several hours at most. Decisions were handed down on the spot, with brief down-to-earth explanations.

The rulings of the Hebrew Peace Courts were considered a prime example of the revolution the Jewish people were undergoing and of the Zionist national revival. The decisions were rendered in Hebrew by modern Zionist Jews who hoped to create a Jewish national home in Palestine, inhabited by a new and independent Jewish society. Accordingly, the judges based their decisions largely on commercial practices and other customs that had developed in Palestine, on their own precedents (although precedents were not considered officially binding), on the legal standards of European legal systems with which the Jews of the Yishuv were familiar, and on traditional Jewish legal sources, with which most members of the society were acquainted, even if they were not well versed in them. Both the judges and the parties to disputes considered these sources to be authoritative.[6] Even so, most of the parties involved were not religious and had only limited traditional educations, and as such based their arguments on the few compendiums of *halakhah* (Jewish law) that were relatively accessible to laypeople, rather than on the much larger, scattered, and less accessible responsa literature, in which rabbis issued rulings on questions brought before them. The main sources were the Talmud, Maimonides's *Mishneh Torah*, the *Hoshen Mishpat* section

funding and organizing Jewish settlement. It was headed by Arthur Ruppin, who was also the first chief of the Hebrew Peace Courts. After World War I, the Palestine Office's functions were transferred to other institutions – first to the Zionist Commission, which served as a liaison between the British military government and the Yishuv, and then to the Zionist Executive and the Jewish Agency Executive.

4 Naor, *Tales from*.

5 Dickstein, *A History*, 28–34.

6 In this respect, the Hebrew Peace Courts resembled other Jewish judicial bodies, such as the courts established in displaced persons camps in Germany after World War II. See Brot, "Between State," 62–63, 68.

of Rabbi Jacob Ben Asher's *Arba'ah Turim*, and Rabbi Joseph Karo's *Shulkhan Arukh* and the commentators on that work.

But, as in every legal system, as the Hebrew Peace Courts grew, and especially after an appeals system was instituted, it became necessary for the judges to base their decisions on clear sources that were agreed on by all. The demand that the judges substantiate their decisions came from two directions. First, it came from the judges themselves, especially from those on the appeals panels. It is the nature of an appeals court that it does not reexamine the evidence, only lower courts' interpretations of legal rules. The central preoccupation of appeals judges is thus norms and values, not findings of fact. Moreover, the higher the level of the panel, the broader the public that attends to its rulings. Judges on higher benches know that their decisions establish norms and precedents with a wide purview. These considerations led the Hebrew Peace Courts, and especially its highest bench, to lay out the sources for their decisions. The second direction from which the demand for substantiated rulings came from the litigants. They based their legal arguments on sources from their varied system of values and culture, and insisted that the court address the arguments each side made and discuss the halakhic and other sources in which the arguments were embedded.[7]

The understanding of the need for justifications based on an organized body of norms increased during the 1920s. At that time, Jewish jurists from Europe and others of broad legal knowledge immigrated to Palestine. These people recognized the need to create an ordered legal system based on a clear and binding set of norms and values. Especially prominent among them were members of the Hebrew Law Society, who sought to fashion a modern Jewish-Hebrew legal system based on a supplemented and secularized version of the halakhah. They saw an urgent need to create a body of norms – a codex, in fact – according to which the judges would rule. Paltiel Dickstein (later Daykan), one of the two most prominent figures in the Society, was the moving force behind the attempt to create a body of binding norms for the Hebrew Peace Courts.[8] Upon his arrival in Palestine, he was appointed court secretary, and later to the post of chairman of the Supreme Hebrew Peace Court in Tel Aviv.

7 Hacohen, "Hebrew Law," 152–163.

8 Dickstein (1885–1969) was a scholar of Hebrew law. Born in Lithuania, he studied law in Odessa. After immigrating to Palestine in 1921, he joined the Hebrew Law Society and the Hebrew Peace Court in Jerusalem. A founder of the Tel Aviv School of Law and Economics, he was awarded the Israel Prize in Jurisprudence in 1957.

This brought the cultural problem to the fore, baring the meta-cultural tension that in the end defeated the Hebrew Peace Courts. As time passed, it became evident that the Hebrew Peace Courts lacked an organized, binding, and agreed-on set of legal norms to be used in rulings – neither laws, directives, nor precedents. The eclectic collection of norms noted above served at most as a collection of guidelines, but none was obligatory. As such, there were many cases in which the judges could not find sources to base their rulings on, and simply decided, as best they could, on the basis of their consciences and common sense. This way of doing justice was acceptable while the Yishuv was small and relatively undeveloped, but it became problematic as the Jewish community grew in numbers, complexity, and diversity. In a small and relatively homogeneous society, it is generally not necessary for judges to provide detailed justifications of their rulings. In such a community, the judges, litigants, and the public share the same culture and system of values. The community thus supplements and interprets judicial rulings on its own, intuitively, according to the view of the world that all its members share. Furthermore, in a small and uniform community, disagreements and interpretive disputes are relatively easier to resolve because there is greater social pressure to do so. As a community grows, develops, and diversifies, the boundaries of the common culture blur and disagreements increase, both because there are more people and because they do not always share the same way of life and outlook. It thus becomes harder for litigants and the community to understand intuitively judicial decisions when the judges do not explicitly present the reasoning behind them. There is no common ground for filling in the blanks. Just as a more complex society shifts from law based on custom to law based on legislation, it also shifts from brief, unwritten, and unsubstantiated judicial decisions based on common sense to judgments based, even if only in part, on reasoned rulings anchored in a stable system of written norms of which the public has knowledge.

Without a guiding system of norms, a court system cannot offer the certitude, stability, and uniformity of judgment that are vital to any behavior-directed normative system, a system of justice and law in particular. According to Mordechai Ben-Hillel Hacohen, a writer and public figure of the time,

> Mr. [Menachem] Ussishkin is incorrect when he says that the Hebrew Peace Courts lack procedures. The bylaws of this institution are fixed and firmly observed, and the Supreme Peace Court oversees it. In this regard there is nothing to criticize. What, then, is the problem? *No fixed law stands before it, and its judgments emerge in accordance with the sensibilities of those who sit in the judges' seats*, and in regard to the people who are chosen for this, "most

of them are without education and without juridical experience," as Mr. Ussishkin says, and they are "connected only to the broadest and most abstract principles of justice and integrity."[9]

The advocates of the Hebrew Peace Courts considered this problem at their second national convention, in 1927, realizing that the institution was in decline. The convention resolved that "the time has come to establish fixed rules and procedures based on Jewish law and the needs of our time and our outlook."[10] Notably, the lack of a clear set of norms and legal texts would soon also become a problem for the Comrades' Courts, the arbitration system of the Histadrut, the workers' organization founded by the labor movement in Palestine in 1921.

As Hacohen noted, at first the Hebrew Peace Courts and the Comrade's Courts endeavored to solve the problem by creating clear procedural rules, a familiar and accepted initiative in the history of law. Legal systems based on courts, but lacking a well-developed system of laws to guide them, achieve the needed uniformity, stability, and certainty by advanced and relatively inflexible procedures. These ensure that court sessions operate according to consistent rules, thus guaranteeing the system's stability and some level of confidence about the outcome of a trial. It is the method followed since the medieval period by English law, which was court-based, and the Yishuv did the same. Historical research has shown that, over time, the Yishuv judicial systems grew more and more formalistic as they sought to create organized and advanced procedures and gave an ever greater role to lawyers, who frequently raised procedural claims. That was resented by many members of the Yishuv, who liked the community nature of the Hebrew Peace Courts and the "fraternal" character of the Histadrut's Comrades' Courts. But it was a necessary step that was meant to maintain the public legitimacy of these bodies.[11]

But in the absence of a stable and binding system of norms, a procedural framework alone is insufficient. The problem was that no set of accepted Hebrew-Jewish norms existed in Palestine or the Jewish world. Those that the litigants and judges based themselves on derived from sources that were not considered binding. On the contrary, they were much disputed in the Jewish public. For example, while there was generally no opposition to the Jews of the Yishuv using the halakhah as a source for their arguments, it was not clear

9 Hacohen, "Hebrew Law," 154 (emphasis added).

10 Dickstein, *A History*, 73.

11 Shamir, *Colonies of Law*, 77; Shamir, "Lex Moriendi." For the Histadrut's Comrades' Courts, see Bar-On and De Vries, "In the Procrustean Bed." The Haganah's judicial system faced a similar issue. See Stern, "Between Militia."

whether, given the modern secular nature of the Zionist community in Palestine, traditional Jewish law was binding or rather simply one that could guide and offer inspiration to the judges. Moreover, it was not even clear how the halakhah could be used as a "guiding" legal source.

The judges of the Hebrew Peace Courts, most of whom were not religious, did not see themselves as bound by religious law. In general, they read halakhic texts freely, and had no compunctions about interpreting them as they saw fit and even diverging from them so as to make them applicable to the society they lived in. One example is *Shochat v. Gluskin*, heard before the Supreme Hebrew Peace Court in January 1923. It involved a claim of fraud in a contract to construct a house. The contractor who made the charge of fraud based his claim in part on Jewish laws relating to that offense. The respondent claimed that the halakhic laws of fraud apply only to chattels, not land, and that the contractor could therefore not invoke them. The Supreme Hebrew Peace Court ruled that the Hebrew Peace Courts were not bound by all the details and fine points of the Talmudic general principle. In other words, the court claimed that it was guided but not bound by halakhah, which it was permitted to interpret, change, or even categorically reject. The court's anchor in the decision was not halakhah, but rather the societal interest in defending against contract fraud. Accordingly, the court decided that the halakhic laws of fraud would apply in this case, even though land rather than chattels was at issue, and that the contract was thus void.[12] This reading, and many other similar ones, raised the hackles of halakhic gatekeepers, leading to severe conflict between the Hebrew Peace Courts and rabbinic courts, as well as parts of the religious population.[13] In general, rulings of this sort did not disturb most of the Yishuv, made up of secular Jews. The more pressing problem was that litigants had no way of knowing what norms would be invoked by the Hebrew Peace Courts in their decisions in any given case. As the Yishuv grew, its economy and commerce became more complex, and as Yishuv society became more heterogeneous and stratified, this problem became more acute and demanded immediate resolution.

While jurists influenced by the Haskalah believed that they had the ability to fashion a system of national legal norms, and took up the task energetically, legislation is a complex and lengthy labor, involving debates over values, culture, and politics. With all their good will, these modern Jews, in Palestine and elsewhere, were not able to reach agreement on what the nature of Jewish-Hebrew law ought to be, nor even what it should be called. It was that

[12] Israel States Archives (hereafter ISA) P/76. Cited in Shamir, *Colonies of Law*, 73–74.

[13] Dickstein, *A History*, 51–52; Shamir, "Lex Moriendi."

problem that doomed the Hebrew Peace Courts to slow decline and oblivion. They disappeared not because of a culture war but because of a meta-cultural decision, not because their judges and staff engaged in endless debates over culture and identity but because the Yishuv as a whole – its institutions, leadership, and elite cohort – decided that the time had not yet come to address the questions of identity and culture that needed to be decided in order to create a body of legal rules that would bind the courts. The Yishuv and its leadership preferred to do without its own independent judicial system so as to avoid descending into a culture war.

The upshot was that, while the Mandate authorities recognized the Hebrew Peace Courts as an arbitration system and provided them with the means to enforce their decisions,[14] and despite the fact that the courts were funding and supported by the National Council and Jewish local authorities, the Jewish public gradually abandoned them. From the mid-1920s onward, the number of cases the courts addressed diminished steadily, until, by the beginning of the 1930s, they were for all intents and purposes irrelevant.[15] Even the Jewish national institutions and many Jewish local authorities (led by the Tel Aviv municipality) preferred to use the Mandate courts rather than to litigate in the local Jewish courts.[16] In Tel Aviv, for example, the number of cases brought before the Hebrew Peace Courts declined from 1,480 in 1923 to just 247 in 1932, a period in which the city's population quadrupled from 13,000 (at the end of 1922) to 52,000.[17] The nadir came in 1933, when the Hebrew Peace Court in Jerusalem was terminated and the activity of the courts in other parts of the country dwindled drastically.

Paltiel Dickstein claimed that the principal reason for the decline of the Hebrew Peace Courts was the "casting off of the national yoke in a large part of the Yishuv." Other reasons he offered were the increasing efficiency of the Mandate courts and the growing number of Jewish lawyers, who preferred to work within a formal legal system.[18] Later it was argued that the courts failed largely because of opposition from elite groups in the Yishuv, among them

[14] The Arbitration Ordinance (1926) authorized District Courts to ratify the rulings of arbitrators, such that the latter would receive the force of a court ruling and enforced by the Execution Office.

[15] Dickstein, *A History*, 36–38; Shamir, "Lex Moriendi." Haifa was an exception. While the number of cases brought before it also dwindled, the Hebrew Peace Court in that city continued to be an accepted place to litigate, especially by members of the Old Yishuv in the lower city. See Kidron, *Between Nationality*, 162–179.

[16] Dickstein, *A History*, 33–38; Shamir, "Lex Moriendi."

[17] Shamir, *Colonies of Law*, xii. On the development of Tel Aviv in these years, see Biger, "The Development."

[18] Dickstein, *A History*, 35–36, 62–68.

rabbinic courts, Yishuv leaders, Jewish lawyers, and the Mandate legal system and government. According to Ronen Shamir, the Hebrew Peace Courts constituted an ideological and institutional opposition to the legal model accepted by those elites, because they were popular rather than formal, did not use complex procedures, and did not require representation by a lawyer. Furthermore, they made free and secular use of halakhic sources, thus challenging both rabbinic courts and the Zionist narrative, which sought to establish a state and create a new Hebrew culture, different from that of the Diaspora. For that reason, Shamir claimed, these elites did not make any effort to support the Hebrew Peace Courts when the larger public turned its back on them.[19]

The claims like those of Dickstein and Shamir, who stressed the circumstances that led to the failure of the Hebrew Peace Courts, are based on the assumption that, with a bit of good will and cooperation, the courts could have regained their place as a vibrant communal arena of legal arbitration. These two scholars were not the only ones to make that claim. Similar arguments repeatedly appear in Israeli historiography, also with regard to the lack of success of other legal institutions. For example, the same argument is made with regard to the failure to enact laws of Israeli-Jewish-Hebrew content, the failure to promulgate a constitution for Israel, and the lack of an academic institution devoted to studying and fashioning Israeli-Jewish-Hebrew law. In this view, these failures were due largely to contingencies – war and the lack of resources, a simple lack of effort or good will, or the opposition of elite groups or of a particular institution to a national initiative in the legal field. For example, it was the opposition of the Mandate regime, lawyers, the rabbinic establishment, or the Yishuv leadership that doomed the Hebrew Peace Courts, or the opposition of the Hebrew University of Jerusalem to establishing a university-level school of law and economics in Tel Aviv.[20] The failure to establish an Israeli legal code based on traditional Jewish sources was thus seen as the cumulative result of contingent failures, some of them caused by simple lack of attention.[21]

But the early and ringing failure of the Hebrew Peace Courts indicates that the ultimate inability to establish an Israeli legal system based on Jewish-Hebrew content has a more profound cause. It lies in the inability to agree about what is Jewish, what is Jewish culture, and what is Jewish law. In the

[19] Shamir, "Lex Moriendi."

[20] Shamir, "Lex Moriendi," 179 (arguing that the failure of the Hebrew Peace Courts was caused by the opposition of the Rabbinic Courts and the Jewish Bar). Cohen, "The School"; Cohen, *Academia in Tel-Aviv*, 23–75 (arguing that the failure of the Tel Aviv School of Law and Economics was caused by the opposition of the Hebrew University of Jerusalem).

[21] See, for example, Harris, "Absent Minded."

absence of such agreement, it is impossible to develop a binding system of "Jewish" norms, and in the absence of such a system, the Hebrew Peace Courts could not provide the people of the Yishuv with predictable, stable, and coherent rulings, thus sealing the courts' fate.

In fact, the interesting point in this sad story is that there was no guiding hand that put an end to the courts. Shamir has a point when he claims that various elite groups opposed the Hebrew Peace Courts for their own reasons. But the fact is that it was the Jewish public at large that brought the system to an end. The steady decline in the number of cases filed with the courts shows that the public voted with its feet in favor of the Mandate courts. Even though the Hebrew Peace Courts were autonomous Zionist courts that promised quick and efficient adjudication by Jewish judges, the people of the Yishuv preferred the formalized British system, based on a clear system of substantive and procedural norms – despite their non-Jewish origin – along with binding precedents and an efficient system of enforcement and implementation. Even when relations between the Yishuv and Great Britain worsened, the Jews in Palestine viewed Great Britain as an exemplar of a democratic and legalist society that could teach them how to conduct themselves in law and society.[22] The nadir that the Hebrew Peace Courts reached shows that even people of national consciousness and pride turned their backs on the Jewish courts and preferred the stable, efficient, fair, and advanced Mandate system. The courts' failure can also explain the Israeli leadership's decision, at the time of independence, to leave the Mandate legal system in place and maintain its functioning and efficient institutions, despite the fact that the sources of the Mandate norms were foreign and did not express Jewish identification.

Yishuv's society rebuff of the Hebrew Peace Courts indicates that intellectuals who demand that we "grapple sincerely and boldly" with questions of identity and culture simply do not represent society as a whole. Yes, human beings are animals in the grip of nets of meaning that they have themselves woven, but, as Abraham Maslow's theory of the hierarchy of needs shows, most human beings do not think about their identities and cultures on a daily basis. They seek first to provide themselves with their basic requirements, before turning to address their identities. The people of the Yishuv always recognized the importance of having a stable, fair, and efficient legal system.

[22] See, for example, Ben-Gurion's speech, November 1, 1947, p. 19. Ben-Gurion's Archives (hereafter BGA), Speeches and Articles; Minutes of the Israeli Provisional Cabinet, December 12, 1948 (Debate between Ben-Gurion and Minister Yitzhak Gruenbaum on privileging English over European law). On Anglophilia and the partiality of the justices of the early Supreme Court for English law, see Oz-Salzberger and Salzberger, "Secret German," 185.

They created the Hebrew Peace Courts at the end of the Ottoman period not only for national reasons, but also so as to offer a stable and fair alternative to the decaying Ottoman imperial court system. In the 1920s they turned their back on their "national" courts when they realized that the system could not offer certainty, stability, and legal coherence at a level approaching that offered by the British. This was not the result of a cultural war, nor was it the behavior of a public that was ignorant and lacking in national consciousness, as Dickstein implied. On the contrary, most of the Jewish public in Palestine during the Mandate period was mobilized in the Zionist project and of high national consciousness. Yet this same public, which battled for Jewish labor and for Hebrew language, education, and culture, abandoned the Hebrew court system when it realized that it operated in uncertain conditions and could not effectively perform the fundamental social role played by a judicial system. The people of the Yishuv came to prefer the courts of the alien colonial regime, operating under foreign laws.

The story of the Hebrew Peace Courts thus offers the first example of a meta-cultural decision against the very attempt to conduct a cultural discourse, or struggle, about law. This decision did not find expression in incisive articles like those written by Lillienblum, nor in political decisions like those made by Herzl. Rather, it was the result of the practical decisions made by thousands of individuals – each day, many Jews chose to refrain from conducting a cultural discussion of what Jewish-Hebrew norms should be used by the Hebrew Peace Courts, and took their suits to the Mandate courts instead. But the consequence of these practical decisions was identical to the determination made by Zionism's founding fathers to avoid cultural debate, because they understood that such a polemic would be detrimental to realizing the goals of Zionism and to the functioning of a legal system.

It is also the first example in this book that the legal field is different from other cultural fields, such as literature and art. The law is not an appropriate arena for questions of identity and culture. It must rule on and direct behavior, whereas questions of identity and culture cannot, by their very nature, be decided one way or the other. Finally, it is also the first example that advocates of cultural Zionism were never able to offer a real and functional purely Jewish alterative to fair and efficient modern Western law.

3

The Hebrew Law Society

An Abortive Attempt to Fashion a Jewish-Hebrew National Code of Law

Jurists inspired by cultural Zionism maintained, from the beginning of the twentieth century, that the Jewish nation's rebirth in its native land should be accompanied by a parallel revival of its national law. Like Ahad Ha'am, they called for beginning the task of the cultural fashioning of a Hebrew-Jewish-Zionist law prior to the establishment of a Jewish state.

The advocates of a national Jewish law revival were motivated not only by cultural Zionism but by two other factors. The first was the emerging awareness, by the huge Jewish community in Russia at the turn of the century, that law was an important tool of political and social change. As part of a gradual process that began in the mid-nineteenth century, and which gained traction in the wake of the legal reforms of Czar Alexander II in 1864, Jews began to make massive use of the law to demand their rights and to defend themselves against bias and other injuries. More and more Jews began to go into the legal profession, which became open to Jews in 1889, gradually replacing the traditional pleaders who represented Jewish interests to state and local authorities. Some of them, like Heinrich Sliosberg, Maxim Vinaver, and Oscar Gruzenberg, became prominent attorneys in St. Petersburg.[1] Jews brought tens of thousands of petitions and lawsuits to Russian courts and administrative

[1] Heinrich Sliosberg (1863–1936) was a non-Zionist Jewish attorney and social activist who studied law in St. Petersburg. He represented many Jews in the Russian capital and throughout the country in suits against the authorities to the extent that it was said that "Sliosberg's steadiest client for many years has been the Jewish people." He served as secretary to the Jewish banker Baron Naftali Hertz Ginzberg. Following the Bolshevik revolution, he emigrated to Paris, where he died.

Maxim Vinaver (1863–1926) was a Russian non-Zionist Jewish attorney, journalist, and social activist who received his legal education in Warsaw. He served as a member of the first Duma (Russia's parliament) for the Constitutional Democratic party (known as the Cadets), while also helping to found the League for the Attainment of Full Rights for the Jewish People in Russia (the Folksgrupe); he later became one of the leaders of the Jewish group of delegates

bodies. When the czar consented to the establishment of the Duma following the revolution of 1905, Jewish candidates and slates ran for office, hoping to use the Duma to improve the position of Jews, but the new parliament never emerged as an orderly and effective body. While only some of these political and legal efforts were successful, they are evidence of a change in the political-civil thinking of the Jews of Eastern Europe, and of a new realization that the law could be an important means of bringing about social and political change. No less importantly, they realized that the law could be used to defend and promote Jewish collective interests and rights, and national rights, too, as some of them grasped.[2] Even if most of the important Russian Jewish attorneys at the time were not Zionists, some of them cooperated with Zionist Jews, including politically, as with the establishment of the League for the Attainment of Full Rights for the Jewish People in Russia in the run-up to the elections to the first Duma in March 1905. In the cultural-legal arena, Sliosberg and Paltiel Dickstein, who would later become the moving force behind the Zionist endeavor to revive Jewish law, established, in 1913, the Branch for the Study of the History of Jewish Law, under the aegis of the Jewish Society for History and Ethnography, founded by Simon Dubnow. Zionist jurists were thus well acquainted with, and influenced by, the view of Jewish jurists in Czarist Russia that the law could be a social and national instrument.

A second factor in the resurgence of interest in Jewish law was the romantic national-historicist conception of the law that developed in Europe at the beginning of the nineteenth century, in response to the universalist tenor of the Enlightenment. The law of each nation, in this view, was a particular historical-cultural construction. The advocates of the historical view of the law acknowledged, of course, that there are universal norms common to every proper legal system, with similar patterns of action, deriving from the social ends of the law. But beyond this, they argued, every legal system had its unique norms and institutions shaped by the specific interests, values, culture, and history of each society. To fashion a better system of law, and to better

to the Duma. He also helped found the Jewish Society for History and Ethnography. Following the revolution he emigrated to France, where he died.

Oscar Gruzenberg (1886–1940) was a Jewish jurist and political leader in Russia who began as an opponent of Zionism but later became a supporter. He studied law in Kiev and became a well-known attorney in St. Petersburg. He defended the victims of pogroms in many trials, and is remembered especially as leading, with Vinaver, the defense of blood libel defendants David Blondes (1900) and Mendel Beilis (1913). He left the Soviet Union in 1926 and died in Nice. In 1950, his remains were brought to Israel for reburial.

2 Nathans, *Beyond the Pale*, 311–366.

interpret, enforce, and use the law, it was thus necessary to be acquainted with the history of the society in question and to understand how its laws emerged from its history. Historical currents in the law developed in Europe, from England in the west to Russia in the east. The most influential of these was the German Historical School of Legal Studies (*geschichtliche Rechtswissenschaft*) founded by the German jurist Friedrich Carl von Savigny. Savigny died in 1875, but his historical theory continued to be extremely influential after his death, and toward the end of the century its influence grew in Central and Eastern Europe, along with the rise in nationalism and the late wave of Romanticism in those regions. These views had a major impact, for example, on the theories of the German jurist Josef Kohler, whose comparative legal studies in turn inspired many Jewish jurists at the turn of the century.[3] The concept of a national law growing out of the nation's spirit and history excited young Zionists who encountered them in their legal studies at Central and Eastern European universities.[4] As Assaf Likhovski has noted, "Hebrew law was born out of an affair between German professors and Zionist students."[5]

Zionist students from Eastern Europe founded the Democratic Faction in 1901, calling on Herzl to address the issues of Jewish culture and identity. About a decade and a half later, a group of young Jewish jurists from Eastern Europe demanded that Jewish national law be based on a reinterpretation of the glorious Jewish legal tradition. These young people, advocates of Hebrew culture and Jewish nationalism, sought to revitalize Jewish law, which until that point had largely been an object of study rather than actually put into practice; to the extent it was used, its scope was limited. This was to be done, they said, by reconstruing the rabbinic legal tradition in conformance with the laws of modern political communities. After several years of writing and discussion,[6] World War I and the Balfour Declaration impelled these young jurists to take action. In December 1917 they founded, in Moscow, the Hebrew Law Society, dedicated to the renaissance of Jewish law.

[3] Likhovski, "Hebrew Law," 339; Radzyner, "Hebrew Law."

[4] Radzyner, "Hebrew Law," 105–106; Edrei, "Why Teach," 468–471.

[5] Likhovski, "Hebrew Law," 341.

[6] See, for example, Samuel Eisenstadt's open letter of 1910, published in *He'atid* (5670–5671), p. 192. It was later printed under the title "Chronicles of the Jewish Law," in Eisenstadt, *Zion with Justice*, 11; see also his call, in another open letter, in 1916, to establish a "scholarly society for the study of Hebrew law" (later republished in *Zion with Justice*, 31, referenced in Radzyner, "Hebrew Law," 144). See also ibid., p. 105, note 55. As already noted, in 1913 Dickstein and Sliosberg founded the Branch for the Study of the History of Jewish Law of the Jewish Society for History and Ethnography, which had been founded by Dubnow. A collection of articles issued by the Branch was lost during World War I.

It was this organization that coined the term "Hebrew law," which would become the focal point of dissension over identity and culture for a century to come.[7] The term would later acquire profound national, cultural, and religious connotations. For example, it would be argued that the words "Hebrew law" were chosen deliberately to express the resuscitation – or invention – of a Jewish national law, so as to depict it as a new Hebrew creation distinct from the law shaped by the Exile, and so as to differentiate it from Jewish law, or at least to fence off, within the halakhah, an area of practical law.[8] But these are all later readings given to the term, at a time when it was the subject of controversy. The founders of the Hebrew Law Society in 1917 seem to simply have translated word for word the Russian term for "Jewish law" (*Еврейское право, Evreyskoe parvo*). In many European languages, the terms "Hebrew" and "Jew" are synonymous.[9]

The moving forces in the Hebrew Law Society were two non-religious Zionists with religious, general, and legal educations: Samuel Eisenstadt, who had studied law in Switzerland, and Paltiel Dickstein, who had done his legal studies in Odessa.[10] They formulated the Society's goals in keeping with their own biographies: "to study in particular law in its Hebrew national form, as it developed over our nations thousands of years of existence in Palestine and the Exile, and to collect the material necessary to continue this development and for new work in our land."[11] The Society's stated goals show that the Hebrew law enterprise was founded on the principles of cultural

[7] Amihai Radzyner notes that the expression appeared in the mid-nineteenth century in a book by Rabbi Zecharia Frankel, but the Zionist jurists from Russia, Eisenstadt most notably, were the first to use the term to refer to modern national Jewish law. Radzyner, "Hebrew Law," 99–100.

[8] Likhovski, "Hebrew Law," 348–350.

[9] In English the words "Jew" and "Hebrew" are not used synonymously as often as they are in Continental languages. This may be why the London chapter of the Hebrew Law Society, founded in 1925, called itself the Society for Jewish Jurisprudence, English branch. For a similar translation from Russian of the Hebrew word *mamlakhtiyut*, see Kedar, "Ben-Gurion's *Mamlakhtiyut*."

[10] Samuel Eisenstadt (1886–1970) was a jurist, scholar and advocate of Hebrew law, author, intellectual, and social and cultural activist. Born in Belarus to a family of Maskilim and socialists, his father was one of the early members of Hovevei Zion. He moved to Palestine in 1925, where he worked as a lawyer and lectured on Hebrew law at the Jerusalem Law Classes, the law school run by the British Mandate administration in Palestine. Among his other social and cultural projects were the founding of the Labor Movement Museum and Archive, the founding of the Tel Aviv School of Law and Economics, the founding of the Hamishpat legal publishing house, and the founding of the legal journal of the same name. He was also a peace activist and active in the League for Human and Civil Rights. On his life, see Ofer, *Man of Vision*.

[11] Eisenstadt and Dickstein, "Our Mission," 6.

Zionism: (1) the need to prepare a suitable legal (and cultural) foundation for the society to be established in Palestine; (2) the need to collect and study the legal and cultural resources that the national spirit had produced, prior to carrying out the Zionist project; and (3) the need to adopt and adapt these resources to the modern secular world by amending them and supplementing them with modern legal norms and values. These were the same principles that guided the national cultural projects that Ahad Ha'am had called for, principal among them the *Otzar Hayahadut* encyclopedia, which in the end he was unable to publish.[12] It was thus a dynamic enterprise that viewed itself as a bridge between Jewish heritage and legal-cultural innovation that would produce a sovereign Jewish community in Palestine.

The snag that would eventually frustrate the Hebrew law project is obvious. Eisenstadt's and Dickstein's Ahad Ha'amist position was not accepted by many other Zionists. Most importantly, it ran counter to the view of the religious Zionists. They also hoped for a revival of Jewish-Hebrew law, but stressed that it would be just that, a revival, not the creation of a new Hebrew law. They hoped that the Jewish spiritual and political awakening would spur new halakhic rulings that would become the living law of the Jewish people in their land. While most religious thinkers – jurists, rabbis, and other intellectuals – advocated new rulings, they stressed that these must be produced with the accepted halakhic tools – interpretation, legal fictions, and rabbinic regulations. As one might expect, religious jurists and thinkers also differed among themselves as to the extent of their flexibility. Some were closer to the extreme that feared modernity and the changes it required, while others recognized that the establishment of a civil society and state posed challenges to halakhic adjudicators and the need for creative, innovative, and tractable solutions. The range of opinions was broad, but all of them opposed the non-religious initiative to fashion a modern Jewish-Hebrew legal system.[13] It should be noted that, in many cases, the dispute was not about the final way the law would look, but rather on the ways of getting there, and the question of who had the authority to legislate. Most secular and religious jurists agreed, for example, that in the Jewish state women should have the same inheritance rights as men, but many on the religious side insisted that the law should not be worded in a way that diverged from the halakhah (according to which women generally do not inherit). Instead, inheritance rights for women should be anchored in ordinances (i.e., by authoritative decrees issued by

12 Ahad Ha'am, "Treasure of Judaism."

13 For religious Zionism's anguished confrontation with Hebrew law, see Radzyner, "Hebrew Law"; Stern, "What Is Jewish."

governmental authorities and not by the legislature) or judicial fictions. They also demanded that the law be drafted by halakhic decisors, or at least made with their blessing.[14] Whatever the case, even prior to the establishment of the Hebrew Law Society it was clear that a chasm separated religious and secular camps regarding the proper way to put a national Jewish law code into place. As such, rabbis and religious jurists worked in parallel with their religious colleagues to revive Jewish law, but along a different path. Among the most prominent of them were Asher Gulak, Chaim Tchernowitz, and later Simha Assaf and Avraham Haim Freimann.[15]

The Hebrew Law Society in Moscow could not operate in the violence and chaos that followed the Bolshevik revolution. It first moved to Kiev, then Odessa, but when it proved impossible to work there as well, its members resolved to carry on their project in Palestine. But even before its most important figures made the move (Dickstein in 1921 and Eisenstadt in 1925), a "legal society named 'Hebrew law'" registered itself in Jerusalem. It was not the same organization as the Russian one. According to Radzyner, the first

[14] On battles like this one over the law of inheritance, see Radzyner and Friedman, "Israeli Legislator," 181–221.

[15] Asher Gulak (1881–1940) was born in Latvia and attended traditional religious schools. He studied law at Dorpat University in Estonia. From 1926 to his death he taught Hebrew law at the Hebrew University of Jerusalem and was one of those who laid the foundation for the academic study of this field. He wrote some forty books, most notably *Yesod Hamishpat Ha'ivri* (*Foundation of Hebrew Law*) in four parts, the first of which was published in 1913; the full work was published in Berlin in 1922.

Chaim Tchernowitz (1870–1949) was a Hebrew author, rabbi, teacher, lecturer, and opinion journalist with close ties to cultural Zionism. While serving as Odessa's chief rabbi he grew close to Ahad Ha'am's Zionist circle, and began to publish his articles in Ahad Ha'am's periodical, *Hashiloah*, signing his pieces "Rav Tz'air" ("Young Rabbi"). Later, in 1902, he founded a kibbutz (commune) of young religious seminary students in his special style, integrating traditional Jewish study with Zionism. He studied at the universities of Bern, Berlin, and Würzburg. He moved to the United States in 1926, where he taught at the Jewish Theological Seminary.

Simha Assaf (1889–1953) was a rabbi, historian, and judge with a religious education. Born in Belarus, he moved to Palestine in 1921. He taught at the Hebrew University beginning in 1925 and served as the university's rector from 1948 to 1950, and was appointed to the Israeli Supreme Court's first bench on the strength of his expertise in Jewish law. He wrote many books on the history of the halakhah, especially on the Gaonic period.

Avraham Haim Friemann (1889–1948) was a rabbi, judge, and scholar of Hebrew law. He studied law at the University of Marburg; upon completing his studies he was appointed to the District Court of Königsberg, where he served until he was dismissed in 1933, after the Nazis came to power. That year he moved to Palestine with his family, where he taught at the Hebrew University from 1943 until he was murdered in an attack on a convoy to Mt. Scopus in April 1948. He was one of the moving forces in the Hebrew law project in Germany and Palestine, and the author of many works in that field.

initiative to found it came in 1918,[16] but it was finally established at the end of 1920, apparently at the inspiration of Yehuda Junovitz, a founder of the Moscow Society who arrived in Palestine that year.[17] Another branch was founded in London in 1925.[18] The dispute between the two camps, and the geographical dispersion of the Jews, meant that each branch operated independently and took on a character of its own.

Amihai Radzyner has shown that the Israeli society and the London branch were of a more conservative and religious cast than the one in Moscow. The Jerusalem society called itself a "Torah-scientific society,"[19] while the London branch termed itself the Society for Jewish Jurisprudence, English Branch, eschewing the word "Hebrew." When other members of the Russian society arrived in Palestine, they formally joined the local society, and Dickstein founded another branch in Tel Aviv, which he headed. But the tensions between the views of the veterans of the Moscow society and the members of the Palestinian organization were apparent to all. For that reason, Eisenstadt's and Dickstein's major cultural and educational projects in the legal field were independent, accomplished without any connection to the Palestinian society. Such was the case with the law journal *Hamishpat*, which Eisenstadt founded independently in 1927, with no connection to the Society's periodical *Hamishpat Ha'ivri* (although Dickstein was co-editor of the latter as well). The same was true of the World Hebrew Law Conference that Dickstein and Eisenstadt organized, on their own, in 1934, over the strident objections of the Hebrew Law Society, which went so far as to issue a statement making it clear that it was not sponsoring the conference.[20] So also was the Tel Aviv School of Law and Economics, another initiative of Dickstein and Eisenstadt, not of the Society.[21]

Ostensibly, the Hebrew Law Society in Palestine was a success. Many of the Yishuv's prominent jurists joined it, and it also enjoyed the support of no few intellectuals and rabbis. Among these were Gad Frumkin, the Jewish justice on the Mandate administration's Supreme Court; Mordechai Eliash, one of the most important lawyers in the country and later Israel's first ambassador to

16 The claim is made in Frumkin's autobiography, *A Judge's Path*. In Radzyner, "Hebrew Law," 148.

17 So Radzyner argues there.

18 On the London Society, see Radzyner, *Mishpat Yehudi*.

19 Ordinances of the Hebrew Law Society, Jerusalem 1921, 3–4. The Central Zionist Archives (hereafter CZA), A417/1, book no. 20.255. Cited in Radzyner, "Hebrew Law," 149. And see generally there pp. 144–152.

20 Radzyner, "Hebrew Law," 162–176.

21 On the Tel Aviv School of Law and Economics, see Cohen, "School of Law and Economics."

Great Britain; and Norman Bentwich, a Zionist who was the Mandate administration's first attorney general.[22] The Society had three branches in Palestine, in Jerusalem, Tel Aviv, and Haifa (although the later branch seems not to have been active), as well as the branch in London. The members organized a national convention in 1926 to discuss the revival of Hebrew law, lectured before a variety of audiences, put out a journal, *Hamishpat Ha'ivri*, produced legal studies (even if not all of these were published by the Society itself),[23] and began (despite their desire to shape a specifically Hebrew law) to translate global legal literature into Hebrew. Some members also worked for the Hebrew Peace Courts.

But a closer look reveals that the Society's projects were not all that successful, and suffered much the same fate as the Hebrew Peace Courts. The works of the Society's members had few readers, and the journals ceased publication. Lectures stopped, and the handful of conferences did not provide impetus for important accomplishments in Hebrew law, or even for its study. The Society had no impact at all on the Common Law in Palestine, nor on the legal field during the Mandate (recall the decline of the Hebrew Peace Courts and the normative confusion that accompanied their work), nor after the establishment of the state. Hebrew law did not even become a fruitful area of research at the Hebrew University or among intellectuals.

True, different versions of it were studied at the Hebrew University of Jerusalem and, later, at the Tel Aviv School of Law and Economics, but the field remained marginal as far as most Jewish jurists were concerned, to the point that it became reduced to a narrow historical study of commercial law in the halakhah, far removed from what the founders of the Hebrew Law Societies in Moscow and Jerusalem had envisioned. Neither did the Tel Aviv School of Law and Economics fare well. While it operated up until independence, and later was one of the three institutions on which Tel Aviv University was founded, a close look shows that it was rickety from the start. The Hebrew University, the Mandate administration, and the Jewish Bar Association never recognized its high academic level, and its graduates were not permitted to practice law without completing their studies at another institution. It remained a "high school" (*Hochschulle*) for legal training, never becoming, as its founders hoped, an academic and cultural center that would fashion, disseminate, and instill Hebrew law in the Jewish society then being built in Palestine.[24]

22 Likhovski, "Hebrew Law," 343; Radzyner, "Hebrew Law," 150.

23 For example, Gulak's important four-volume work.

24 Cohen, "School of Law and Economics"; Cohen, *Academia in Tel-Aviv*, 23–75.

Moreover, not only did the Hebrew Law Society's projects not go well, but the Zionist movement and the Yishuv were, for all intents and purposes, indifferent. While members of the society tried to give the impression that their operations were influential and broad in scope, in sober historical perspective it is clear that the Yishuv leadership did not share this view at all, and unambiguously preferred to cooperate with the British legal system, which provided justice fairly and efficiently. The single national conference organized by the Hebrew Law Society, in 1926 in Jerusalem, was not attended by representatives of the Jewish national institutions nor by those of any political movement. Mizrahi, the religious Zionist party, was the only one to bother to send official greetings to the conference's participants.[25] Most of the country's attorneys did not take part in the Society's projects, despite the nationalist rhetoric that many Jewish lawyers used, and the fact that some of them were members of the society. They preferred to operate in the framework of the Mandate system, which they viewed as advanced, fair, and efficient. Jewish lawyers restricted the national-cultural elements of their behavior to an effort to insist on using only Hebrew in the courts and other Mandate institutions, and to specific battles to gain legal recognition from them for national cultural symbols, such as municipal bylaws establishing Friday night and Saturday as the official day of rest in Jewish towns and cities.[26] The larger public was also indifferent, in contrast with their efforts on behalf of Hebrew language and culture, or for Hebrew labor and the purchase of Jewish-produced products. They held marches, demonstrations, and other protest activities for these latter causes, but not against Jews who took their litigation to Mandate courts or against laws instituted by the English. Very few people bothered to attend the lectures on the revival of Hebrew-Jewish law, or to buy the few books and periodicals published in the field. In the absence of public support, and in the wake of the decision by most members of the Society to stop paying their dues, the project to revive Jewish-Hebrew law went bankrupt by the second half of the 1930s. The Society was unable to pay its debts (in particular, the loans it had taken to finance the fifth volume of the journal *Hamishpat Ha'ivri*). As a result, the few public lectures in Tel Aviv were canceled, and the journal ceased publication (after appearing at irregular and lengthy intervals). The Society officially shut down its activities in 1938.[27]

25 Radzyner, "Hebrew Law," 152.
26 Likhovski, *Law and Identity*, 155–161.
27 Radzyner, "Hebrew Law," 163.

At first glance, it looks as if the decline in support for the project of Hebrew legal revival, or innovation, was a product of demographic and social changes in the Yishuv. The Yishuv grew rapidly during this period as western countries limited immigration into their territories, so waves of middle-class Jews from Central and Eastern Europe headed to Palestine. Many of these newcomers lacked deep Zionist consciousness, and they were thus sometimes called the "no choice" immigrants. The demographic and capital growth that arrived from Europe and North America set in motion accelerated urbanization and led to the rapid development of manufacturing, commerce, agriculture, academic activity, and art in the Yishuv. The law needed to provide for the needs of this economy, and for those of a swiftly developing society, leaving no time for a deep discussion of consciousness and culture. These years were thus marked by the massive anglicization of law. The changes sweeping the country required the British to update the existing law and adapt it to the socioeconomic and cultural circumstances that took form in the territory.[28] The Zionist movement was concerned at the time with seeking practical political solutions, in light of the semi-official anti-Semitism of East European countries and the Nazi rise to power, and of the Arab Revolt that broke out in 1936 and the first proposals to partition Palestine. The consideration of questions of national culture was set aside.

The waning of the revival project must, apparently, also be attributed to cultural elements. The 1930s were not only a high point in the Yishuv's economic and social development, but also a period that shaped the identity of the Yishuv into a modern Western one. The immigration of middle-class Jews from the cities of Central and Eastern Europe, the Yishuv's economic and social development, and British support for these changes considerably reinforced the perception of the Jews in Palestine that they were part of the West.[29] The calls of advocates of cultural Zionism and of Hebrew law project to take up and reconsider the question of the new Jewish-Zionist identity no longer spoke to the Jewish masses in Palestine. With the country developing so rapidly, the Jews of the Yishuv felt confident in their Jewish

[28] Likhovski, *Law and Identity*, 168–169.

[29] Likhovski, *Law and Identity*. Likhovski notes that the reinforcement of the Yishuv's Western European image of itself was also expressed in a change in its attitude toward Oriental culture. The immigrants' encounter with the actual "Orient" (rather than just its Romantic image) and with Arab opposition to the Zionist project (which reached violent acmes in the disturbances of 1929 and then again in the Arab Revolt) led many members of the Yishuv to abandon attempts to adopt an Oriental identity; they came to prefer a European identity with "Mediterranean accents." These changes in attitude toward the cultures of the East and Europe were expressed in art, music, architecture, and in the law as well.

identity and their close links to modern Western culture. While they were a minority in Palestine, they were building an advanced "Hebrew" society with its own educational systems, cultural institutions, literature, art, theater, and music. While questions of identity and culture did concern them to one extent or another, they saw no need to express them specifically in the field of law, as the Mandate regime provided them with a functional and well-developed legal system that they generally did not view as alien or discriminatory against them.

I propose a broader explanation for the failure of the Hebrew Law Society. It was defeated by a combination of cultural factors, such as those that Likhovski and Radzyner posit, with a meta-cultural factor – the Yishuv's refusal to launch a culture war that would involve an attempt to fashion the contents of a national Hebrew-Jewish legal system. Given this refusal, the legal revival project was doomed. The Hebrew Law Society was paralyzed because of ideological tensions and struggles that tore it apart from within. The broader Jewish public, and the Zionist movement, did not extent a helping hand at the time of the crisis because they realized that the Hebrew law enterprise was hopeless, confused, and internally divided, and because the public was relatively indifferent to questions of identity and culture.

The tragedy of the story of the Hebrew Law Society lies in the fact that its death was foreknown. Modern Jewish history shows that the societies in Moscow, Jerusalem, Tel Aviv, and London had no chance from the start of bringing about a renaissance of Hebrew law, that is, of creating, for a sovereign Jewish society, a modern legal system based on the 2,000-year-old Jewish legal tradition. It was an ambitions and hopeless project for the same reason that most other cultural projects of the cultural stream of Zionism failed – since the beginnings of the processes of secularization and enlightenment that affected Jewish society, Jews no longer agreed about how to define their culture and identity. The Hebrew Law Society was founded after nearly a century of debate about culture between religious and non-religious Jews, between Maskilim and conservatives, between Orthodox and Reform Jews, between those who sought to update a culture based on Jewish tradition and revolutionaries who demanded an entirely new Jewish or Hebrew culture. Furthermore, the Society was founded some twenty years after the cultural polemic that shook the Zionist movement for more than a decade. In short, by the time the Society came into being, the Zionists, and in fact all modern Jews, were battle-tried and battered; it was already clear what potential for destruction was contained in the debate over Jewish culture. It was already clear that no clear resolution of the question could be achieved, and that the debate was harming the Zionist movement and was detrimental to its efforts to further Zionism's goals and to the development of the Yishuv. It is hardly surprising, then, that the Society did not gain any real support, or even any real attention from the national institutions, the Yishuv elite, Jewish lawyers, or the public at large. On the contrary, the burden of proof that the Hebrew law project was both possible and not fraught with danger lay on the Society itself.

The Hebrew Law Society thus had to make do with its own resources, both economic and intellectual. As noted, money ran out when the Society's members refused to continue paying dues and asked to leave. On top of that, the Society exhausted its intellectual forces in internal ideological debates over the nature of Jewish-Hebrew law and the proper way to revive and further it. It withered and the Yishuv, its elites and its leadership, extended no help. Once again it was a meta-cultural decision. The multiplying needs of the growing Yishuv made the need for a functioning and effective legal system acute. It was clear to the people of the Yishuv that the debates of the members of the Hebrew Law Society would not lead to the creation of a mature national law system, and might in fact impede that very goal. It would be detrimental to achieving Zionism's goals and to the Yishuv's growth. They thus turned their backs on the legal revival project, along with the pointless cultural debate it involved, and stuck to practical legal solutions.

The Yishuv was right. The Hebrew law revival may have been a heroic project, but in practical terms it was impossible to achieve, for the two reasons I pointed out in my introduction, generally cultural and specifically legal in nature. The cultural reason was that, for the previous 250 years, there had been no agreement among Jews about the right way to define Judaism in the modern world. This dispute made it difficult to define Jewish law and to agree on the proper way to revive, develop, and adapt it to modern society. The second reason touches on the law itself. Law is a social system meant to adjudicate a society's differences regarding values and culture. To promulgate a Hebrew code of law, one based on Jewish-Hebrew values, the members of the Hebrew Law Society would have had to take a position in the cultural polemic and formulate that position in a list of clear-cut legal rules. This need to take a stand and legislate would in turn lead to a dispute over a series of practical political issues, which rendered the Hebrew Law Society's mission impossible. Among the first of these problems was the problem of authority. What body was empowered to assemble the Jewish legal heritage, reformulate it, shape it into laws, and decide points of dispute?

In all this, the cultural polemic within the Hebrew Law Society was a microcosm of that of modern Jewish society as a whole. For an understanding of how modern Jews, Zionists in particular, wrestled with issues of identity and culture, the tensions and disputes that ripped apart the Hebrew Law Society offer an object lesson. Here I offer but a brief account of the various points of friction, to show just how high, and perhaps unscalable, the barriers loomed then, and still loom today, to reaching a determination of who is a Jew and what Jewish culture is, both prerequisites for establishing what Jewish-Hebrew law is. It is these barriers that stand in the way of those who seek to integrate Hebrew law into the legal system of a modern democratic state.

Before doing so, two comments are necessary. First, these disagreements are not paradoxes, or problems that could not be overcome theoretically; rather, they are practical difficulties. In the existing social and political circumstances, however, they are not amenable to clear and feasible solutions. Legal systems are designed to make binary decisions between lawful and unlawful, innocent and guilty, a characteristic that makes it even more difficult to conduct a dialogue and reach compromises and consensus on such questions. Second, the Hebrew Law Society's short life and death indicate that it was the project of a small group of intellectuals, shepherds without flocks, which held no interest for the larger public and leadership. The disputes I will recount were disagreements among intellectuals, by which I mean people whose central preoccupation, and identity, was the production, dissemination, and interpretation of texts, whether religious, legal, philosophical, literary, or otherwise. The disputants were divided among themselves regarding the proper cultural model to be used in fashioning Hebrew law and Hebrew culture – for example, whether the model should be religious or secular, traditional or modernist-revolutionary. They were, however, united in their modernist belief in the need to shape culture and in their concern that their generation was one of cultural decline. Therefore, if a rooted Jewish legal system and culture was not developed, the Zionist project and Jewish society would have no future. That being the case, all parties to the debate shared a sense of urgency and believed that they were engaged in a national project of critical importance. Not only could the project not be delayed, but it needed to be accomplished in advance of other Zionist endeavors – political and economic, for example – or at the very least had to be pursued in parallel with those efforts. This was the fundamental difference between the promoters of the Hebrew law project and the rest of the Yishuv. Both the Zionist leadership and the Yishuv elite believed in the fundamental idea of modernism, that societies may be shaped in accordance with enlightenment values; but they did not share the sense of urgency and anxiety of the Hebrew law advocates. Rather, they thought, it would be wrong to give the cultural debate priority over state and society building. The Hebrew law activists thus had no allies among the larger public and its leaders.

The major fault line in the Hebrew law community was the secular-religious divide. Most of the founders of the Hebrew Law Society in Moscow were secular Jews who sought a revival of Hebrew law through its adaptation to the needs of a modern Jewish nation-state in Palestine. In other words, they sought to secularize the law. While they wished to base the laws of the Jewish state on the legal principles and rules to be found in traditional religious law, they were secular in the sense that they did not consider themselves bound by the halakhah or by its rabbinic decisors. As they saw it, the halakhic literature was a national historic cultural asset that belonged to them as Jews, and that it was their right – indeed, in a certain way, their duty – to use it for their contemporary needs in whatever way seemed to them fitting. For them, the legal principles to be found in the halakhah were building blocks that could and should be cut and shaped in new ways to build a modern secular structure. Furthermore, it was clear to them that when the traditional Jewish building stones provided insufficient, meaning in cases where halakhah as it stood was undeveloped (e.g., in the fields of constitutional law and the laws of modern financial instruments) or where the halakhah was not appropriate for modern circumstances (e.g., inheritance), traditional Jewish law needed to be supplemented by appropriate norms formulated in the accepted manner of modern legal science. The position of the Society's founders in Moscow was thus much like the position taken by Ahad Ha'am with regard to ownership of Jewish cultural assets and the need to secularize and adapt them to modern circumstances. In this regard, Likhovski is correct when he maintains that, while the members of the Hebrew Law Society of Moscow used the term "revival" of Hebrew law, they were in fact inventing Hebrew law by creating a new legal corpus. While this corpus made use of and carried on halakhic norms, it used them to construct a new Jewish cultural-legal structure.[30]

The Society's religious members opposed this idea of "renewing" Jewish-Hebrew law, and certainly secularizing or recreating it. In their view, the Hebrew law initiative was a cultural project to found the law of the Jewish state on the halakhah, which they considered to be the national law of the Jewish people. The religious advocates of Hebrew law agreed, of course, that the halakhah as it stood did not always answer to the needs of a modern state. It thus needed to be interpreted and adapted to these new circumstances. But they stressed that this adaptation should be accomplished only by the methods recognized by the halakhah itself. This was true both with regard to adapting the form of the halakhah, meaning its codification, and with regard to the

[30] Likhovski, "Hebrew Law"; Radzyner, "Hebrew Law," 96–99, 144–147.

interpretation of its substance. Both these processes had to be accomplished in familiar and accepted halakhic ways, through interpretation, legal fictions, and the promulgation of rabbinic edicts of various types.

This larger difference of approach engendered a large number of more specific disagreements. First, the two groups differed on the question of authority. The worldview of the secularists was democratic and dynamic, stressing the autonomy of the individual. The individual human being had the right and duty to legislate for himself and to maintain an ongoing dialogue with the traditions into which he was born. According to the religious jurists, however, God was the ultimate source of the halakhah, and the authority to develop and interpret it was invested solely in authorized halakhic decisors, who did so in the accepted traditional way.[31]

Second, the two sides differed over whether, in fact, a distinct Hebrew law existed. This was a theoretical dispute over whether Hebrew law was no more than a body of legal rules, or a broader normative system that included Hebrew-Jewish values, principles of creation, and interpretations that cannot be separated from the legal aspect of the halakhah.[32] Most critically, however, it was a religious-halakhic debate. Many of the religious jurists maintained that laws governing relations between people or between citizens and the government could not be separated out from the larger sea of halakhah, which was a holistic system that could not be separated into component parts. According to this position, obedience to Hebrew law derived from and required obedience to the halakhah as a whole; the system's legal rules could not be adopted without also accepting the faith and tradition of religious observance.[33]

Third, the two sides differed on a range of methodological issues touching on how to renew or adapt Jewish law. These were, first of all, questions regarding the Jewish sources themselves. Secular Zionists demanded that priority be given to early halakhic sources, from the biblical through the pre-Talmudic period, which came from an era of full, authentic, and "pre-exilic" Jewish life. This was the period in which the exemplary works of Jewish law and morality were composed. The religious Zionists, in contrast, opposed this approach and demanded recognition for the great halakhic works produced from the pre-Talmudic era through the present day. Another methodological difference was over how to engage in law. The secularists demanded the use of academic and "scientific" tools that had developed in Europe – scholarly

[31] For the various aspects of the dispute over authority among religious and secular jurists, see Likhovski, "Hebrew Law," 352–353; Radzyner, "Hebrew Law," 117–124.

[32] Likhovski, "Hebrew Law," 354, 359–361; Radzyner, "Hebrew Law," 105–110, 124–132.

[33] Radzyner, "Hebrew Law," 100–105.

analysis, the use of the sociology of law to "translate" social values and interests into law, the use of comparative and historical approaches, the legislation of structured legal codes, and other academic analytic practices. The religious jurists, for their part, maintained that the halakhah could be modified and moved forward only by halakhic decisors using traditional means.[34]

There were also serious disagreements within the religious and secular camps. Religious members of the Hebrew Law Society disputed just how much innovation, creativity, dynamism, and boldness was permissible in adapting Jewish law to the needs of a modern state. These disputes were much like the debates, over the generations, between conservative rabbinic authorities and those who were more flexible and dynamic in their approach. But the huge force of secularization and modernization in the twentieth century, as well as the urgent need that emerged in Jewish communities to adapt the halakhah to life in modern secular democracies governed according to the rule of law, caused believing Jews to be faced with an extremely difficult problem.[35] In practice, they demanded that the halakhah change in a way and to an extent with no precedent in Jewish history, so as to produce a new halakhah, perhaps even a new Judaism, along the lines of the fundamental change brought about by the "Rabbinic revolution" that followed the destruction of the Temple in 70 CE.[36] Quite naturally, secular Jews do not consider such a revolution problematic; indeed, many religious Jews also recognize that the halakhah must change profoundly in adapting it to modern life. But many other Orthodox Jews are not prepared to accept such a wide-ranging revolution in the halakhah, certainly not one explicitly framed as such. At most, they are willing to agree to limited changes accomplished in the accepted ways, even if these small changes eventually constitute together a comprehensive revision. The modern Hebrew law project thus, by its very nature, finds itself colliding inexorably with the belief systems of Orthodox Jews.

[34] Likhovski, "Hebrew Law," 351–352, 359–360; Radzyner, "Hebrew Law," 133–144; Radzyner, "Between Scholar."

[35] The Israeli state is secular in two senses. First, most of its population is secular, made up of people who do not feel themselves obligated to obey the halakhah and its decisors; second, the modern democratic state is the realization of a fundamentally secular idea – that of the sovereignty of the human being, according to which people are free to shape their lives as they see fit, and are not subject to any outside authority.

[36] The destruction of the Temple required Jews to change their religious rites, and even their conception of their religion, from one based largely on the Temple service in Jerusalem (and less so at other temples or pilgrimage sites, such as the Jewish temple in Alexandria) to the rabbinic conception of Judaism we know today, which was a rather marginal view among the Jews of Second Temple times. For more on this, see Stroumsa, *End of Sacrifice*.

The rabbinic and political leaders of religious Zionism have held, from the dawn of Zionism to the present day, to the position termed the "integrative model." They have sought to integrate parts of Jewish religious law into Israel's state laws, and understood this project as both religious and Zionist-nationalist.[37] But in officially, explicitly, and consistently supporting the integration of Jewish into Israeli law, religious Zionist leadership has actually hidden its head in the sand. It has not grappled with the problems that the Hebrew law project presents to the halakhah, out of a messianic hope that somehow, perhaps by miracle, the project will get implemented without bringing about major changes in the halakhah as it currently stands.[38] Despite the religious Zionist leadership's longtime support for the integrative model, Orthodox Zionists really had only two real options – to entirely abandon the idea of reviving or renewing Jewish law and making it the law of the Jewish state, or to see it as a cultural-national, rather than religious-halakhic project. That would mean a project that preserves religious symbols in national law, while the law itself would not owe its authority to the halakhah and would not act in accordance with halakhic principles.

Most Haredim and many religious Zionists in the end rejected the idea of reviving Hebrew law, arguing that, in practice, the adaptation of the halakhah to a modern secular (and certainly democratic) state is simply impossible under current circumstances. That being the case, the project should be set aside, and the laws of the state of the Jews should be treated like the law of other countries, while waiting for future changes. In this view, the standardization and codification of the multitude of halakhic rulings is a difficult task that does not sit well with either the practice or the pluralistic philosophy of the halakhah. Furthermore, the halakhah is silent with regard to many issues that concern the modern state, its economy, and society. To update the halakhah in these areas is to contend with difficult practical and political problems. Whatever the case, the religious opponents of the Hebrew law project argued, the secular concept of the revival of Hebrew law is unacceptable because, from a religious viewpoint, the halakhah is holistic, eternal, and universal, such that no particular part of it can be carved out under the rubric "Hebrew law," to be transplanted into a secular legal system. In a secular democratic state, there is no way to bridge over the gaps between regarding the

[37] Stern, "What Is Jewish," 16–19.

[38] Since independence, this policy has found expression in ongoing attempts to impress the halakhah on Israeli law on various levels: a legal provision that refers to the halakhah to establish an entire area of law (marriage and divorce) and attempts to establish halakhic principles as binding principles in Israeli law or to insert religious norms into specific pieces of legislation.

secular democratic concept of the authority to legislate, based on the ideas of individual sovereignty and autonomy, and the view that the citizenry is source of legal authority. In the halakhic-religious view, God is the source of law, and only authorized interpreters may say what the law is.[39] The deeper significance of this claim is that the Hebrew law project is fundamentally secular in nature (at least in a political sense), one that explicitly rejects the religious force of the halakhah by replacing divine authority with that of the secular legislator. Izhak Englrad, later a justice on Israel's Supreme Court, put it this way: "The true significance [of the incorporation of religious law by the Knesset] is the ascendance of the legislative body over religious law in an explicit rejection of the super-human force of the halakhah.... Selective incorporation is an explicit rejection of the sacred nature of the halakhah, and thus has anti-religious significance."[40]

In contrast, other religious jurists enthusiastically supported the project of reviving Hebrew law for cultural-national reasons, principally the belief that the Jewish religion and the halakhah are the foundation of Jewish culture, even in a largely secular society. For that reason, it is fitting for the legal system of a Jewish state to be based on "Hebrew law," based on halakhah, which is the Jewish people's "national law." Even though this cultural approach is not detached from a religious-messianic hope that the cultural project will, in the end, reinforce religion and instill it deeply in Israeli society, these religious supporters were well aware of the religious, political, and practical difficulties that made it impossible to establish the halakhah as the law of the state of Israel. This was the approach taken, for example, by Avraham Haim Freimann and Moshe Zilberg; its most eminent advocate after independence was Justice Menahem Elon.[41] The latter later offered this summation of the cultural position: "It is not the aspiration for *religious* achievements that guides the scholars and sympathizers of Hebrew law, but rather the potent and healthy desire for *legal achievements* for the legal system of a young state – achievements drawn from the rich and wonderful legal and cultural heritage that is the birthright of the Jewish state and its citizens" (emphasis in the original).[42]

39 For the early debate, see Radzyner, "Hebrew Law," and his many sources; Shamir, *Colonies of Law*, 39–40. For the latter debate, see Englard, "Integration of Jewish Law"; Englard, *Religious Law*; Leibowitz, "Separation of Religion"; Edrei, "Why Teach," 472–474; Stern, "What Is Jewish," 19–20.

40 Englard, "Integration of Jewish Law," 119.

41 Freiman, "Jewish Law"; Silberg, *Inner Harmony*; Elon, *Jewish Law*, vol. 4; Radzyner, "Hebrew Law," 81.

42 Elon, "Foundations of Law," 252–253.

Two points of dispute arose among secular Jews (and among those religious ones who viewed the Hebrew law project as a cultural-national one). The first had to do with the past and the question of what was worthy of preservation; the second looked to the future with the question of how Hebrew law ought to be shaped. The first issue included the debate over the boundaries of Hebrew law: Did it coincide with the halakhah, or did it also express Jewish morals, the Jewish "spirit," or the larger Jewish heritage?[43] Here also belong the discussions of the question of what substantive sources comprised the Jewish law. That is, what were the sources within the halakhah – the Mishnah and Talmud, or also post-Talmudic sources? And what about Jewish heritage in the form of non-halakhic sources, Jewish literature in all its variety, or political thinking? Finally, there was the question of how to render these Jewish sources accessible to the broader public, religious and secular, that was not familiar with them.

The second point of disagreement had to do with the question of how a modern Hebrew law should be fashioned. Under this heading came the methodological disagreements that I addressed above, regarding the proper way to adapt the halakhah to modern circumstances – among them the most suitable way to conduct research into Hebrew law; how best, in practice, to assemble and codify it; how to integrate Jewish sources of various types; and how to integrate them with sources from foreign legal systems, such as Roman and modern law.[44] One issue that deserves broader attention is the issue of legal borrowing of norms from other systems.

The advocates of Hebrew law were preoccupied first and foremost with borrowings from Western legal systems, meaning the synthesis of Jewish law with Western law. They had to decide whether to keep Europe in mind or set it aside. Europe was the place from which most of the members of the Yishuv, at that time, had come to Palestine, and it was also the *lieu de mémoire* to which they were connected by sentiments of identity and culture. Beyond this, European culture was seen by everyone – new and veteran immigrants, from Europe and elsewhere – as the highest and most progressive culture that should be learned from and which the Yishuv should seek to be part of. (The multicultural views accepted today began to emerge only in the 1960s, in parallel with decolonization and the rise of the discourse of identity.) Most members of the Yishuv thus saw themselves as Western and European in that sense, and wanted their legal system to be part of that culture. For example, they wanted it to express the ideas of democracy and rule of law, to embody

[43] Likhovski, "Hebrew Law," 354, 368–370; Radzyner, "Hebrew Law," 105–110, 124–132.

[44] Likhovski, "Hebrew Law," 354–357, 364–368.

the concepts of property rights and freedom of contract, and the principles of Western criminal law. The advocates of Hebrew law thus unambiguously believed that the principal source of inspiration, and for supplementing Jewish norms, would be European law – Roman law and the European and American national laws that developed from it. They thus took it upon themselves to translate parts of the *Corpus Iuris Civilis*, the important Roman legal work composed during the reign of the Emperor Justinian.[45] Some of them urged the Mandate administration and its judges to deepen and broaden the process of anglicization of the law of Palestine, on the grounds that the Ottoman law used in Palestine was backward and inappropriate for modern conditions.[46]

Yet Europe also signified the wretched Jewish past and future threats against them there. For many Jews, the Romans (i.e., the "early Europeans") were those who destroyed the Hebrew-Jewish community of the Second Temple period, and their European descendants were those who embittered the lives of the Jews for two thousand years, until forcing them to flee the continent to any place that would take them in. For these reasons, Ze'ev Yavetz, one of the founders of Mizrahi, the religious Zionist movement, claimed, "We have no place in our court, in our return to our land, for Roman law, the product of the spirit of the people who exiled us from our land."[47] As anti-Semitism grew in Europe, and especially after the Nazi rise to power, a tide of disgust with Europe rose in the Yishuv. In 1938 Moshe Zilberg declared: "No one could conceive of tying the first steps of the Hebrew nation to the intellectual products of the German genius."[48]

Attitudes toward the East were also equivocal. Immigration to Palestine, meaning a return to the East, was perceived as a return not only to the physical Zion but also to Zion as an idea and ideal. In this sense, the return to the ancestral land integrated into the belief of the Jewish national movement that the political framework they would establish would enable to the Jews to found an exemplary society that would be a light to the gentiles. The Land of Israel was not just the place where the prophets of the Bible had preached social justice, but also part of the region that had been the cradle of civilization and endowed humankind with agriculture, writing, the city, and other revolutionary scientific and technological inventions, not to mention monotheism and biblical ethics. The empires of the Middle East and ancient Mediterranean and the Muslim empires that replaced them had also had

45 Likhovski, "Hebrew Law," 344; Radzyner, "Hebrew Law," 109.
46 Likhovski, *Law and Identity*, 157–158.
47 Yavetz, "Hamizrahi," in Radzyner, "Hebrew Law," 109.
48 Silberg, *Inner Harmony*, 198.

sophisticated legal systems that could serve as inspirations and models for imitation. The return to Zion was thus seen as a part of a broader process of the decline of Europe and the rise of the East, and many in the Yishuv believed that the Zionists, who had a share in Western civilization, while also recognizing the greatness and potential of the East, were the people most suited to lead an Oriental renaissance. In 1910, Samuel Eisenstadt issued an open letter:

> History calls us . . . look to the shores of the Arab Sea and the rivers of India! The great and ancient peoples of the east are awakening from generations of slumber and fighting for their freedom. The roar of national awakening thunders in the world of the ancient cultures . . . a new and enlightened society is taking form on the shores of Asia . . . the law of the peoples of the east is awakening . . . the east longs and yearns to be revealed as a forceful and original eastern law . . . that suckles and is nourished by the source of Eastern religion, which can complete and organize Eastern life. To this eastern society, to the secret of the nations, to the soul of which our soul is close, and our sentiments to their sentiments, we must bring our sophisticated law, the law of the ancient Semite people, first and foremost to the enlightened peoples of Western Asia.[49]

The passage shows just how awash the young Eisenstadt and his colleagues were with Orientalist perceptions, with mixed contempt and fear. Alongside their Middle Eastern romanticism, the immigrants from Europe also arrived with a sense of superiority over Eastern law and culture. The East was seen as a region that had declined and degenerated over time, to the point that it lagged far behind European culture. In such circumstances, it was hard to depict Hebrew law as nourished by and integrated into Eastern law. On the contrary, Hebrew law and culture were not seen as something that could beneficially influence the people and law of the east. Eisenstadt's letter was written in 1910, when he was still in Russia. His encounter with Palestine almost expunged, among most members of the Hebrew law project, all Orientalist romanticism. The national struggle between the Jews and the Arabs reinforced their negative attitude toward the east and toward its inhabitants and law.[50]

Aside from their ambivalent attitude toward foreign cultures, the Hebrew law advocates grappled with practical issues. What was the significance of legal borrowing? Should rules and legal institutions be adopted (e.g., specific

[49] Eisenstadt, "Chronicles," 31.

[50] Likhovski, "Hebrew Law," 363–364. It should be noted that Eisenstadt was a lifelong advocate of binational cooperation.

laws, or models of courts), or should only principles and values be taken from foreign legal systems, while norms, procedures, and legal institutions were shaped locally? Which legal tradition was most appropriate for the conditions in and culture of the Yishuv and the Jewish state? If Western law was chosen, then which of the two Western legal traditions, the Anglo-American or the Romano-Germanic one that developed on the continent? And within either of those traditions, should preference be given to the law of a specific country – for example, France, Germany, Italy, England, or the United States?

The members of the Hebrew Law Society thus differed on many profound legal questions. They all wanted a national Jewish-Hebrew legal system, but did not agree about what materials would be used in its construction, nor on the way to construct this new legal edifice, nor about who would be the architects and builders. The Society's problem was that it could not limit itself to an academic debate over these questions. On the contrary, it was founded with the purpose of shaping legal norms, building legal institutions (e.g., to assist the Hebrew Peace Courts), and crafting the whole cloth of a legal system that would stand ready for the Jewish state when it was founded. But this practical need, the need to create clear, detailed, and explicit legal norms (laws and regulations) added further difficulties to those caused by ideological tensions and infighting.

The practical need to formulate clear and explicit legal norms precluded, for Zionist jurists, the simple solution that became a safe haven for many Jewish intellectuals and public officials who addressed the question of Jewish culture. They avoided explicitly defining "Judaism" and asserted the abstract claim that the essence of Judaism was to be found in the general moral principles enunciated by the prophets and which had since appeared in Jewish texts over the generations.[51] Such a vague, general definition of Judaism enabled them to avoid disputes because those general principles were not in dispute. Paltiel Dickstein, for example, repeatedly demanded that Hebrew law be committed first of all to the spirit of the prophets rather than to the dry letter of the halakhah,[52] and humanist Israeli jurists, both religious and non-religious, today take similar positions and propose making Jewish heritage (especially the writings of the prophets) a moral compass and critical standard against which Israeli law should be measured. Two generations later, Ruth Gavison would write:

[51] Katz and Kedar, "Judaism."
[52] Dickstein, "Commercial Deception," 150–151; Dickstein, "Hebrew Law of Peace," 149.

> I hope that in another generation, when the Jewish children of today are sitting on the bench of the Supreme Court, they will know how to express Kant's Categorical Imperative in the "Jewish" language of Hillel the Elder. When they want to strike down collective punishment, I hope they will be able to invoke the Jewish maxim: "Each by his own sin will die," not just universal literature on the subject; that after terrible terror attacks they will be able to weigh Nahman Bialik, that "revenge such as this, the revenge of the blood of a small child, Satan has yet to create." I would hope that secular liberal Jews will choose to express their commitment to human rights by saying that: "A man created in the image [of God] is endearing"; . . . that Judaism is rich enough to help us deal with the whole range of issues presented in this world. It can inspire us and it can permit us to invoke our own sources when we come to deliberate and decide the cases that we face, in courts and in life.[53]

But, unlike intellectuals, educators, or political leaders, jurists cannot simply make a general declaration of moral principle. They must, in the final analysis, draft explicit rules of behavior and resolve specific conflicts. They must write constitutions, laws, contracts, and tax regulations, or preside over trials to reach reasoned rulings as to which side is right. The practical need to translate Jewish values into clear legal rules paralyzed the Hebrew Law Society and brought an end to the attempts to make Hebrew law into the living law of a modern society. The Hebrew Law Society collapsed before World War II, a decade before Israel was founded.

So it was that the attempts to fashion a Jewish national legal system during the Yishuv period failed. As early as the beginning of the 1930s it was clear that an independent Jewish court system would not be accepted by most of the Jews in Palestine, and the Hebrew Law Society's limited, intermittent, and conflict-ridden initiatives to create, or revive, Jewish national law were going nowhere. Ideological tensions paralyzed the Society from within and put paid its efforts to craft a Jewish-Hebrew national system of law. Furthermore, the Society's members eventually realized that the Hebrew Peace Courts and Hebrew Law Societies would not be saved by the public or the Yishuv leadership. The actual devotees of the Hebrew law project were, it turned out, few in number. Yes, most of the Jewish public and most Zionists supported the idea of national law in theory, but they took no part in the efforts to revive that national law, withheld their support from the Society's projects, and displayed no real interest in them. That was the case with the public at large as well as with the leadership and most intellectuals. In fact, the

[53] Gavison, "Democracy and Judaism," 356–357. And see also Stern, "What Is Jewish," 44–58.

Hebrew law project was, when it came down to it, a conflict-riven and confused enterprise, with but a handful of supporters and influence of only a symbolic sort, on the periphery of Zionist activity. No real functional and effective "Jewish" alternative to the British legal system ever emerged, and so the British system was adopted by Israel.

The effort to create an independent Jewish-Hebrew law system was, as a result, channeled into two narrow efforts that did not arouse cultural controversy between groups in the Yishuv. The Hebrew law project became a "law in Hebrew" project. Jewish lawyers expressed their national identities by insisting on litigating in Hebrew in the Mandate courts and other institutions. The revival of the Hebrew language was not a matter of controversy in the Yishuv (or among Diaspora Jews), and their insistence on using Hebrew in the courts was seen as both legitimate and achievable.[54] Second, Hebrew law became a field of academic study, without any pretentions that it would actually be implemented any time soon. Courses in Hebrew law were offered at the Hebrew University of Jerusalem (even though it did not have a law faculty at the time) and at the Tel Aviv School of Law and Economics. The advocates of Hebrew law hoped that the protected environment of the academy, shielded to a certain extent from political and cultural pressures and from the immediate need to reach decisions, would make it possible to address the issue in depth and develop it to the point where it could offer a legal system for the Jewish state.[55] These two channels presaged what would happen after independence. The Israeliness of Israeli law would find expression principally in linguistic ways (the formulation of all laws and legal documents in Hebrew) and in formal ways (e.g., by crafting an Israeli code officially independent of foreign codes), while the debate over the Jewish-Hebrew-Israeli substance would be relegated to the academy.

54 Likhovski, *Law and Identity*, 156–158.
55 Likhovski, *Law and Identity*, 161–166.

4

Why a Jewish-Hebrew System of Law Was Not Instituted at Independence

Zionist history seemed to be on fast forward during the turbulent years that followed World War II and the first years after independence. A spotlight shone briefly on the issue of crafting a national law code, but it soon went out. The period just before and after the establishment of the state are of importance here because it was then that the hope to promulgate an original Israeli legal system collided with the real world. Never in the history of Zionism had the debate over the nature of law been so full of drama and pathos, and never had so many people listened to such grand speeches about the need for the new state's laws to be based on the Jewish people's rich legal heritage. The leaders of the Yishuv and the state, the chief rabbis, and senior jurists, among many others, spoke out about the issue.[1] The disappointment was as deep as the language was lofty. All aspirations to fashion an original national law shattered on the shoals of reality. The passionate debate was incongruous with the facts on the ground. The historical moment at which the most dogged declarations about the need for a Jewish-Hebrew legal system were voiced was also the moment at which it was clearer than ever that Israeli society did not have the time or the human and other resources to take up the subject. Cultural polemics would delay, perhaps even put at risk, the creation of a functional legal system and the ability to grapple with the other enormous challenges that Israeli society faced. But, at the same time, jurists and representatives of the public also recognized that they urgently needed to be able to

[1] The issues of the legal journal *Hapraklit* from the two years preceding and following independence offers a sense of just how broad the debate was. The editors printed not just proposals and articles on the subject by jurists, but also the entire texts of speeches by national leaders and figures in the legal field. One example is a speech given by David Remez on the eve of independence: "We will certainly make it our goal to draw everything possible from our wellsprings, so as to water the field of law in the Jewish state." Minutes of the Legal Council, January 5, 1948, 2, ISA G-110/40. See also the speech of Dov Yosef there.

cope with a wealth of other issues – a difficult war, the pressing need to obtain international recognition, massive immigration, a severe economic crisis, and cultural and social problems deriving from these. That was what impelled the state leadership's important meta-cultural decision not to insert controversial provisions about identity and culture into Israeli law. Zionist leaders from Hovevei Zion to Herzl and onward had the healthy instinct to place cultural debate out of bounds. The result was a semi-official policy of tacit disregard for these matters that held until the 1980s, and which in large measure holds today.

Under Ottoman and British rule, the Yishuv, along with its political and intellectual leadership, could view the question of creating a national law as a theoretical one, almost something belonging to some future messianic age. This enabled them to ignore, in large measure, the fact that crafting such a system was extremely problematic. Once colonial rule reached its end and a Jewish state was about to be founded, however, the public had to address directly what Israel's law and legal system would look like. The British would be leaving, and it would no longer be possible to depend on their efficient and fair courts and governing institutions while putting off the question of a Jewish law for the land to the indefinite future. Quite naturally, the need to create a legal system for the state-to-be restarted the debate over the nature and substance of Israeli law. The question of its Jewish or Hebrew nature became acute. The question was: What would be Israeli about Israeli law?

The establishment of the state was a hugely emotional event for the Yishuv and the Jewish people as a whole, all the more so because it so closely followed the Holocaust and the young state's fight for its life. Even people who generally disliked pathos and emotional and religious language found themselves caught up. The successful establishment of an independent Jewish state was perceived as a pivotal event in Jewish history and as testimony to the human capacity for overcoming the greatest difficulties, whether physical, political, economic, or cultural. Many believed that, just as a "now or never" opportunity to found the Jewish state had presented itself, there was a window of opportunity to overcome cultural and political disagreements (and among religious Jews, halakhic disagreements as well) and to carry out a Jewish law revolution. The hope was that the founding of the state would require Israeli society to view Jewish law not as an academic subject or abstract idea, but rather as the living law of a fully sovereign modern national community.[2] On the one hand, independent Israelis would not want to continue to use foreign

[2] See, as one example among many, Globes, "Hebrew Court."

law; on the other hand, the new political, social, and economic reality would make it imperative that Jewish law become a functioning, up-to-date system fit to serve a national society with a secular majority and a large non-Jewish minority.[3]

Yet it soon became very clear that the establishment of the state had not eliminated the cultural disputes that had plagued the advocates of Hebrew law and the Zionist movement from the time of its origin. There could be no doubt that the elation at the founding of the state had not resolved those disputes. An indication of the coming dissension came during the initial discussions, on the eve of independence, of what sort of legal system needed to be crafted for the new country. There was not even agreement on what the Jewish people's national legal heritage should be called, as different speakers used different terms. Many contemporary Israeli jurists assume that the term "Hebrew law" had been in use by the members of the Yishuv, or at least by the jurists and intellectuals among them, since World War I. But that would belie the fact, already noted, that the public at large, and even the great majority of Yishuv jurists, did not participate in the activities of the Hebrew Law Society and took no interest in revitalizing Jewish national law. When the discussions commenced, the veterans of the Hebrew Law Society were chagrined to hear the person who had been assigned to prepare the law and legal system for the state-to-be – Dov Yosef, a leading attorney and doctor of law – using the term "Jewish law" rather than "Hebrew law." For example, at the beginning of 1948, Yosef made it clear that a decision had to be made as to "whether we will institute Jewish law as the foundation of state law, or instead take the laws of the government of Palestine as a basis and supplement it with laws appropriate to an enlightened and advanced country."[4] The fact that there was not even a consensus about what to call the Jewish-Hebrew-Israeli law that was the subject of the discussion shows just how much confusion there was, and what points were up for debate.

It turned out that the elation and feeling of brotherhood that pervaded at the time of independence (further reinforced by the war) could not be harnessed to the project of creating a Jewish-Hebrew legal system for the new country. Furthermore, the harsh conditions of Israel's initial years further impeded the endeavor. As time passed, it transpired that the new Jewish state

3 The call to renew Jewish law was directed not just at legislators and jurists, but also at religious halakhic decisors, who were expected to understand that it was their duty to lead a religious revolution with regard to the way the halakhah was viewed. In this view, the halakhah had to be adapted to the needs of a sovereign and largely non-observant Jewish society.

4 Minutes of the Legal Council, January 5, 1948, 3, ISA G-110/40. It should be noted that, during the Mandate, Yosef opposed the Hebrew Peace Courts.

was facing huge challenges, and even the most avid advocates of the Hebrew law enterprise realized that, under the circumstances, it would not be possible to put in place such a system on short order; the state would have to maintain, to a large extent, the Mandate regime's legal system.

Many in the Yishuv and the Zionist movement supposed that the international situation that followed World War II might well lead to the establishment of a Jewish state. But no one was prepared for how quickly it happened. Even those who did try to make preparations for the eventuality that a state would be declared in a short time – Ben-Gurion, for example – focused on more pressing issues, such as forming an army, and did not turn their attention to establishing a legal system. The rapid pace of historical events and the uncertainty that surrounded it made the situation worse. The United Nations General Assembly passed the decision partitioning Palestine into Jewish and Arab states on November 29, 1947; war broke out immediately thereafter. In the meantime, the British were unsure whether to accept the resolution and, if so, how to implement it; the indecision ended when parliament ordered a hasty withdrawal by May 15. These and other events left little time for the Yishuv leadership to set up a legal system, much less to institute a new, advanced, modern, Jewish system. The field of law was more problematic than others because there was no institutional continuity. The Yishuv and Jewish national institutions had operated under British law, which proved itself efficient and fair. They took no real part in the effort to fashion an independent Jewish legal system. It was thus now necessary to create such a system out of thin air. Only at the end of 1947 did the Jewish National Council, the Yishuv's executive organ, establish a legal department, headed by Zerach Warhaftig,[5] which was followed by a similar department in the Jewish Agency (the top Jewish national institution in Palestine, serving as the executive arm of the World Zionist Organization). In the wake of the United Nations decision, the National Council established a Situation Committee charged with coordinating and overseeing the preparations for the state. It also appointed a Legal Council to advise the Situation Committee and, principally, to plan the legal system and prepare the legislation required for the establishment of the state and the operation of its institutions.[6] The jurists

[5] Zerach Warhaftig (1906–2002) was a politician and jurist, and a signer of Israel's Declaration of Independence. Born in Belarus, he was a leading Zionist in Poland, representing the religious Hapoel Hamizrahi party. After immigrating to Palestine in 1946, he served as legal counsel to the National Council, in the first nine Knessets, and twice as minister of religions. He held a doctorate in law from the Hebrew University of Jerusalem and served as a lecturer in Hebrew law at that institution from 1948 to 1963.

[6] Karp, "The Legal Council."

who served in the National Council's and the Jewish Agency's Legal Departments, and those who took part in the Legal Council, were stirred by the magnitude of the hour and their role in this revolution in Jewish history. They also knew that time was short. Yet the war made it difficult for the Legal Council's committees to do their work, simply because their members were scattered among Jerusalem, the Tel Aviv area, and Haifa, and it was sometimes dangerous, even impossible, to travel. The Arab rejection of the UN resolution and the ambivalence that Great Britain and the United States displayed over whether to carry out the letter of the decision by sticking to its timetable for Britain's evacuation and the establishment of the two states created another layer of uncertainty, making the work of creating a legal system for the new state even more difficult.[7]

That being the case, it was clear from an early stage that the Legal Council would need to address only the essential work of establishing a functional legal system, which meant that it would have to be based on that of the Mandate system. Any attempt at a sweeping introduction of new laws, procedures, and institutions would inevitably be extremely disruptive, both legally and socially. The high-sounding rhetoric about doing just that might have been sincere, but it was apparent to all that the dream of instituting a Jewish-Hebrew system of laws and norms could not be realized in the near future. No one knew at the time when, exactly, the state would be declared, but everyone estimated, correctly as it turned out, that it would happen within a few months. Moreover, everyone realized that, in an open and democratic society like the Yishuv, an entire system of law could not be imposed from above, without public deliberation ending in a democratic decision, even if the laws were claimed to be good and proper Jewish ones.[8] As such, the Jewish-Hebrew-national character of the law would be expressed in the fact that the legal system would be staffed by Israeli Jews who would speak and write in Hebrew and interpret the law in an "Israeli way," even if the laws themselves had been originated by a foreign imperial regime, Ottoman or British.[9]

The decision to carry the Mandate administration's legal system over into the new state should not be seen as a deliberate act of adopting Western

[7] Harris, "Absent Minded," 44–50.

[8] In most of the best-known instances in which comprehensive new law codes were instituted, they were imposed on the public by non-democratic rulers. The Austrian, French, German, and Italian codes, to name a few, were imposed by "enlightened" absolute rulers, or in the transitional periods between revolutions or wars of liberation and the establishment of a democratic government.

[9] Likhovski, *Law and Identity*, 166–168 (Likhovski calls it "the second death of legal revival"); Likhovski, "The Time"; Globes, "Hebrew Court."

culture, for three reasons. First, Mandate law had to be left in place to prevent legal and social chaos, no matter where it came from. Israel was no different in this respect from other postcolonial nations that adopted the legal systems, and even the language, of their colonial rulers, because there was no consensus about culture and law in their societies. These nations wanted to avoid turmoil and culture wars between different population groups. Second, there was no real Jewish cultural-legal alternative available. By that I mean that there was no commonly accepted version of Jewish law that could be applied and put into operation by an efficient and fair legal system appropriate to a modern mass democratic society. Third, most of the Israeli population did not see Mandate law as culturally foreign, for the simple reason that most citizens saw themselves as proud Jews who were part and parcel of European civilization. Western law was not alien, imposed by a foreign ruler; rather, they too had a stake in it.

The advocates of Hebrew law realized that, under the circumstances, it would not be possible to institute a comprehensive legal system based on Jewish foundations. Three options thus remained on the table. The first was to legislate as many laws based on Jewish law as possible, or at least to add Jewish chapters or sections to existing laws. The second was to insert into the new country's declaration of independence or constitution, when they were drafted, a general declaration that Jewish (or Hebrew) law would be one of the sources of legislation for the new country (or perhaps even the principal source). The third was to have Jewish-Hebrew law serve as the country's residual law, meaning that it would apply in cases where there was a legal lacuna, that is, in instances in which judges did not find an answer to a problem brought before them in existing law or precedent.

The first option was discarded fairly quickly. True, following World War II, the advocates of Hebrew law were reinvigorated by the prospect that a Jewish state would soon come into being. While the Hebrew Law Society did not resume its activity, any number of "Hebrew" legislative proposals were drafted in different areas of law, and a number of proposed constitutions were written.[10] But these enthusiastic attempts were not successful – none of them ever became the law of the land. There was simply not enough time or human and other resources to scrutinize the suggestions in a serious way and to conduct open democratic deliberations about them. The second possibility fell by the wayside for similar reasons – it was not clear when a constitution would be promulgated and what it would contain, nor was it clear exactly how

[10] Radzyner, "A Scholar," 315, note 196; Likhovski, *Law and Identity*, 166–167.

the state would choose to declare its independence and what the legal force of that declaration would be.[11] Even at this early juncture, it seems to have been clear to jurists and public figures who were involved in the matter that such a formal declaration, as vague as it might be kept, would be no more than empty language that would nevertheless set off severe cultural dissension.

The advocates of Hebrew law realized that the most practical possibility was the residual law option. Section 46 of the fundamental Mandate law, the Palestine Order in Council of 1922, stated that, in the case of a lacuna in the law, judges were to refer to English law. The proposal discussed by the Legal Council was to strike this section and legislate in its place an Israeli provision that would instruct judges facing a lacuna to refer to Jewish (or Hebrew) law. In a series of articles he published following the UN partition resolution, Paltiel Dickstein argued such a provision could be easily passed and would not disrupt the legal system or society. It was obvious, he claimed, that there would be only a few such lacunas, meaning that the provision would not cause a disruption in the existing law, but it would be of high declarative value, and would accustom the legal system and the public to the idea of referring to Hebrew law. It would, he said, serve as a "modest avowal" that would make it possible, over time, an increasing use of Hebrew law.[12] Indeed, when this proposal was made (apparently by Dickstein) in February 1948 in the Legal Council's Sixth Subcommittee (which was charged, in part, with considering the place Jewish law would have in the new country's legal system), it was accepted unanimously. Participating in the meeting were Dickstein; Moshe Zilberg, a future Supreme Court justice; Felix Rosenblüth, who would change his name to Rosen and become Israel's first minister of justice; along with Warhaftig of Hapo'el Hamizrahi and Nahum Nir of the left-wing party Mapam, both of whom would chair the Knesset's Constitution, Law and Justice Committee. While the subcommittee convened in Tel Aviv in the absence of its members from Jerusalem, who could not get to that city because of the fighting, those present were a heterogeneous group that included religious and non-religious figures and representatives of both the left and

[11] In fact, this constitutional issue came up during the first year of independence. The Supreme Court ruled that Israel's Declaration of Independence was not a constitution, but rather a statement of the credo of Israel society. See HCJ 5/48 *Leon v. Acting District Commissioner of Tel-Aviv* [1948] IsrSC 1 58.

[12] Radzyner and Friedman have shown that Paltiel Dickstein apparently first proposed making Hebrew law the Jewish state's residual law in two articles he published in *Hapraklit*. Dickstein, "A Jewish State"; Dickstein, "Proclamation." And see also Harris, "Absent Minded," 34–35; Radzyner and Friedman, "Israeli Legislator," 226–236.

the right. That suggests that the idea of making Hebrew law the country's residual law was both practical and had broad support.

Historians who have examined the issue all agree with Dickstein and maintain that it this was indeed a proper and practical possibility that could have placed Israeli law on a Jewish legal foundation. They attribute the ultimate failure to do so to specific historical circumstances or particular figures who interfered with and halted the initiative.[13] Some assert that, in the end, the proposal was not accepted because the decision makers in Jerusalem, which was cut off from Tel Aviv at the time, disregarded it; because of delays in establishing legal institutions; and because of other chance circumstances.[14] Others blame the failure to adopt Jewish-Hebrew law as the country's residual law on Haim Cohn, who would later serve as attorney general and deputy chief justice. They claim that Cohn, one of the Legal Council's five secretaries,[15] opposed the idea and maneuvered between the Tel Aviv and Jerusalem members to neutralize the decision made in Tel Aviv. Cohn did not include the recommendation in the final report the subcommittee submitted to the Legal Council's chairman, Dov Yosef, and it was not included in the end in the Provisional State Council's Law Number 1, nor in the Law and Administration Ordinance, 1948, the two formal laws that provided the legal basis for the transfer of authority from the Mandate to the sovereign Israeli state. These historians all presume that the integration of Jewish law into Israeli law, certainly in the form of the residual law proposal or as a general (if vague) formal declaration, was not only desirable but also possible at that time. In fact, however, the residual law proposal was a sham solution, far more perilous than it was beneficial.

There are two reasons. First, the very existence of lacunas in law, and of the concept of residual law, is a subject of controversy among legal scholars.[16] Second, such a declaration is dangerous because, the minute it is included in a formal legal text, it ceases to be merely symbolic and becomes a binding norm. A declaration that Jewish (or Hebrew) law is the formal source of Israeli legislation requires the Knesset to legislate in accordance with it, or at the very least in its spirit, even if the Knesset does not know how to do so. A legal declaration that "Hebrew law" is Israel's residual law requires judges to rule

[13] The claim is similar to that made by legal historians about the Hebrew Peace Courts and the Hebrew Law Society. These failed because of contingencies and "local" conflicts.

[14] Harris, "Absent Minded," 44–52; Elon, *Jewish Law*, vol. 4, 1617–1618.

[15] On the Legal Council's five secretaries, see Karp, "Legal Council."

[16] I address this issue at length in Chapter 7.

according to Hebrew law in certain cases, even if it is not clear what "Hebrew law" means and whether doing so is at all possible.

Experienced jurists with expertise in legal theory and practice have, with good reason, taken exception to these proposals, and have voiced their opposition despite their support, in principle, for basing Israeli law on Jewish law. One such figure was Rabbi Avraham Haim Freimann, who had served for nearly a decade as a district court judge in Königsberg, Germany, and devoted many years of his life to the study, teaching, and advancement of Jewish law. He warned against an over-hasty decision to establish Jewish law as the future state's residual law. "Replacing the English Common Law with Torah law, and revoking all the special rights of foreign subjects [another subject that came up at the same meeting], are far-reaching changes and should not be decided on rashly," he said.[17] Moshe Smoira, a senior Jewish attorney during the Mandate period, who would later be appointed the first chief justice of Israel's Supreme Court, had spoken in support of basing Israeli law on the Jewish legal tradition. Yet he was skeptical of the logic behind the repeal of Section 46 and making Jewish-Hebrew law the country's residual law. He wondered, at a meeting of the Legal Council that addressed the subject, whether "this proposal has been made at Mr. Warhaftig's personal discretion, or does it express the official position of the [national] institutions?"[18] Haim Cohn took a similar position. On the eve of independence, he drafted an inheritance law proposal based on Jewish law (which never passed) and frequently thereafter addressed Jewish law as a Supreme Court justice and legal scholar. But despite being an enthusiastic supporter of reviving Jewish-Hebrew law, and calling himself the "last of the Mohicans" of the Hebrew Law Society,[19] he also firmly opposed declaring Jewish law the country's residual law.

It could be argued, at least with regard to Smoira and Cohn, that at one stage they advocated a Hebrew law revival simply as lip service to the national cause, for public consumption. But, in this view, these two men, raised in Germany, were in fact devotees of Western law and actually opposed the entire idea. That is a claim on the cultural level, one that views the failure to implement Jewish law as mainly the result of a culture war between East and West or between religious and secular Jews. In other words, opposition to declaring Jewish-Hebrew law as Israel's residual law had cultural-religious motives. But this hypothesis is problematic for two principal reasons. First,

[17] ISA, G-119/6.

[18] ISA, G-110/38.

[19] But see an opposite position on Haim Cohn's attitude to Hebrew law, in Radzyner and Friedman, "Israeli Legislator," 233.

the claim that there was a culture war is overly simplistic. It does not properly describe the complex positions of the parties to the debate, and creates camps that are in large measure imaginary. There were never really two contending factions, "Jews" versus "Hellenizers," the latter preferring Western culture and "universal" values to Jewish ones. With the exception of small and marginal groups, most Israelis then, and still, identified as Jews. Moshe Smoira, and certainly Haim Cohn, truly believed that the Jews are a nation with an ancient and glorious legal tradition that they should have pride in and use. Yet, at the same time, they were secular Jews who did not accept the authority of the halakhah and its rabbinic decisors. They opposed what they saw as attempts to impose the halakhah, as it stood, or to recognize the authority of halakhic decisors to make law for the state of Israel.

Second, the culture war claim is simplistic also in that it disregards the enormous legal difficulties – discussed above – involved in the ostensibly simple solution of declaring Jewish-Hebrew law to be Israel's residual law. For these reasons, both religious jurists, such as Freimann, and secular ones, such as Smoira, opposed the idea.

A better understanding of this opposition to the repeal of Section 46 and to making Jewish-Hebrew law Israel's residual law is to view it as a meta-cultural position. In other words, these were clear-headed jurists who understood the serious ramifications of such declarative legislation on customary law, and recognized the hazards that such provisions create for courts, the rule of law, and in the end for society as a whole. Smoira and Cohn in fact stood with the semi-official Zionist policy from Herzl's time, in that they sought to muffle cultural conflict and to keep disputes about identity and culture out of formal legal documents.

Another look at the brief discussion of whether Jewish-Hebrew law should serve as Israel's residual law shows that what was at stake was not a simple declarative act, but a complex and dangerous matter. The snares the law set became apparent in the legislative memorandum that Warhaftig prepared for the Legal Council. Warhaftig, recall, had supported Dickstein's proposal to revoke Section 46 of the Mandate law, which specified that English law would serve as the Mandate administration's residual law, and to replace it with one assigning that role to Jewish law. Warhaftig put it this way in paragraph 7 of his memorandum. Israeli judges would rule "according to the laws that were in force on the day before the termination of the Mandate, and in accordance with the foundations of Torah law and principles of justice and integrity."[20]

[20] ISA, G-111/3; G-110/38. This was a legal memorandum accompanying the law governing the transition from Mandate to state. The Law and Administration Ordinance, 1948, was drafted on the basis of this memorandum and later additions to it.

A quick comparison of Dickstein's proposal with Warhaftig's memorandum shows just how different they are. The former spoke of a secularized Hebrew law of the type promoted by the Hebrew Law Society of Moscow, while the latter, a religious jurist, spoke of Torah law.[21] The problem runs even deeper, given that Dickstein and Warhaftig represented only two opinions along a much broader spectrum of conflicting opinion. The potential for a culture war is plain. It was for this reason that experienced jurists and common-sense politicians opposed the proposal to apply Jewish (or Hebrew) law in Israel, even if only in the form of a general declaration or as residual law.

In the end, Israel did not state, in its declaration of independence, constitution, or law, that Jewish or Hebrew law would be the source of its law, or even have the status of residual law in cases of legal lacunas. The young state chose, at its founding, to circumvent the dispute that would be involved in grounding Jewish-Israeli identity in law.

[21] Dickstein, "A Jewish State"; Dickstein, "Proclamation"; Harris, "Absent Minded," 34–35; Radzyner and Friedman, "Israeli Legislator," 226–236.

5

A Hebrew Constitution for the Jewish State

How the Cultural Dispute Prevented the Promulgation of a Written Constitution

The refusal of jurists and public leaders, on the eve of independence, to address the question of the Israeli (or Jewish-Hebrew) nature of Israeli law, even by means of an ambiguous general statement, was one of the important explanations of why the young nation did not promulgate a written constitution.[1] At first, their position was not in line with society as a whole; Israelis largely agreed that the new country needed to adopt a constitution. As time passed, however, it became ever clearer that drafting and enacting such a document would involve large-scale cultural-political discord. As a result, many retreated from the position that what was required was a single and overarching document with a formal preamble. Instead, they came to support the idea of passing a constitution piece by piece, in documents that would eventually comprise a constitution.

A written constitution presented two problems to those who sought to base the state of Israel's laws on Jewish legal and cultural heritage. The first was that it is difficult, perhaps impossible, to formulate laws of Israeli-Jewish content, because there is no consensus about what constitutes such content. Precisely for this reason, achieving that goal was a delicate and dangerous matter that had the potential to ignite cultural and political dissension. In this regard, the question "What is a Jewish-Israeli constitution?" is no less difficult to answer than the question of how to enact a Jewish-Israeli contract, inheritance, or penal law.

The second problem is unique to the constitutional case. It grows out of the fact that modern political culture sees a constitution as the fundamental text of a polity and its legal system. A constitution establishes the state's political and legal order, and serves as a central civic and cultural symbol. It is the cultural

[1] Kedar, *Ben-Gurion and the Constitution*, 86–121; Kedar, "The Roots"; Yanai, "Politics and Constitution-Making."

and symbolic importance of a modern constitution that made enacting one in Israel impossible. Each political party wanted the text to articulate its ideology and culture, and each wanted to limit the place the constitution would give to other ideologies and cultural symbols. Under the circumstances, the Cabinet and Knesset feared that the debate over the substance of a constitution would deteriorate into cultural and perhaps even civil war. They resolved instead to enact a constitution piecemeal, meaning one without a preamble, consisting of separate articles passed individually. Such a process would sidestep dangerous cultural debate. I will address the general difficulty of enacting laws of Jewish-Hebrew content in the next chapter. Here I focus on the special difficulty presented by an Israeli-Hebrew constitution, and on the meta-cultural decision not to enact a written constitution as a unitary document.

At the head of the opponents of enacting a formal written and entrenched constitution ("entrenched" meaning one that can be changed only through a difficult and complex procedure, such as a special majority or referendum) stood Prime Minister David Ben-Gurion. The position of Israel's first prime minister grew largely out of his fear that the ideological and cultural dispute over the contents of the constitution would be futile and gratuitous and divert Israeli society from realizing the goals of Zionism and the crucial task of building up the state and society. Conflict over a constitution would plunge Israel into a maelstrom of discord and political battles over culture and identity that would be detrimental to the country's fragile sense of civic unity. Ben-Gurion repeatedly warned, when the issue of a constitution was discussed in the Knesset and by Mapai, his party, that Israelis needed to focus on buttressing state and society and should not get caught up in dangerous legal wrangling. "It is a pointless debate that will take up our time in the Knesset and the press, for no purpose, and distract us from actual action," he maintained.[2]

Ben-Gurion was not alone in these concerns. On the contrary, the danger of cultural conflict was highlighted at the very start of the Knesset plenum's debate on the constitution issue, on February 1, 1950. The opening speech was made by the chairman of the Constitution, Law and Justice Committee, Knesset Member Nahum Nir of Mapam, a prominent supporter of a written constitution. His speech showed just how politically and culturally charged the subject was, and how hard it would be to draft even a preamble. Twice in his speech Nir stressed a constitution's enormous symbolic importance. "The country's constitution," he declared,

[2] Minutes of the Constitution, Law and Justice Committee, July 13, 1949, 13.

> is important for us, because we want to say, in the country's constitution, what has been characteristic of the nation in the past, present and future, how we arrived at this state ... you, the religious block, believe that we have achieved what we have achieved by virtue of "the Rock of Israel" [God]; Herut [the right-wing Revisionist-nationalist party] will hold to its belief that we reached this moment thanks to the decision in January 1944 to eject the English from the country ... the labor movement in this country will maintain its belief in one thing: that the state was founded thanks to the fact that the labor and pioneer movement created the conditions for founding this country.[3]

Perhaps because there was no way to avoid it, Nir underlined the principal problem that faced the Knesset – the ideological-partisan fervor of many of that body's members, which prevented them from agreeing even on a preamble. The language used by Israel's legislators demonstrated that it would be impossible to get Knesset approval for even a formulation very similar to the declaration of independence, written less than two years before.[4]

The beginning of the debate gave a good indication of where it would end up. But Nir's speech also pointed to a solution – a piecemeal constitution, one that, according to another Knesset member, Moshe Unna of the religious Hapo'el Hamizrahi party, would have "no framework, no preamble."[5] This would sidestep the need to make the historic decisions about the issues raised by Nir.

Ben-Gurion, Nir, and others were not overstating their concern. Other members of the Knesset, the press, and the public at large were intensively caught up in issues of identity and ideology. The constitutional debate during Israel's early years was not about the structure of government or human rights; rather, it was symbolic and full of pathos, addressing Zionist and Jewish history, and questions of identity, culture, and ideology. The constitution's ideological content was then seen as no less, and perhaps even more, important than explicitly guaranteeing human rights. Contemporary Israelis viewed the constitutional battle largely as a struggle to determine their country's identity.[6] The contenders believed that the constitution would determine

3 Knesset Records, February 1, 1950, 718–719.

4 Knesset Records, May 8, 1950, 1306–1307 (MK Aharon Zisling).

5 Unna, *Separate Ways*, 254. Many Knesset members spoke about the preamble of the constitution. See, for example, a speech by Meir Vilner of Maki (the Communists), Knesset Records, February 14, 1950, 800–804. Notably, many members of the left-wing opposition, all of whom favored a constitution, sound much like the speech Ben-Gurion made against a written constitution to the Constitution, Law and Justice Committee on July 13, 1949.

6 Yanai, "Politics and Constitution-Making," 111–112; Rozin, "Forming a Collective Identity."

the Jewish state's image for many years to come, which was why they so fervently debated it. For example, the religious press was very much concerned with the issue of whether the constitution would mention God or divine providence, seeing such a reference as emblematic of the Jewish religion's standing in the state.[7]

Ben-Gurion closely followed the lively polemics in the press and on the street, as well as the discussions within each party and in the Knesset. The dissension in his own party and the Knesset was all he needed to grasp the highly charged emotionalism of the issue. He realized that the members of the different parties viewed the constitution as a programmatic document, a credo that would express their worldviews, not a legal document that established the principles of citizenship, laid down the structure of government, and guaranteed human rights. Ironically, Ben-Gurion, who was adept at evoking pathos and who loved to hold forth on Jewish history and the nature of the Jewish nation, took his colleagues to task for conducting what he said was a pointless, grandiose, and even religious discourse.[8] He had voiced his fear of hyperbolic fractiousness that could deteriorate into a culture war as early as the end of 1948, during a session of the Provisional State Council devoted to the import of meat. He did not address the constitution directly, but highlighted the difficulty of reaching consensus on formal legal-constitutional principles during a period of demographic flux and other major changes, and the danger that the attempt to establish principles, rather than to seek pragmatic compromises and solutions, could lead to culture war:

> Unfortunately, in this matter [the importation of meat], Mr. Shapira [Minister of Absorption and Health, of the United Religious Front] has mixed in a second issue, which is perhaps more important in itself than that of kosher meat. But many, and perhaps all of us, think that this is not the time to decide this issue, which is that of the relationship between state and religion.... And we, in any case many of us ... believe that, while this is a very important question, there are at present much more urgent matters before us, and they must be solved before this *Kulturkampf* takes place in our midst.... I doubt whether we are allowed, as we find ourselves in the midst of a bitter struggle for survival (and I am not certain that our struggle for survival will end even if this war does formally) to make decisions about religion and state. We are facing the difficult tasks of massive immigration, of settling the conquered territories, of housing, and the like. Is this the right time to argue among ourselves about religion and state? The issue is undoubtedly important, and

7 Radzyner and Friedman, *The Religious Community*, 84, note 239.
8 Rozin, "Forming a Collective Identity"; Rozin, "From We to I," 44, 47.

> the Jewish people will resolve it when the appropriate time comes.... For the time being, let us deal with what joins us all together.[9]

Half a year on, Ben-Gurion spoke in the same vein to the members of his Knesset faction. "Do we need yet another metaphysical disputation ... with Mapam [the Marxist, pro-Soviet party] and Herut and with Yitzhak-Meir Levin [leader of the ultra-Orthodox Agudat Israel Party]? Do we have that much time at our hands? Don't we have more important things to do?"[10] About a month later, he said much the same to the Knesset's Constitution, Law and Justice Committee:

> The constitution issue will send us off on a detour. We really like having theoretical arguments: one will demonstrate his commitment to the dignity of the Jewish people, another to the socialist revolution, a third to popular democracy, and yet another to the pioneering spirit. It is an empty debate that will futilely take up our time in the Knesset and in the press while distracting us from practical matters. But if the majority thinks otherwise, the majority will do as it thinks best.[11]

Ben-Gurion did not oppose discussing the question of Israel's Jewish identity, but he tenaciously refused to give the identity debate a toehold in legal documents. In fact, few political leaders (certainly not those who served in active leadership positions rather than serving only as theoreticians and spiritual guides) addressed issues of identity and culture as profoundly as Ben-Gurion did. He understood very well that the weaving of webs of meaning is important, not only on the personal psychological plane, but also on the social and civic level. Shared stories and symbols grant meaning to individuals and society; in fact, they create societies and bid them together. He knew, for example, that it would be impossible to promote democracy and a republican mindset that connects citizens if individuals do not feel emotional bonds to other citizens and to the civic institutions that connect them. Such bonds must be based on perceptions of a common identity and culture. He thus convened conferences to discuss Jewish identity, argued the issue on the pages of daily newspapers and in periodicals, corresponded and held dozens of meetings with intellectuals and young people who were interested in these questions, and impelled the Ministry of Education to draw up a curriculum

9 Provisional State Council Records, vol. 2, December 16, 1948, 24–25.
10 Minutes of Mapai Knesset faction and the party secretariat, June 14, 1949, 23, BGA.
11 Minutes of the Constitution, Law and Justice Committee, July 13, 1949, 13.

for teaching Jewish heritage.[12] Nevertheless, he consistently refused to ensconce matters of identity and culture in legislation, all the more so in a constitution.

Ben-Gurion's policy was in keeping with the Zionist movement's long-standing opposition to the cultural Zionism of Ahad Ha'am, specifically the movement's insistence on giving priority to the creation of a Jewish legal state over cultural debate about the character and identity of the Jewish people. Like other Zionist leaders before him, Herzl most notably, Ben-Gurion preferred to carry out the Zionist program and build a Jewish society and state over an internal debate about the nature of Judaism. In particular, he opposed attempts to formalize culture, meaning to determine Israel's character or a particular definition of Jewish culture in formal legal and political arrangements. He believed all his life that the culture and identity of Jews in Israel would be shaped not by an academic debate, but first and foremost by living a life in common.[13] It was a dynamic and ongoing process, with no end point and no destination. Ben-Gurion stated his position on culture in a long programmatic article, "Zionism's Mission at This Moment," written in 1941:

> History consists of stages, there is a chronology, but is there an end and a "final goal"? Who can make boundaries for the generations to come? In what respect is our capacity better than those of the generations that preceded us? We do not live according to what they said, and the generations to come will not live according to what we say. Each of us must do in his time what is incumbent on us, so that we may reach a higher stage than where we stood when we began . . . and as long as no regime has ever been established that is founded on the Jewish imperative "love your neighbor as yourself," we will not be idle and we will not rest. And perhaps this, too, is not a "final" goal, for no one knows the human spirit.[14]

It was not only that Ben-Gurion and others in the labor movement thought that it was illogical to address Jewish identity in the Jewish state's constitution. It was also the position taken by Ben-Gurion's rival Ze'ev Jabotinsky. In a speech he gave in 1937 to the Royal Commission that was addressing the issue of partitioning Palestine into a Jewish and Arab state, Jabotinsky said:

> I do not believe it desirable that the constitution of any country contain special sections explicitly guaranteeing its "national" character. It is my belief

12 Kedar, *Mamlakhtiyut*, 236–247; Ohana, *Messianism and Mamlachtiut*; Letter from Ben-Gurion to Minister of Education Zalman Aranne, November 7, 1955, BGA: Correspondence.

13 Kedar, "Equality and Partnership."

14 Ben-Gurion, "Zionism's Objectives"; Ben Gurion, "Reply to the Disputants."

> that one sign of a good constitution is that we find very few such sections. The natural and best way is for the "national" character of a state to be guaranteed by the simple fact that it has a specific majority. If the majority is English, the state is English, and there is no need for any special guarantees. That being the case, when I say the words "Hebrew state," I mean a commonwealth, or land, enjoying a sufficient measure of self-government in its internal and external affairs, which has a Jewish majority.[15]

Jabotinsky's remarks testify to the modern dynamic thinking of the Zionist movement. The role of a political (or national) movement is not to nail down a conception of culture for future generations, but to create a flexible political-civic framework and political and economic conditions that enable the public to freely shape and express its culture, and change it as it wishes.

When the Israeli state was born, it became evident that it would be very difficult to resolve ideological and cultural differences in a civic framework. In a state based on law, fundamental arrangements need to be anchored in legal documents that are implemented according to orderly and transparent processes.[16] Indeed, when Ben-Gurion realized that a constitution would, far more than furthering the Israeli state and society, become a point of ideological and cultural contention over the nature and character of the Jewish people and Jewish state, he grasped that seeking to enact one would present a clear and present danger to the Zionist project. The danger, as he saw it, was no less serious than that of Ahad Ha'am's demand to conduct a "spiritual" inquiry into the nature of Judaism in the modern age. Ben-Gurion knew that any such ideological debate would be long and rancorous, because it would make it much more difficult for the contending parties to accept formal legal documents; it would be much easier for them to accommodate themselves to unwritten compromises growing out of an awareness that these were necessary if all parties were to live together in a common society. He was particularly

[15] Jabotinsky, *Works*, 224.

[16] At least since the 1930s, religious Jews had also argued that the future Jewish state should enact a constitution. Zerach Warhaftig, for example, was heavily involved in writing such a document prior to independence, and then chaired the Provisional State Council's Constitution Committee. Some of the draft constitutions submitted to the Council, most notably that authored by Leo Cohen, which served as the basis for the deliberations of the Council and the Knesset, were written by religiously observant Jews. It was only toward the end of 1948 that the religious leadership took a clear position in favor of postponing the promulgation of a constitution to some later date. The motivation was not opposition to the principle of a constitution, but rather their concern that a constitution enacted at the time of independence might well set in stone religion-state relations that they did not accept. See Goldberg, "Religious Zionism"; Goldberg, "When Planting Trees"; Radzyner and Friedman, *The Religious Community*, 57.

concerned that the preamble to a constitution would raise issues such as who had "created" the state, and that the desire to have the constitution define Jewish and Israeli identity would be a divisive point of dispute. The upshot would be that the constitution that was finally arrived at would be a lamentable document that would do nothing to promote a sense of civic-republican community and which would not be to the credit of Israeli democracy. What it certainly would not be was an edifying text that would serve as the cornerstone of Israeli civil society. As he saw it, keeping the cultural debate on a low flame would contribute to underlining shared responsibility and partnership on the social, cultural, and civic levels.

This dynamic approach, which opposed setting matters of culture and identity in constitutional stone, was consistent with the opposition of many in the labor movement to an entrenched constitution. Both the opposition to an entrenched constitution and opposition to including definitions of identity in such a text grew out of a rejection of a static, "religious" concept of culture and law. By that I mean the idea that there are sacred values that cannot be changed and which ought to be safeguarded in texts or procedures. Ben-Gurion summed up his view at a meeting of the Mapai Knesset faction called to discuss the need for an entrenched constitution:

> A younger generation always arises, one more aware and deliberate and sharp, and what was sufficient for us will not satisfy it and will not bind it in any way – nor should it be bound. Not only are we not permitted to bind it, but we cannot succeed in doing so. It will break through [the bonds] because it is much younger than you are.[17]

This applies both to the debate over an entrenched constitution and to the issue of including definitions of identity and culture in a constitution. Ben-Gurion understood that the desire to ensconce specific cultural or ideological concepts in a foundation document grew out of the disputants' fears that the Jewish culture that they subscribed to was in danger of vanishing, that the Jewish nation was in decline. They thus sought to stand in the breach and defend the culture that they knew by anchoring it in a legal-constitutional document. For Ben-Gurion, that was anti-democratic. It was an approach that did not respect human autonomy and which misconstrued the dynamic and evolutionary nature of human culture.

The opponents of a formal written constitution, led by Ben-Gurion, thus did not reject establishing the structure of government, citizenship, and human rights in a positive legal way, that is, in a written law. What they

[17] Minutes of Mapai Knesset faction and the party secretariat, June 16, 1949, 25, BGA.

repudiated was doing so in the form of a formal constitution. For this reason, the Knesset resolved to enact a constitution piece by piece, without a solemn preamble that would address questions of identity and culture in Israel. This compromise was in keeping with Zionist policy from the time of Hovevei Zion and Herzl, which scrupulously and consistently negated cultural Zionism, and with the position taken by Israel's Ministry of Justice and the country's legal elite, which until the early 1980s refrained from including any explicit language on the state's Jewish identity and culture in Israeli legislation. It is this legislative policy that I will address in the next chapter.

6

Jewish Law and Legislation in Israel

As independence approached, many tried their hand at drafting proposals for laws in different areas. These drafts were generally written with great enthusiasm and a sincere desire to found the Jewish state's legal system on Jewish cultural and legal heritage, even if they were not fashioned strictly according to the halakhah.[1] As I have already noted, none of these private initiatives ended up turning into an Israeli law (and certainly not into a national constitution). For the advocates of reviving Jewish-Hebrew law, this was further evidence of a culture war between Judaism and the West, and that secular Western culture had shunted aside authentic Jewish culture. In fact, however, there had never been a relevant model of Jewish law that could have been put into operation in Israel. Even more to the point, there had never been a culture war between Judaism and the West in the Israeli legal field. Rather, there was a meta-cultural political effort to avoid a dangerous *Kulturkampf*. In the state's early days, it became clear that there was no consensus about how to define Jewish law and heritage, or on the ways to use them as a foundation for Israeli law. That being the case, public debate of these issues would be virulent and trenchant. The political leadership, Ministry of Justice, and legal system as a whole consequently chose not to enter into a cultural debate in the framework of the legislative process. Instead, the Israeli nature of the country's laws would be expressed in other ways – institutional, legal, and symbolic.

An interesting test case that explains the Israeli legal system's deliberate policy of steering clear of questions of culture, religion, and identity in law is the enactment of the new country's inheritance law (formally called the Succession Law, 1965). There was an urgent social need to change the outdated and problematic inheritance laws that Israel had received from

[1] Radzyner, "A Scholar," 315, note 196.

the Mandate, and as such it became one of the first important branches of law that the young state sought to put in place. In fact, the first drafts of the law were composed even before independence. For this reason, the inheritance law suffered from a "cultural pediatric disease" that later laws avoided. The law's initial draft was written at a time when many jurists still believed that Israeli law could be based in large measure on the halakhah. Its chronological primacy and the earnest effort to base it on halakhah put it at the center of a scathing cultural and political conflict, one of precisely the kind that Ben-Gurion and many other members of the political and legal elite sought to avoid in the matter of the constitution. The history of the inheritance law thus offers an interesting – and sobering – glimpse of the kind of dangerous culture war and associated political struggle that was liable to break out around the constitution question. The story of the successive forms the legislation took, and of its final enactment, demonstrates quite well why the state of Israel did well to turn its back on private bills of a "Hebrew" nature that were written on the eve of independence. It also offers a very good explanation of the Justice Ministry's semi-official policy after independence.[2]

It was clear to jurists under the British Mandate that inheritance law required a complete overhaul. Mandate law in this area was a jumble of Ottoman and British provisions, most of them based on the laws of different faith communities. It was not appropriate for the economic and political life of a modern polity, in particular because it discriminated against women and girls.[3] Consequently, in January 1948, Dov Yosef, chairman of the Legal Council, asked Haim Cohn, one of the Council's secretaries, to prepare a draft of a new inheritance law.[4] Rabbi Isaac Halevi Herzog, the Yishuv's and later the state's chief Ashkenazi rabbi, also sought to revive the Jewish laws of inheritance.[5] Cohn's initial draft of parts of the law were circulated prior to independence, and the first full draft was released about a year thereafter.

Yosef seems to have assigned Cohn to write the draft because of the latter's biography, and because Cohn had already published a proposed law governing wills.[6] Cohn came from a devout family in Lübeck, Germany, abandoned religious observance during his twenties, and became a prominent voice against religion and the political influence of the religious community and their political parties. Despite this, Cohn retained a profound respect for

2 Radzyner and Friedman, "Israeli Legislator," 181–214.

3 Radzyner and Friedman, "Israeli Legislator," 202, note 132.

4 ISA G-110/40; Radzyner and Friedman, "Israeli Legislator," 188.

5 On Rabbi Herzog's proposed law, see Radzyner and Friedman, "Israeli Legislator," 182.

6 On Cohn's proposed law on wills, see Radzyner and Friedman, "Israeli Legislator," 175, 181–185.

and interest in Jewish heritage, learning, and law, and believed that these should serve as the basis for Israel's laws. Furthermore, Cohn had, since his youth, seen himself as one of the only people who could actually take on this task. He boasted great expertise in the halakhah and halakhic thinking, production, and interpretation, and was committed to the Hebrew law project of Dickstein and Eisenstadt. After independence, and late in his life, Cohn viewed himself as the last acolyte of Ahad Ha'am in the legal field, a committed secularist who remained dedicated to the preservation of Jewish heritage and the revival of Jewish law in the spirit of the Hebrew Law Society of Moscow. He was indeed a relic in an area that came to be divided between the national-religious jurists who for all practical purposes took over the Hebrew law project (even if they were deeply divided among themselves about the goals and feasibility of the project) and the secular "culturists" who were enthusiasts of the idea but lacked serious knowledge of the halakhah (and who were, like their religious counterparts, unable to reach a consensus about what constituted Hebrew law and Jewish culture). Unlike them, Cohn had both the required knowledge and the commitment and enthusiasm.[7]

Following Cohn's participation in the First World Congress of Jewish Studies, held in Jerusalem in 1947, he took up the complicated subject of inheritance law, beginning with the issue of testate succession.[8] It was a classic Hebrew law project, ostensibly a direct consequence of the secular Hebrew Law Society of Moscow's credo. He deliberately gave his first article on the subject the title "Proposed Rabbinic Rulings in Inheritance Laws." In this early period of his efforts, Cohn wanted to show that he was not a halakhic reformer but rather a codifier of existing provisions of Jewish law.

His proposed law of testate succession actually prompted few reactions. His first proposal seems to have been disregarded for two reasons. First, he drew it up prior to the UN partition decision, meaning that the issue was still a theoretical rather than a practical one at the time. That made it possible for Cohn to dodge, to a certain extent, the question of who had the final authority to generate law in the Jewish state. Did that power reside in the legislature and national courts, or did it lay in the hands of traditional halakhic decisors? Second, his proposal addressed only testate succession, not all of inheritance law. As such, Cohn grappled largely with technical halakhic difficulties of a

7 Cohn, "Looking Ahead," and see Cohn, "Yesterday's Concern."

8 Inheritance law has two parts, testate (dealing with a person who wills the division of his property after his death) and intestate (when the deceased has not left a will). In these latter cases, the law of inheritance, along with judicial rulings and the legal customs that derive from it, determine how the property will be divided.

type that the halakhah had addressed over many generations, such as the proper way to prove that a commitment has been given to grant possession in a will.[9]

Cohn's second draft, however, aroused the ire of halakhic authorities and leaders of the religious public. He composed it during the two months prior to independence, while serving as secretary to the Legal Council and in close contact with the Yishuv's legal and political elite. The second draft differed from the first in two principal ways. First, with independence approaching, the question of institutional authority was on the table. While Cohn himself did not directly address the issue in his proposal, it was clear that it would be necessary to decide the question of who would determine what the law was in the new state. Second, Cohn expanded his proposal into a comprehensive law of inheritance, both testate and intestate. He thus had to take the bull by the horns and address the fact that the halakhah, as it stood, was incompatible with contemporary social and political values and modern economic life. In particular, he needed to deal with the halakhah's unequal treatment of girls and women and with its principle of primogeniture, in which the eldest heir is given preference. On these issues, and several others, Cohn indeed diverged from the halakhah; his draft treated male and female heirs equally, as it treated the parents of the deceased and their descendants (if the deceased had no children). It also did away with the preference for the eldest son. After independence, Cohn was appointed director-general of the Ministry of Justice and state attorney, and about two years later to the post of attorney general. His proposal served as the basis for proposals for inheritance laws that the Justice Ministry drafted during the 1950s.

Cohn was a freethinking Jew who did not see himself bound by the halakhah and its rabbinic decisors. For him, Jewish law was a cultural asset that belonged to all Jews, who could use it in a free and dynamic manner, not a code of divine origin to be interpreted and expounded only by rabbinic decisors. Furthermore, he was also an enthusiastic modernist and Zionist. He viewed the Zionist project as a modern one, an expression of the sovereignty of the autonomous individual, a member of a society that legislates for itself according to the demands of changing values and the dynamic needs of life. Even though he was prepared to adopt not only the substance of the

9 Premodern legal systems dealt with the question of how to guarantee that a pledge to transfer possession was freely made. The three principal ways of ascertaining this are a ceremonial declaration that changes the legal situation (*verba solemnia*), a written assurance, or the symbolic transfer of an asset by the buyer to the seller at the time the latter takes upon himself the obligation to transfer the object or property he is selling to the buyer; in halakhah this procedure is referred to as *kinyan sudar*.

halakhah but also its ways of thinking and innovation, Cohn differed from his religious colleagues on at least two important matters. First, he thought that the halakhah as it stood should be changed wherever it was incompatible with modern life and values. He maintained that the halakhah of his time had lost the creativity that had been one of its traditional hallmarks, and was unable to accommodate to the dynamism of human life out of fear of modernity and secularization. Unlike most modern halakhic authorities, Cohn thought that the methods of halakhic innovation and interpretation familiar since the Second Temple period could be harnessed to renew Jewish law while adhering to its style and fundamental values. In the case of inheritance, for example, he thought that a modern law could remain faithful to the general principles of the tradition without needing to adopt the whole web of provisions that had been derived from these principles over the course of many generations. As such, he had no compunctions about fashioning entirely new provisions deviating from the halakhah as it stood, when the halakhah contradicted modern values.

Second, Cohn believed that Hebrew and Israeli law were permitted, indeed obligated, to take inspiration also from foreign legal systems and ways of thinking, and to import legal solutions fashioned elsewhere that better fit the modern world than existing halakhah. Jewish law had always been profoundly influenced from the outside, he argued, but halakhic decisors generally refused to recognize that it was legitimate to want to bring Jewish law into accord with the laws of the rest of the world. Halakhic decisors did not accept the desire to be part of the global community of nations as a legitimate motive for changing Jewish law; on the contrary, the opposite was true.[10] Cohn quickly found that rabbis, religious jurists, and religious communal leaders stridently opposed his proposals.

The reactions of rabbis and religious jurists to Cohn's proposals can be divided into three groups. Some, most prominently Avraham Haim Freimann, accepted Cohn's draft in principle because, in their view, the Hebrew law project was a national-cultural rather than a religious one. Cognizant of Cohn's divergence from the halakhah, they may well have seen it as a contribution to the revival and renewal of Jewish law. After all, the draft was largely based on the halakhah, and made innovations and adapted Jewish law to modern conditions in places where everyone agreed that such innovation was necessary.[11] Others, like Zerach Warhaftig, categorically rejected the

[10] Radzyner and Friedman, "Israeli Legislator," 181–186.

[11] Radzyner and Friedman, "Israeli Legislator," 191–194. The authors point out that Freimann offered many other criticisms as well. For example, he thought it was too "capitalistic." But he did not reject

proposal on the grounds that it clearly deviated from the halakhah, and indeed did so openly and explicitly, rather than through the use of fictions or *takanot* (singular: *taknah*), rabbinic edicts that provide solutions to problems that standard halakhic reasoning cannot solve. This group demanded the formulation of an alternative proposal consistent with the halakhah and its accepted means of innovation, but never offered one.[12] A third group, the most prominent member of which was Rabbi Shlomo Goren, Chief Military Rabbi of the Israeli Defense Forces (IDF), criticized the draft's deviation from the halakhah, but focused on procedural issues. They agreed that the halakhah urgently required revision on the matters of inheritance by women and primogeniture. But at issue was the proper way to do so. Goren argued that, in a Jewish state, the Knesset could not enact a primary law (what he called a "constitutional law") that explicitly diverged from the halakhah. Such laws should accord in their provisions to halakhic status quo. The necessary changes should be made in the form of secondary legislation or administrative regulations that would grant inheritance rights to women and girls.[13]

The potent symbolism of the law and the cultural-political debate that it aroused long delayed its enactment. Despite the urgent social need for a comprehensive modern inheritance law in Israel, and despite the fact that the legislative process began on the eve of independence, a new Israeli law of inheritance went into force only in 1965. The saga of its enactment offers an object lesson in what would have happened if the Knesset had decided to enact a constitution for Israel as a single formal document.

The conflict over Cohn's draft law prompted the top officials in the Justice Ministry, led by Cohn and Uri Yadin, head of the Future Legislative Planning Department, which later became the Legislative Department, to abandon the effort to base Israeli law on the halakhah to every extent possible. Instead, they decided to draft legislation according to the needs and values of Israeli society. The halakhah and Jewish heritage would serve as only one of many sources of inspiration. According to Cohn, after the inheritance law affair, he tried "to bring Hebrew law into Israeli law not by the main road, but by detours,

it out of hand because it deviated from the halakhah. A similar position seems to have been taken by Moshe Unna, a member of the Knesset representing the Religious Kibbutz Movement. See Unna, *Separate Ways*, 96–101.

12 Radzyner and Friedman, "Israeli Legislator," 194–197.

13 Radzyner and Friedman, "Israeli Legislator," 208. It should be noted that Rabbi Goren was not responding to Cohn's proposal, but rather to a draft succession bill later produced by the Justice Ministry, based on Cohn's proposal.

through the back door."[14] This new policy was already evident in the supplementary material to the inheritance law drafted by the ministry in 1952:

> We have seen Hebrew law as a major, but not mandatory or sole source. Our proposal is not a codification of the norms of Hebrew law, not as they are found in the *Shukhan Arukh* and its commentaries, not even with adjustments to current needs. In those places where the proposed law deviates from Hebrew law, we have not used legal fictions, but have rather stated the matters directly, freely styled, unfettered by traditional formulations (such as the form of a will), but in the final analysis we have sought to keep our proposal as close as possible to Hebrew law, and in some matters – among them the most fundamental, such as maintenance from an estate – we see our proposal as a kind of extension of Hebrew law.[15]

Cohn, Yadin, and others would later relate that the Legislative Department did not really seek "to keep . . . proposal[s] as close as possible to Hebrew law," and did not see Jewish law as a principal source of inspiration for legislation. Instead, it turned to Jewish law only when it accorded with the present needs and values of Israeli society. Such was the case with the inheritance law, they claimed, as well as with other laws. According to Yadin, "It transpires that the call 'bring us Hebrew law' is a nice and desirable slogan, but its transformation from the abstract to the practical runs into many problems. It may well be that the time has not yet arrived, and that we do not yet have the jurists and scholars who are able to take up this heavy task."[16]

In this, Yadin voiced the policy that the Legislative Department has followed to this day. Israel enacts laws in accordance with its needs and values. Israeli law has a wide range of sources of inspiration. As the country is a modern industrialized society, the Ministry of Justice takes under consideration similar relevant arrangements in other industrialized countries. This does not mean that the halakhah (now referred to as Hebrew law) does not serve as source. Indeed, in 1959 the ministry established the position of special adviser on Jewish law, later expanding that post into a small department that is meant to provide the drafters of legislation in the Knesset and ministry with the relevant halakhic material and positions. The halakhic position on issues that require legislation is indeed brought before the staff that formulates laws, but the quotes above show that the halakhah is taken into consideration only

[14] Shashar, *Haim Cohn*, 110.

[15] Succession Law proposal (1952), Explanatory notes, 6–7, ISA, GL-21864/2.

[16] Yadin, "The Succession Law," 194. For Cohn's similar ideas, see Radzyner and Friedman, "Israeli Legislator," 219–221.

when it is consistent with current social and economic needs, as the legislators understand them. In other words, the Ministry of Justice and Knesset do not see the halakhah as a primary source of inspiration, above others, and certainly not one that binds them. At times it looks as if the ministry examines draft legislation's accordance with Jewish law only when the drafts are already in nearly final form. The authors of the draft and the minister of justice make a point of underlining those places in which the proposal resembles halakhic arrangements, even if those arrangements were not actually inspired by the halakhah but were rather an original idea formulated in Israel or inspired by the laws of another country. The upshot of this way of working is that Jewish law has indeed a presence in Israeli law at some level – whether symbolically, or in the form of general principles, or on the concrete level of a specific arrangement – but this limited presence does not generally satisfy the advocates of the Hebrew law project.[17] Justice Menachem Elon, a scholar of Jewish law who served during the 1950s in the Legislative Department and later as the ministry's first adviser on Jewish law, put it this way:

> Although a considerable number of Israeli statutes are based on principles of Jewish law, that number, relatively speaking, is meager and much smaller than it need have been; and, in fact, various laws are in conflict with Jewish law for no good reason.[18]

Indeed, the disciples of cultural Zionism in the legal realm have criticized this policy. In the 1950s, veterans of the Hebrew Law Society, both secular and religious, protested,[19] but once they aged and passed on, the critique about the negligible place of Jewish law in Israeli law has come largely from jurists, scholars, and public figures hailing from the religious community. Religious members of the Knesset (from both the Haredi and national religious parties) repeatedly voice it in Knesset debates of all types, and call for a more massive assimilation of Jewish law ("Hebrew law" is the literal translation of the term they used) into Israeli law. An example is the platform of the National Religious Party in the elections to the Fourteenth Knesset, in 1996: "The movement will endeavor to found the law of the state of Israel in the principles of Hebrew law, and will act to promote the dissemination, study,

[17] On the place of Jewish Law in Israeli legislation, see Elon, *Jewish Law*, vol. 4, 1624–1729; Rakover, *Jewish Law*.

[18] Elon, *Jewish Law*, vol. 4, 1627.

[19] See, for example, Eisenstadt, "The New Codification."

and integration of fundamental Hebrew law in all the country's systems of legislation and law."[20]

Beyond the leadership of the religious public, another small and homogenous group has been vocal in its criticism of the paucity of Jewish law in Israeli law – progressive religious Zionist academics. They decry the fact that, despite the declarations of justice ministers and the ministry staff, Jewish law does not truly serve as a source of Israeli legislation, neither primary or central. Legislation that is presented as being based on Jewish law, they charge, is not actually so based; in fact, it sometimes contradicts the halakhah. These critics complain that the ministry does not explicitly acknowledge that it does not really see Jewish law as a source of inspiration for Israeli law. The ministry only uses it in a limited declarative and symbolic way.[21]

On the face of it, this testifies to a culture war between religious and nonreligious Israelis, between the advocates of modern Western culture and Jews who seek to preserve their "authentic" tradition and make it the cultural basis for the society in their old-new land. Painting the issue in the colors of a culture war is no doubt aided by the critique I mentioned above of the Justice Ministry's legislative policy. It seeks to create the impression that there is, in fact, a clearly defined and agreed-on Jewish-Hebrew option. In other words, it presumes that all differences of opinion on the nature of Hebrew law and the debate over it are only about the most effective and proper way of introducing it into Israeli law. The criticism of the Justice Ministry is clear and confident, and creates the impression that what is at stake is an eminently possible project that requires only goodwill and the mobilization of jurists and intellectuals to further it. This criticism is gentle and restrained, and does not include a demand to make Jewish law the only source of Israeli law. Rather, this group wants it to be the first source of inspiration for legislation. Its members demand "only" that Israeli law not be "in conflict with Jewish law for no good reason."[22] In other words, wherever it is possible to apply Jewish law, it should be applied. This depiction of the Hebrew law revival project as practicable, possible, and worthy creates the mistaken impression that the project has not been implemented because of a lack of goodwill on the part of elected officials and the Justice Ministry's senior staff. It is a small leap from that to a picture of the Hebrew law debate as another aspect of the culture war between, on the

[20] Cited in Stern, "What Is Jewish," 18, note 11.

[21] See, among many publications, Katz, "Role of Hebrew Law"; Lifshitz, "Israeli Law"; Lifshitz, "One Derives" (claiming that the Israeli law on unjust enrichment is not based on the halakhah despite its title); Radzyner and Friedman, "Israeli Legislator," 215–221. And see also Elon, *Jewish Law*, vol. 4, 1625–1627; Rakover, *Jewish Law*.

[22] Elon, *Jewish Law*, vol. 4, 1627.

one side, a Western-secular "Hellenizing" group lacking all empathy for Judaism and, on the other side, the guardians of the embers of authentic Judaism. But the truth is that there is not, and has never been, a real possibility of basing Israeli law on Jewish law.

The policy of muting cultural disputes by keeping cultural issues off the table became, after independence, the position of the national government. According to that position, cultural conflict was a danger to the Israeli republic for two reasons: first, because cultural dissension could easily deteriorate into discord over the question of authority, and even into a situation in which some Israelis did not recognize the authority of state institutions and the law of the land. Second, fierce ideological, cultural, and religious debate over the questions "who is a Jew," "what is a Jewish state," or "what are Jewish law and Jewish culture" could dissolve civil and national solidarity and partnership in Israel. State institutions therefore made it unambiguously clear that in the sovereign state of Israel, the question of Jewish law, like the larger question of the Israeli character of Israel's laws, was not a question that involved the *authority* of the Knesset, the cabinet, and the courts; at most, it was a cultural question regarding the content of the laws. Haim Cohn put this succinctly during the debate over his proposed inheritance law: "There is no dispute that the Knesset decides . . . the question is [only] to what extent the Knesset, when it legislates, should make use of Hebrew law. The question is not the Knesset's right to enact laws."[23] It was also necessary to make it clear that state institutions would not allow the flames of the cultural debate to be fanned, thus endangering the stability and security of Israeli society and Israeli law, even at the price of muting the cultural debate and attempts to integrate Jewish culture and law into Israeli law. Cohn, clearly echoing Ben-Gurion, told the participants in a discussion of the inheritance law: "The Ministry of Justice formulates legislative proposals in a way that it finds the most fitting to the matter at hand, and it is not its goal to revive Hebrew law. To the extent that the rulings of Hebrew law are appropriate, they are inserted into laws. The Ministry of Justice will continue to act in this matter as long as it has not received [other] instructions from the cabinet."[24]

Another important Zionist point emerges from what Cohn said, one that is connected to the other two. Most of those who insist on imbuing Israeli law with Jewish law have done so from a vantage point identical to Ahad Ha'am's.

[23] Minutes of a public meeting regarding the Succession Law proposal (1952), February 9, 1954, ISA, GL-21864/2.

[24] Minutes of a public meeting regarding the Succession Law proposal (1952), February 9, 1954, ISA, GL-21864/2. Compare to the words of Ben-Gurion: "The sovereignty of the nation is in the hands of the Knesset, not the Rabbinate," Knesset Record, March 5, 1951, 1244.

They believe in the existence of some sort of ongoing Jewish nature (even if one that develops, changes, or becomes secularized over the generations). Aside from the great difficulty of defining this Jewish core, the position holds that culture (and law) are static and essential, and that there is some sort of fundamental Jewish culture that each generation shapes and expresses in a new way, pouring "old wine into new vessels." This view is simply inconsistent with the modern dynamic and autonomous conception that is the basis of Zionism, according to which all human beings (and thus also Jews of this generation) are born into a specific tradition, but are nevertheless permitted – even required – to shape their lives and their futures by themselves. Both the Knesset and the Ministry of Justice of the Jewish state were committed to this fundamental Zionist republican worldview. As such, they could not agree that cultural assumptions could restrict, in advance, their ability to legislate. This is not a view that denies Jewish identity and culture, but rather a meta-cultural position that insists on sovereignty and refuses to be constrained by a religious or cultural "dead hand." According to this position, Israeli culture is a branch of Jewish culture, but it is not subordinate to it and may take from that culture what it wishes and neglect those parts that do not fit its needs. Jewish-Israeli society is not even required to imbue old Jewish symbols with new content – for example, to endow holidays and the Sabbath with new meaning. "The dead cannot praise God" (Psalms 115:17), Ben-Gurion frequently declared in his speeches. The culture of the present, he meant, is an evolutionary product that, of course, begins in past traditions; it is rooted in tradition whether it wishes to be or not. But it is the right and obligation of each generation to engage in constant reinterpretation of that tradition, and to change it if that is required. Along the same lines, Israeli law is rooted in Jewish law, but not subservient to it, neither to its substance nor to its templates of thought. Israeli law should not artificially preserve ancient beliefs and symbols simply "because they are there." It is the sovereign-autonomous enterprise of Jews who are bold enough to think for themselves and to legislate for themselves as they see fit.

The story of Haim Cohn offers a good illustration of this position. The failure of Cohn's initiative to write a modern, progressive law of inheritance based largely on the halakhah cured him of his "Ahad Ha'am syndrome." He woke up from the illusion that it would be possible to gain a consensus for basing Israeli law, in a profound way, on Jewish legal heritage. His personal background as the scion of an important rabbinic family who had nevertheless abandoned religion, and the speed and resoluteness with which he switched from supporting the Hebrew law project to opposing it, cast him in the role of a Jewish apostate contending with traditionalists. But a careful reading of what Cohn wrote and said, and a close examination of the policy pursued by the Legislative Department that operated under him in his role as attorney general, shows that this view is mistaken. Cohn remained an advocate of Hebrew law, which he studied and thought about throughout his life. He frequently referenced Jewish law both as a judge and as a legal scholar. The change in his conduct did not result from a change of attitude with regard to Jewish law, but rather from the change in his role and his position. He began as a private attorney who studied Jewish law for his own edification. Later, he became a senior official in the Israeli state's legal system – first as one of the five secretaries of the Situation Committee's Legal Council, then as state attorney after independence; not long afterward, he was appointed attorney general, a post he filled until 1960, when he was appointed to the Supreme Court. He also served, briefly, as justice minister. His national posts *required* him, in the simplest sense of the word, to act in accordance with the policy of cultural muting that had been semi-official Zionist policy at least since the inception of the World Zionist Organization. After independence, Cohn in fact became the person who, by virtue of his position, was responsible for ensuring that conflict over Israeli culture and identity would not jeopardize the operations of the Israeli legal system, that is, the rule of law and democracy. The national responsibly placed on Cohn's shoulders, as the person responsible for the state prosecution, the Legislative Department, and for providing legal counsel to the cabinet and ministries, positioned him at important decision-making crossroads where the danger that cultural conflict could ignite, and deteriorate into a culture war, or even a civil war, was clear and present. Cohn himself sat in on meetings where the question of whether Hebrew law was the law of the Torah was debated, whether it was appropriate for Israeli law to take inspiration from German or English law, and other similar issues. In these discussions, the arguments were no longer theoretical matters appearing in scholarly articles; they were now arrows that different political camps were firing one at the other, with the potential for making it impossible for the legal system to operate.

Cultural conflict in the legal field is dangerous not just to society but also to those involved in it, particularly those on the secular side. Even though Haim Cohn was one of the Hebrew law revival movement's greatest champions, he came to be perceived, from the end of 1947 onward, as one of the greatest nemeses of that project, and continues to be seen as such to this day. He is depicted as the person who thwarted it, as a dissembler on the issue who spoke glowingly about Jewish law even as his actions prevented Jewish law's penetration of Israeli law. Later, Chief Justice Aharon Barak would suffer a similar fate. Yet Barak's life project was, and remains, the creation of an independent Israeli-Zionist legal system and legal theory. He was the first jurist bold enough to make Jewish heritage Israel's residual law; as a Supreme Court justice he bravely grappled with issues of identity and culture. Yet, in much of Israeli society, Barak is seen as anti-Zionist and anti-Jewish. The flame of conflict over Jewish culture and identity can inflict heavy burns.

Israel's Ministry of Justice does not in any way take an "anti-Hebrew" or "anti-Jewish" position. On the contrary, it operates in accordance with a Zionist policy that seeks to muffle conflicts over culture and identity. This policy finds expression not only in the issue of assimilating the halakhah (Jewish law) into Israeli law, but in other areas as well. For example, the ministry delays the enactment of laws of great symbolic significance until their cultural-identity contact can be excised, or at least blurred. A constitution was not promulgated at the time of independence primarily because of concern that the process of enacting one would lead to a culture war. But the constitution was not the only case when such considerations were applied. In fact, the political solution of enacting basic laws instead of a constitution is identical to the solution that the leaders of the legal system followed when confronting the issue of enacting an Israeli civil code.

Codes are laws of great breadth, made up of hundreds or even thousands of clauses, constructed in an orderly fashion so as to organize a wide area of law. In modern political and legal culture, codes, like constitutions, are seen as symbols of modernization, independence, and national pride. The codification of law (civil law in particular) is, in modern Western culture, viewed as a national-cultural project, not just a legal one, of the first order. Codes, like constitutions, have become such central symbols in European (and world) culture that nearly every new country founded in the last two centuries has immediately written not only its own constitution, but also its own civil code. It was no less clear to the first Israelis that their country would, immediately upon independence, enact its own civil code. But the pressing needs of the hour, and the urgent need for massive legislation, prompted the Ministry of Justice to choose a different approach – gradual legislation of foundational laws in the area of private law (family, inheritance, property, contracts, and other fundamental fields). To this end, it established a Department of Future Legislative Planning, with the principal assignment of shaping an overall legislative policy and drafting the needed civil legislation. The intention was that, at some future point, these laws would be united into a complete Israeli civil code of the type that most other countries have. The civil laws were enacted gradually in the 1960s and 1970s (it was called, in legal terminology, "the new civil legislation"), and the project of uniting it into a single code began in the 1980s. The obvious similarity between the Justice Ministry's decision to enact civil legislation gradually and the Knesset's decision to enact basic laws over an extended period of time shows that both bodies were thinking along the same lines. The intention was to put off the enactment of a constitution or code to some future date when the issues of identity and culture – so the Knesset and Justice Ministry hoped – would be less fraught.[25] This gradualist strategy would dim, so they hoped, the symbolic and cultural-identity aspect of these texts; it would, for example, create a situation in which Israeli constitutional texts (its basic laws) would lack a formal preamble that would need to grapple with the identity of the Israeli demos. Similarly, it would create a situation in which the compendiums of Israeli civil and criminal law would lack a general section that would have to define the system's general principles, establish the source of residual law, and address other potentially explosive cultural-identity issues. Gradual legislation made it possible to put off the enactment of culturally controversial legislation without detriment to the legislative process as a whole. For example, the enactment of a bill of rights and family law were postponed.[26]

The same silencing policy led the Knesset and Justice Ministry to refrain from making any mention of issues of culture and identity in legislation. In fact, the word "Jewish" and its derivatives is almost completely absent from laws passed by the Knesset.[27] This was not only the Ministry's policy, but also that of the legal system and the entire legal elite. Until the 1980s, both the courts and academic legal studies did all they could to avoid inserting matters of values, ideology, and identity into legal writing and judicial opinions. For example, when the "who is a Jew" question reached the Supreme Court, the justices refused to allow the court to become an arena for working out the Jewish nature of the state and its citizens, for example, in the *Rufeisen* (Brother Daniel) case of 1962,[28] and the *Shalit* case of 1968.[29]

In *Rufeisen*, the Supreme Court, by majority vote, rejected the petition of a Carmelite friar who had grown up as a Jew to be recognized as of Jewish nationality under the terms of the Law of Return.[30] The court's decision rested

[25] Kedar, "Law, Culture," 192.

[26] The "fundamental principles" section has been the major factor delaying the enactment of the Israeli Civil Code tabled in the Knesset in June 2011. Despite the fact that the general part of the law consists of only two brief clauses declaring seemingly uncontroversial principles (e.g., the obligation to act in good faith), the debate over them has prevented the enactment of the bill for many years.

[27] A few laws (the most important of which is the Law of Return) speak of Israel as a Jewish state, but even these have avoided addressing the questions of what Judaism is, what a Jewish state is, and what that state's culture and law need to be. See Rubinstein, "Book Review," 655–656.

[28] HCJ 72/62 *Rufeisen v. Minister of the Interior* [1962] IsrSC 16 2428.

[29] HCJ 58/68 *Shalit v. Minister of the Interior* [1970] IsrSC 23(2) 477.

[30] This was before the addition of clause 4a to the Law of Return, which broadened the class of those entitled to enter Israel under the law's terms to those who were born to a Jewish family.

on a substantive issue, but the justices notably refused to make any positive determination of who is a Jew. They could permit themselves to evade such a substantive issue because it was fairly easy for them to rule that, according to the standard understanding of the word "Jew," as the court put it, "as it is commonly used by the Jewish people today," a Christian friar cannot be a Jew.[31] All the justices stressed that their ruling was not based on halakhic tenets, but rather on the accepted rules of legal interpretation – linguistic interpretation based on the common meaning of the word "Jew" and purposive interpretation that seeks to clarify the "legislative goal that produced the law's provisions."[32]

Shalit raised the question of whether the Interior Ministry was obligated to register Shalit's children as Jews on their identity cards on the basis of his declaration that his children were Jews. They were not, however, Jews according to the halakhah, according to which membership in the Jewish nation devolves in the matrilineal line. Shalit's wife was not Jewish and had not converted to Judaism. A nine-justice expanded bench of the Supreme Court required the Interior Ministry to register the children as Jews, by a vote of five to four. Before the court issued its ruling, Chief Justice Shimon Agranat asked the attorney general, who was representing the state in the case, to propose to the Cabinet that it ask the Knesset to solve the problem. "The court has a feeling," Agranat wrote, "that this subject is, largely, ideological and not legal."[33] Only when the Cabinet refused to do so did the Court proceed to rule in the case. The ruling shows that the justices in the majority categorically refused to enter into an "intra-Jewish" debate over culture and values as applying to the question of who is a Jew. They translated the issue into one of general (rather than Jewish) formal authority. Three of the justices in the majority adhered to the position that the question before them was primarily a formal legal one: "Is the Ministry of the Interior required to register the petitioner's children as members of the Jewish nation according to the Population Registry Ordinance and the Population Registry Law?" They thus based their decision on the formal legal determination that the population registry clerk holds a governmental position, and thus must, like the justices themselves, take into consideration only the civil and legal considerations that emerge from the law that grants him his authority. He may not take into account substantive issues relating to who qualifies as a Jew. True, two of the justices in the majority (Alfred Witkon and Zvi Berinson) took a less formalist position, but in the end

31 *Rufeisen v. Minister of the Interior*, 2455, and see also 2438–2439.

32 *Rufeisen v. Minister of the Interior*, 2438.

33 A report of Gideon Reicher, *Yedioth Ahronoth*, November 22, 1968, 2. Cited in Reitan, "Law of Return," 48.

they joined the opinion of their three colleagues. Justice Witkon ruled that the court should recognize that, in certain cases, the court would have to take a position on ideological disputes, but added that there was no need to do so in this case. Justice Berinson made use of substantive reasoning, according to which halakhic concepts should not be imposed on the Jewish people, certainly not in the state of Israel, where such concepts were not acceptable to the majority of the country's Jews. But, beyond this general assertion, he did not seek to make a positive determination of what Jewish culture is and who is a Jew. Two of the justices in the minority, Chief Justice Shmuel Agranat and Justice Moshe Landau (who would later serve as chief justice), went even further. They based their decisions on their determination that the issue was a cultural and political one that split the Israeli population. As such, the proper solution was to use the Court's authority to exercise its own judgment by not issuing a ruling of any sort. The question of who is a Jew, they argued, is not judicable, because it requires the court to make a judicial decision on a controversial ideological and cultural issue.

The *Shalit* ruling is important for my subject not only because of its substance and the political storm it set off, but because it is a notable case in which Israel's most senior judges voiced their clear support for the semi-official Zionist and Israeli policy that gives preference to the construction of the national-legal framework to engage in a profound, but sterile, discussion of Israeli society's identity and culture. The chief justice and his successor went so far as to explicitly reject the attempt to use the court to resolve ideological disputes over identity, and the rest of the justices took the position that the Court would find ways to avoid addressing this issue.

Like the Zionist movement did early on, Israel's national governing and judicial institutions thus refused to allow questions of identity and culture to impinge on political and legal deliberations. The Knesset and the Ministry of Justice did not base Israel's laws on Jewish law. It was not that they were alienated from Jewish heritage and its legal element; rather, they realized that these could not really be translated into laws, simply because there was no consensus on what constituted Jewish culture, and what were the proper ways to constitute a Hebrew-Israeli legal system on its basis. Even those who sought with all their might to base Israeli law on Jewish heritage did not know how to do so in practical terms. It was not a culture war in which "alienated Hellenizers" defeated "real Jews." Once again, it was a meta-cultural decision to circumvent such cultural conflict.

PART II

The Resurgence of Cultural Conflict

7

Jewish Heritage and a Jewish Democratic State

The Identity Discourse Returns to the Legal Debate

From time of its birth, Israel's political leaders and top jurists chose to avoid engaging, explicitly and materially, in the debate over Jewish culture and identity, wherever doing so was liable to spur cultural conflict or severe political-ideological contention. This changed in 1980, a watershed year for Israeli law. The Foundations of Law Act legislated that year formally retracted what had been a venerable Zionist and Israeli policy and, for the first time in the country's legal history, included a declaration that the residual law of Israel would be "the principles of freedom, justice, equity and peace of Israel's heritage." Recall that a proposal to enact a similar declaration was debated among jurists on the eve of independence, and that the leadership of the legal system refused to further it by bringing it up for discussion in the Provisional State Council. This time, however, the initiative succeeded. Since that time the Knesset has passed other laws requiring courts and other state authorities (e.g., the Central Elections Committee, responsible for running the country's national and local polls) to address the heritage and values of Israel as a "Jewish and democratic state," a phrase included in in Basic Law: Human Dignity and Liberty and Basic Law: Freedom of Occupation, enacted by the Knesset in 1992, and later also in Basic Law: The Knesset, when it was amended in 2002. In 2018 the Knesset approved Basic Law: Israel – The Nation-State of the Jewish People (known also as the Nation-State Law).[1] That same year, the Knesset also amended the Foundations of Law Act by declaring that "the principles of freedom, justice, equity and peace of Hebrew Law" would also be part of the country's residual law. In this chapter my subject is this new legislation, its history, and the debate it aroused in judicial rulings and legal writing. (As the Nation-State Law passed just as this book was

[1] On the problems presented by this law, see Kedar, "On the Danger"; Sussman, "Basic Law"; Gavison, "Constitutional Anchoring."

completed, I will be able to address it only in brief.) In the next chapter, I will address the broader historical and cultural context of the new legislation and the place of law in the fierce cultural debate ignited in Israel by this legislation.

The change in Knesset policy on identity and culture did not take place until the 1980s. Up to that point, the Knesset adhered to its policy of silence on these issues. In the few cases in which it could not avoid deciding pressing political issues, such as those touching on religion and the state, the Knesset found practical compromises. One such case was the flare-up of the "who is a Jew" issue following the Supreme Court's *Shalit* decision of January 1970.[2] The Knesset had no choice but to legislate rules to guide the officials of the Interior Ministry's Population Registry in applying the Law of Return. The Knesset added a clause, 4B, to that law: "For the purposes of this Law, 'Jew' means a person who was born of a Jewish mother or has become converted to Judaism and who is not a member of another religion." But this amendment was a practical and special arrangement, limited to applying the Law of Return. It made no pretense of making a broader statement about Jewish culture and identity in the broader area of Israeli society, as is clearly evidenced by the amendment's legislative history. The amendment was not passed after comprehensive public deliberation about Israeli identity or Jewish culture, nor even about the independence of Israeli law. Rather, it was a specific response to a lacuna in the law made evident by the *Shalit* case. Despite the rubric "who is a Jew," the affair was not about identity. Instead, it was a political-institutional issue of church and state relations, meaning the proper division of power between the state and the religious establishment, in this case the question of who had the authority to determine who could or could not be granted citizenship under the provisions of the Law of Return. There are two testimonies to the amendment being a political compromise regarding power relations between the state and the religious establishment. The first is that clause 4B does not demand "halakhic [Orthodox] conversion," but rather deliberately left that point open so as not to get tangled up in the controversy between the different Jewish religious movements over their differing procedures for conversion. The second piece of evidence is to be found in clause 4A, also added to the law at this time. It addresses the rights of family members and considerably broadens the class of those entitled to immigrate to Israel under the Law of Return to include "a child and a grandchild of a Jew, the spouse of a Jew, the spouse of a child of a Jew and

[2] HCJ 58/68 *Shalit v. Minister of the Interior* [1970] IsrSC 23(2) 477. I have discussed that case at length in Chapter 6.

the spouse of a grandchild of a Jew, except for a person who has been a Jew and has voluntarily changed his religion," none of whom was included in the original law. In other words, clause 4A expanded the purview of the law, while clause 4B restricted it. As the Law of Return definitively impinges on the nature of Israeli citizenship, it also impacts Israeli identity and culture. The church and state problem is indeed connected to the problem of culture, as the demand that religion influence public life in Israel grows out of its central cultural role. Nevertheless, they are two different problems. Even a person who believes that the state should "make no law respecting an establishment of religion," in the words of the First Amendment to the Constitution of the United States, might well agree, and even desire, that symbols and rituals of religious origin find expression in the public space and in the laws of the land (e.g., the specification of a particular day of the week as an official and legal day of rest). But the amendment to the Law of Return did not seek to define the Jewish identity of the state of Israel. In contrast, the Foundations of Law Act and other laws including the language "Jewish and democratic state" do not address the division of authority between the religious establishment and the state. Instead, they enter into the broader Israeli debate over culture and identity. Their entire purpose is to define the Jewish nature ("Jewishness") of the state and its laws.

The Foundations of Law Act emerged from long deliberation over the independence of Israeli law. It was not a debate over the Jewish-Hebrew content of the law, but rather over its formal independence, meaning the question of whether Israeli law was subsidiary to English law. It is ironic that it was this formal debate, which took care not to address questions of culture and identity, that restarted the debate over culture in the law. At stake was the legal force of a provision of Mandate Law (section 46 of the Palestine Order in Council, 1922), which required reference to English law in cases of a lacuna in Israeli law, meaning in cases in which judges did not find an answer to a question before them in statute or precedent.[3] There were three principal positions in the debate. The first was that the Mandate provision had expired of its own accord, as Israel now had an independent and advanced set of laws that rendered any obligation to refer to English law superfluous. The second was that the provision remained binding so long as the Knesset did not repeal it. The third position was intermediate between the other two, substantively closer to the first, but recognizing the force of the Mandate provision in a

[3] I analyze the different positions in this debate more broadly in Chapter 10. For a similar discussion in Pakistan, see Lau, *The Role*, 35–45.

formal sense. That position thus held that, in the final analysis, special legislation would be required to revoke it.

One of the principal participants in the debate was Aharon Barak, then a professor of law at the Hebrew University of Jerusalem.[4] Like many other Israeli jurists, Barak ascribed importance to ensuring the independence of Israeli law. As a member of the committees that drafted two new civil statues that were enacted during the 1960s and 1970s (the Agency Law and the Custodian Law), and as a teacher of law, he believed that Israel could and should fashion an original Israeli theory of law. In the debate over the revocation of section 46, Barak took the intermediate position – he believed that, given the problematic nature of the idea that there are lacunas in the law, and the existence of an advanced independent Israeli legal system, there would not in fact be cases in which Israeli judges would need to refer to English law to fill in gaps in the law. Nevertheless, he agreed that it would be correct to formally repeal the Mandate provision. Barak was appointed attorney general in 1975, and, in keeping with his view of Zionism, he asked the Legislative Department to expedite the preparation of a list of Ottoman and Mandate laws that had expired in the wake of new Israeli legislation and which thus needed to be revoked. He also asked the head of that department to draft a brief piece of legislation declaring the revocation of section 46.[5]

But what began as a modest measure to express the formal independence of Israeli law snowballed into a vehement cultural debate that lasted for almost a decade. In keeping with the minimalist tradition of Israeli law, the original version of the law comprised only two short clauses. One declared that section 46 of the Palestine Order in Council was repealed; the other stated that nothing in the repeal would "impact the law that existed in the country on the eve of the onset of this law."[6] The proposed law did not include a clause establishing what residual law would replace English law, and for good reason. First, from a philosophical and legal point of view, the question of whether there is indeed such a thing as a lacuna in the law is a controversial one. It can be argued that there is no real situation in which a lacuna can occur because there is always some legal norm, written or unwritten, that applies to the case at hand. Even if lacunas do exist, it is hard to know whether a given instance is indeed a lacuna, or instead a "negative arrangement," that is, a situation in which the legislature deliberately decided not to enact a law governing a

4 On Barak, see Kedar, "Scholar, Teacher."

5 For the legislative history of the Foundations of Law Act, see Barak, "Foundations of Law Act," 280–283.

6 Barak, "Foundations of Law Act," 280.

certain situation. Attorney General Barak and Uri Yadin, the head of the Legislative Department, both doubted that there were actually lacunas in the law, and argued that what sometimes seems to be a lacuna is, in fact, a normal dispute over interpretation.

Second, long-serving Justice Ministry officials, led by Yadin, were concerned that determining what should be Israel's residual law would set off a cultural debate. Yadin remembered the trenchant but pointless cultural and ideological debate over the issue that had flared before independence,[7] and he and Haim Cohn were among the principal shapers of the "cultural muting policy" I discussed above. Barak relates that Yadin tried to persuade him not to pursue the formal step of revoking section 46, on the grounds that there was no need to do so. That law, he argued, had been enacted more than fifty years previously, under a colonial administration. It required the judges in the colony to refer to the law of the mother country, but it was irrelevant to an independent state with its own advanced legal system.[8]

Yadin was a jurist of great experience. As one of the secretaries to the Legal Council prior to independence, and the top legislation official since then, he was very well acquainted with legal snares that were not visible to untrained eyes. The residual law issue was one of them. At first glance, it involved an innocuous and risk-free declaration of the guiding values of the legal system, but in reality such a provision was doubly perilous.

The first danger was that what was at issue was a *declaration*, meaning a statement of great symbolic importance. Its symbolic weight was due to the fact that the term "residual law" referred to a set of values and meta-principles that guide society and its legal activity. That being the case, declarations on this subject are generally included in constitutive legal texts, such as constitutions or civil codes. The great symbolism inherent in a declaration about residual law makes the process of formulating and enacting such declarations a cultural and political battleground. That was the central reason that many countries have preferred to sidestep the subject by means of laconic legislation using general and vague language – precisely what Barak hoped to do. So, for example, the laws of some countries instruct that judges should rule in accordance with the general principles of the legal system or with societal values. Others state that judges must rule in accordance with the way that they believe the country's legislators would solve the problem – what is called the

7 Yadin, "Custodian Law," 493–494. And see supra, Chapter 4. Yadin, like Haim Cohn, was one of the five secretaries to the Situation Committee's Legal Council.

8 Yadin, "Custodian Law."

Swiss model.[9] The French civil code takes this one step further. It simply requires judges to rule in every civil case, even in cases where the code is not clear or has a lacuna, but does not instruct them how to do so. In other words, it does not state what the residual law is.[10]

The second danger in a declaration about residual law lies in the fact that it is a *legal* declaration. That is, it has practical binding force. To explain this point, I offer a brief discussion of the proposal declaring that Hebrew law or Jewish heritage is Israel's residual law. Such a legal declaration is not merely a string of words; it is an instruction to act, with twofold meaning. First, a judge who encounters a lacuna would be required to refer to Hebrew law. She would be obligated to do so even if she has no idea what the terms "Hebrew law" or "the principles of Israel's heritage" mean, and even if ruling accordingly would cause cultural dissension or cast her as a taking a side in such a cultural controversy. Second, she would be required to decide what Hebrew law or the principles of Israel's heritage say with regard to the case at hand (in case there is a lacuna in the existing law), and to apply it. Furthermore, the citizenry and state authorities will be required, of course, to obey her decision, meaning accede to her interpretation of Hebrew law, and thus, by extension, to her interpretation of what Jewish-Israeli identity is.

Requiring judges to rule according to Hebrew law is unfair to them, and in the final analysis risky in a civic sense. It is unfair to judges because it demands that they make decisions on matters about which there is no consensus, neither in the legislature nor among the public, and about which therefore they have reached no decision. It ensnares such a judge in an impossible situation – if she renders a decision, a large portion of the public that does not agree with her definition of Judaism and which holds to some other idea of what Hebrew law is will criticize her fiercely. This part of the public will accuse the judge of making a political decision, of politicizing the law. Presumably, observers in the academy and among the public will quickly point out the rickety foundation in Jewish-Hebrew law on which the judge has built her ruling. They will argue, for example, that the judge deviated from the halakhah or used manners of interpretation or reasoning that are not halakhically acceptable.

Or suppose that the judge refuses to decide according to residual law. For example, she claims that there is not really a lacuna in the law, or that she has found a way to interpret the law that does not require her to refer to Hebrew law. In that case, she will be accused of making a mockery of the law, which

[9] Clause 1, Swiss Civil Code (1907).
[10] Clause 4, French Civil Code (1803).

has been enacted by representatives of the people, and thus of democracy as well. The Hebrew cultural purists will condemn her as a self-hating Jew. Either way, such a law erodes the legitimacy of the courts and, in the final analysis, the rule of law, democracy, and Israel's civic culture, because it requires judges to rule on issues of identity and culture about which there is no public consensus. This will paint the courts in political colors and bring them, to their detriment, into the midst of profound cultural and political debates.

Yadin's fears turn out to have been justified. The modest and concise bill that he and Barak drafted grew like a snowball. The draft was disseminated, as usual, to all government ministries in November 1976. Less than a month later, the Ministry of Religions had already voiced its opposition to the brief bill, and suggested adding this clause: "wherever there is a lacuna in Israeli law, Hebrew law will apply." The Ministry of Religions meant the halakhah, not Hebrew law of the sort the Hebrew Law Society of Moscow sought to formulate when it was founded in 1917.[11] It was like a replay of the debate over revoking section 46 that took place just before independence. At the time, Paltiel Dickstein proposed that Hebrew law (in its broad national, not its religious halakhic sense) be made Israel's residual law. Zerach Warhaftig of Hapo'el Hamizrahi then "translated" Dickstein's use of "Hebrew law" into "the foundations of Torah law and principles of justice and integrity."[12] Once a demand had been made to enact a positive statement about what would be Israel's residual law, instead of English law, it was no longer possible to get everything back in the box. For naught Uri Yadin warned that there was no need for an institution of residual law. "We would be better off not addressing the subject and letting Section 46 die a natural death," he argued.[13] The Ministry of Religion's proposal was only the start. Cabinet ministers, members of the Knesset, rabbis, and public figures all began campaigning for their own version of the residual law provision. In his legislative history of the Foundations of Law Act, Aharon Barak used diplomatic language to recount the discussions within the Justice Ministry over how best to word the clause establishing Israel's residual law. It is clear between the lines, however, that the discussion came in response to political pressure from the outside to make Jewish law (halakhah) as Israel's residual law. Pressure in this direction increased after the Likud formed a government in 1977 that depended on the support of the religious-Zionist National Religious Party and the Haredi

[11] Barak, "Foundations of Law Act," 280.

[12] G-111/3 ISA.

[13] Barak, "Foundations of Law Act," 281.

Agudat Israel party. Justice Ministry officials were well aware that there was no workable way to translate halakhah into modern state law, even as residual law, and that contention over the issue would jeopardize Israel's social and legal stability. They thus anxiously sought a formulation that would satisfy the advocates of Jewish law while remaining ambiguous enough not to bind judges or force them into the religion-state or culture conflicts. At first, Barak proposed that Israel's residual law would be the principles of the country's declaration of independence, but this general and vague reference to that document was not sufficiently "Jewish" to satisfy the Jewish law advocates. Barak then turned to Nahum Rakover, the ministry's adviser on Jewish law, for "assistance in finding a formula that will grant [the law] a Hebrew cast. I mean not just language, but also substance, such as the underlined passage from the Declaration of Independence ('it will be based on freedom, justice and peace as envisaged by the prophets of Israel')…. I do not mean a specific reference to Hebrew law [he presumably meant Jewish law or halakhah]."[14] In the end, the Ministry of Justice proposed four alternative proposals in this spirit, which were merged into the final wording. Two more years of turbulent debate passed before the law was enacted by the Knesset on July 23, 1980.[15] The new and very general residual law provision that the Knesset passed did not provide judges with new tools or clear guidelines to aid them in their work when they encountered a lacuna. As such, it was perceived largely as a symbolic measure that did not change legal reality. Yoram Danziger, who would later serve on the Supreme Court, correctly observed that clause 1 of the law was "a symbolic gesture that did more damage than good."[16] It was a symbol devoid of meaning. The meaning of the phrase "the principles of freedom, justice, equity and peace of Israel's heritage" was unclear, and did nothing for the Jewish identity of the state. Yet it fanned the flames of a pointless debate over Jewish law and its application in Israeli law. It was not long before the phrase "Israel's heritage" came before the courts, which had to decide what it meant.

It is not my intention here to get caught up in the meaning of the expression "Israel's heritage" and what it includes and does not include – for example, whether the term is equivalent to Jewish law or denotes something broader. Instead, I want to examine whether and to what extent such a provision is necessary, the scope of its impact on Israeli law and culture, and the hazards it presents. The conflicting claims about how to understand the term "Israel's

[14] Barak, "Foundations of Law Act," 281.

[15] See Knesset Records, August 2, 1978, 3972–3973; February 11, 1980, 1817–1836; March 4, 1980, 2145–2152; July 23, 1980, 4025–4031.

[16] Danziger, "Symbolic Gesture."

heritage" and the use of Jewish law had reached the Supreme Court in two cases that were given additional hearings in 1980, *Handles v. Kupat Am* and *Kenig v. Cohen*.[17] *Handles* dealt with the ownership of an object (in this case, two promissory notes) that a man had found on the floor of a bank's safe deposit box room. Did they belong to the finder or to the bank? The question at issue was whether the safe deposit box room was public space (the Hebrew term used by the parties to the dispute and the judges was *reshut harabim*) or the bank's private property. *Kenig* raised the issue of whether a series of unsigned notes left by a woman who committed suicide should be considered a defective legal will, or more precisely, whether they could be seen as a will created by a person who believed she was about to die (the term used was a Talmudic-Aramaic one, *shkhiv mera*). These two cases are considered important precedents in the law of the restoration of lost property and the law of inheritance, but I am interested not in the Supreme Court's ruling on the matter of law but rather in the debate the cases set off about the Foundations of Law Act and Jewish law. As the terms *reshut harabim* and *shkhiv mera* are ones taken from halakhah, a discussion ensued over the question of whether the court should, or must, refer to Jewish law in deciding the case.

The question was raised by Justice Menachem Elon, one of the leading champions of basing Israeli law on Jewish law in the spirit of the Hebrew Law Society. In *Handles*, Elon concurred that there was no lacuna in the law, only an issue of interpretation, but argued that, in the Foundations of Law Act, the legislature had demonstrated its intent that Jewish law have precedence, even in matters of interpretation. In other words, he argued that the Knesset had, for all intents and purposes, decided that Jewish law was the principal basis for interpretation and source of inspiration in Israeli law. Elon, whose intellectual life's work was the revitalization of Jewish law, had frequently made this claim in his writings and opinions prior to *Handles*,[18] but in this case he maintained that the passage of the Foundations of Law Act bolstered his position. Furthermore, Elon sought to give broad scope to the concept of the lacuna. In his view, legal lacunas exist also in cases in which courts seek to imbue general standards with actual content, terms such as "good faith" and "reasonableness." In *Kenig*, Elon reiterated two previous assertions of his: first, that the Foundations of Law Act and its legislative history clearly imply the primacy of Jewish law as a source of interpretation; second, that the term "lacuna" needs

[17] FH 13/80 *Handles v. Bank Kupat Am*, IsrSC 35(2) 785; FH 40/80 *Kenig v. Cohen* [1982] IsrSC 36(3) 701.

[18] Elon, *Religious Legislation*. And see also the 1973 Hebrew edition of his *Jewish Law*.

to be understood broadly, so as to include the interpretation of ambiguous standards. Legal scholars might debate whether legal lacunas actually exist, Elon wrote, aiming his barbs at Barak and Yadin, but once the Knesset had, in the Foundations of Law Act, recognized the existence of lacunas and declared what the residual law would be in such cases, an interpreter could not evade lacunas or insist on long lists of conditions for their existence. Justice Elon clearly saw the Foundations of Law Act as an opportunity to revive the Hebrew law project. He believed that the new law had not only made Jewish law Israel's residual law, but also created the formal possibility of granting Jewish law primacy in judicial interpretation. He may also have hoped that it would be just a short step from there to requiring Jewish law to be the prime source of inspiration for the Knesset as well.

Elon's position was opposed by Chief Justice Landau and the rest of the judges of the benches who heard the two cases. They contested, in particular, Elon's claim that the Foundations of Law Act gave Jewish law primacy as a source of interpretation. Justice Haim Cohn put this succinctly in *Handles*, reaffirming the accepted legal policy of the Zionist movement and Israeli state from their inception:

> The Israeli legislature uses, by its very nature, many legal terms which also appear in Jewish law, such as "promissory note" [*shtar hov*], "loan" [*milveh*], "attachment" [of collateral, *shi'bud*], "partnership" [*shutfut*], and so on.... But this hardly justifies – and certainly does not require – interpreting these terms in accordance with Jewish law....
>
> This simple approach does not change with the enactment of the Foundations of Law Act, 1980; the need for a link to sources from Israel's heritage does not arise in any way as long as the answer to a question that needs to be decided can be sought and found "in statue, precedent, or analogy." We must first seek solutions to our problems in law, and we must interpret the law according to the rules of interpretation set and used in precedent.
>
> This should not be taken to mean that we must abjure all connection to Jewish law, so long as we can draw from it evidence to reinforce or contradict or material to compare or contrast or wisdom and discernment from which we can learn good values. But this is an option and not an obligation, and while perhaps it is commendable to do so as much as possible, there is certainly no detriment in doing little. And there are judges who stand by the teachings of their predecessors to avoid all *obiter dicta* that are not eminently pertinent to the issue at hand. For them, and those like them, any such diversion into Jewish law is absolutely unacceptable. While I am not of that party, nor can I be so strict with myself when it comes to *obiter dicta*, I cannot, in any case, disregard the fact that references to Jewish law are in the nature of *obiter dicta*.

> Furthermore, [even] if an expression or idiom taken from Jewish law is to be interpreted in its sense in Jewish law, that hardly implies that the substantive commands of Jewish law are to be applied as if they were law enacted by our legislature.[19]

Barak was the only one of the justices to respond also, if only briefly, to Justice Elon's broad construal of the term "legal lacuna." In *Handles*, Barak offered two "cautionary remarks," as he called them, in response to Elon. First, the legal term "lacuna," he wrote, does not extend to the interpretation of standards such as "good faith"; the meaning of such terms is determined by "regular" interpretation, not by filling lacunas. Second, the Foundations of Law Act did not absorb Jewish law into Israeli law as residual law, and certainly did not grant it precedence as a source of interpretation or make it a source of interpretation to which judges were required to refer. "Hebrew law does not apply because it was not absorbed," Barak asserted succinctly in *Kenig*.

As I have already noted, at no point did the discussion among the judges develop into a comprehensive debate over Jewish law, that is, over its definition, extent, and the question of adapting it into Israeli law. Most of the justices disregarded the question entirely. Even Justices Cohn and Barak, who addressed Elon's claims at some length, did not, in their opinions, offer a comprehensive analysis of the issue (as they later did in scholarly articles). They only briefly remarked that Elon's position was not grounded in the language of the law. A survey of subsequent rulings, since the early 1980s, shows that the country's courts followed in the footsteps of the Supreme Court. For the last four decades they have consistently avoided using the vague and problematic Foundations of Law Act.[20]

19 *Handles v. Bank Kupat Am* (Cohn J.), 789–790. For Cohn's ideas, see also "Jewishness of the State"; "Values of a Jewish."

20 The Foundations of Law Act was also addressed by Elon and Barak in HCJ 1635/90 *Jerzhevski v. Prime Minister*, IsrSC 45(1) 749, but the debate there differed only slightly from those in *Handles* and *Kenig*, and in any case was the exception that proves the rule. *Jerzhevski* involved the question of how a political agreement between political parties should be interpreted. Since the law at the time did not address such agreements, Elon argued that there was a lacuna that required invoking clause 1 of the Foundations of Law Act. In contrast, Justice Barak wrote that, while the question had indeed not been addressed in legislation, it was not a lacuna that needed to be filled by means of the provision in the Foundations of Law Act, but rather through the regular process of "developing the [existing] law." Law is not limited to legislation, Barak argued; the issue of a political agreement is part of public law, controlled by precedent and constitutional conventions. Judges use the existing normative bricks of the common law to build and develop the law. For a survey of the few judgments from all courts that addressed

Justice Elon's attempts to invoke the new law immediately following its enactment, and in particular to interpret it very broadly and to read into it statements it does not contain, fundamentally turned the Foundations of Law Act into a dead letter and doomed it to oblivion. Elon hastily invoked the law to rule that "Israel's heritage" means Hebrew law, and that Hebrew law means the halakhah (Jewish law) in its broadest sense, and that the halakhah also needs to be the binding source of interpretation for all of Israeli law. But this broad interpretation had two problems. First, Elon's claims were strained because *Handles* and *Kenig* clearly did not involve lacunas in the common sense of the term (if there can indeed be said to be a common sense of such a controversial term), but rather "only" profound interpretive disputes. That being the case, there was no cause to invoke the Foundations of Law Act. Second, even if there was reason to refer to that law, it was not at all clear that Elon's construal of the law was correct, given that the Knesset had deliberately refrained from referring to Hebrew law (and certainly the halakhah) in the wording of the law, preferring rather to cite "the principles of freedom, justice, equity and peace of Israel's heritage."

It was not until 2018 that the Knesset, in an expedited procedure that allowed almost no debate, appended the words "Hebrew law" before the words "Israel's heritage." Yet it did not define what exactly Hebrew law is, and more specifically did not equate it with the halakhah.[21] Some of the legislators who took part in the debate claimed that this added language was no more than a symbolic amendment, lacking any real content, added to the law for political gain.[22] Presumably this new amendment will not remedy the difficulties in the use of the term Hebrew law that I laid out in Chapter 3. As such, it will not change the fact that most Israeli judges disregard the Foundations of Law Act. The amendment aroused relatively no interest in the media, and did not provoke much public or academic discussion.

The alacrity with which Justice Elon offered his broad interpretation of the term "Israel's heritage" is reminiscent of Zerach Warhaftig's similar haste, just before independence, to translate the vague term "Hebrew law" into "Torah law," immediately demonstrating the danger of cultural conflict for the state that was about to come into existence. No wonder that the most vigorous opposition to Elon's attempt to revive the Hebrew law project came from

clause 1 of the law and the question of filling in lacuna, see Raniel, "Clouds and Winds," especially 75–124. And see also Porat, *Proposal to Amend*.

[21] Knesset Records, November 13, 2017, 142–165; April 30, 2018, 263–341; Minutes of the Knesset's Constitution, Law and Justice Committee, June 26, November 21, December 5, 2017; March 5–6, 2018.

[22] See, for example, MK Yoel Hasson, Knesset Records, April 30, 2018, 280–281.

Justice Cohn in the *Handles* case. Just prior to independence, Cohn had witnessed the strident cultural dissension that followed the attempt to found Israeli law on "Jewish-Hebrew" content. He was well aware of the futility of such cultural battles and their danger to society. After the state was founded he became one of the architects of the cultural muting policy in the legal field; in *Handles*, he came to its defense.

Elon's attempt to use the Foundations of Law Act to revive the Hebrew law idea has been inflated in the telling into a cultural battle of giants between him and Aharon Barak (and less so between him and Haim Cohn and Moshe Landau). In Israel's collective memory, the contention over the Foundations of Law Act is seen as a culture war between religious Israelis, represented by Elon, and secular ones, represented by the non-religious justices; between judges who are attuned to the people and rooted in the national culture and heritage (Elon) and those who claim to be so but who are actually part of a "Hellenizing" elite influenced and inspired by universal values and largely dismissive of local national Jewish culture (Barak and Cohn). Even Barak's theoretical skepticism, from the early 1970s, about the actuality of legal lacunas, and thus of the need for residual law, is perceived as a pretext Barak came up with in order to help him evade referring to Jewish law, which he considered strange and odd.[23] It was of little use to Barak that he had been the initiator and drafter of the Foundations of Law Act, and that he had pressed for its passage over the objections of senior officials in the Ministry of Justice. It was of no help to him that he had been the first jurist in Zionist history to dare move away from the semi-official muting policy and make, in Israeli law, a declaration that the principles of Israel's heritage are Israel's residual law. Nor was it any help that there was no consensus in Israeli society as to how to define Hebrew law (or Jewish law) and what the best ways were to translate it into laws for a modern state.

The fact is that there was never a debate between religious and non-religious justices on the Supreme Court, or between "authentic Jews" and "universalist Hellenizers." It was, once again, a meta-cultural dispute. Justice Elon sought to take advantage of the Foundations of Law Act to set off a cultural conversation about the question of what "Israel's heritage" means, while the rest of the justices stuck to long-standing Zionist policy by refusing to turn the court into an arena for such a fight. The Foundations of Law Act was

[23] Similar charges were levied at Barak even at an academic conference held in his honor when he retired from the Supreme Court in 2006. In his response, he rejected the claim that he was alienated from Jewish culture and law, and stressed that he had been the moving force and drafter of the Foundations of Law Act.

a dead letter as far as the courts were concerned – it was a law that no one used. But outside the courtrooms, it became a central emblem of cultural conflict.

In the academy, the Act at first aroused a fairly lively debate between scholars who plumbed its meaning, the proper ways to use it, and its effect on Israeli law.[24] Even though most academics believed that the new law would not have any profound practical significance, the very fact that a scholarly discourse was underway set off a larger debate over the meaning of the expression "Israel's heritage" and its relationship to the term "Hebrew law," thus restarting, to some extent, the debate over the need or possibility of basing Israeli law on independent Jewish-Hebrew content. The fact that Justices Cohn, Barak, and Elon participated in the academic conversation by publishing articles on the issue contributed to creating the myth that a lengthy cultural debate took place on the pages of judicial opinions and scholarly journals. What was forgotten was that the Supreme Court adhered to the accepted Zionist policy of refraining from cultural debate, and that the academic debate was limited in scope and quickly died down.

Later, in the public mind, the debate over the Foundations of Law Act became linked to the larger debate over the Supreme Court's conduct and the reasoning it used to explain its rulings in its opinions. Beginning in the 1980s, Israel's courts (like courts throughout the world) began taking a more activist approach in their opinions. The Supreme Court no longer had any hesitation about addressing issues that it had in the past refrained from dealing with, from relationships within the family to foreign and defense policy. Neither did it have any compunctions about making explicit the value dimension of its rulings, or discussing the distributive consequences of its decisions.[25] Its conduct and new ways of writing opinions gained the Court the reputation of being unafraid to take part in debates over culture and politics or to shape public policy. The cultural debate that ostensibly took place in the court over "Israel's heritage" was perceived, in error, to be just one more of the cultural-political debates in which the courts were involved.

Finally, the brief discussion of the Foundations of Law Act has, in Israeli collective memory, been bound up with another, later debate, that over the nebulous expression "Jewish and democratic state," first included in Israeli

[24] Procaccia, "Foundations of Law"; Kirschenbaum, "Foundations of Law"; Elon, "More About"; Ben-Menahem, "Foundations of Law"; Shochetman, "On Analogy"; Shifman, "Jewish Law"; Deutch, "Jewish Law"; Maoz, "Place of Jewish Law"; Barak, "Foundations of Law." Cheshin, "Jewish Heritage"; Barak, "Values of Israel."

[25] Mautner, *Law and the Culture*, 54–98.

legislation in 1992. Despite the difference between these two debates, and even though the matter at issue with the Foundations of Law Act was much more limited, and the debate in fact ended almost before it began, the earlier controversy is now seen as a preview of the great cultural polemic that has raged in Israeli society since the 1990s. Since then, Israelis are accustomed to view Israeli society through the distorting prism of the tension that allegedly exists in the expression "Jewish and democratic state." Consequently, the refusal of the justices to be dragged into cultural polemics over the expression "Israel's heritage" has been interpreted as taking a stand in the Israeli culture war between the "Jews" and the "democrats." The limited debate over "Israel's heritage" has come to be seen as the prehistory of the much larger one over the meaning of "Jewish and democratic state."

The journey toward the Jewish and democratic state began in the mid-1980s. Until that point no Israelis doubted that they lived in the Jewish nation-state. All they had to do was look around them to see it – they lived in an independent country with a Jewish majority and rich Hebrew culture. As is the case in every age, of course, intellectuals and educators were, in the 1980s, lamenting that the country's culture and spirit were waning and inferior to previous generations. They largely attributed the decline to that of the labor movement and the Likud's rise to power.[26] But Israeli society did not feel the need for a legal declaration that Israel was the Jewish nation-state. To put it another way, Israelis did not sense that their country's Jewish character was threatened. Even if such a fear entered the mind of some individuals, the classic Zionist view still prevailed, according to which the way to guarantee that the state was a Jewish state was not by means of nebulous political or legal pronouncements but by maintaining a sovereign entity in which Jews were a majority and thus could freely sustain Jewish culture. Nevertheless, for reasons that I will explain in the next chapter, in the 1980s the Knesset felt a need to bolster the identity of the Jewish nation-state by means of legal declarations included in the country's Basic Laws.

The first step in reinforcing Jewish identity in Israeli law (in fact, the second step, the first being the enactment of the Foundations of Law Act) was taken in the mid-1980s, in an amendment to Basic Law: The Knesset. The amendment was passed in the wake of a Supreme Court ruling of 1984, voiding a decision of the Central Elections Committee to disqualify two political parties from contesting that year's election – Kach, a religious-nationalist faction led by Rabbi Meir Kahane that advocated racist policies such as revoking the

[26] For a survey of this pessimistic view and its effect on the law, see Mautner, *Law and the Culture*, 127–142.

citizenship of the country's non-Jews, and the Progressive List for Peace, a joint Jewish-Arab list accused of denying the Jewish people's right to a state of their own.[27] In its ruling, the Court reiterated the principle of defensive democracy that it had first asserted in the *Yeredor* ruling of 1965. In that decision, the Supreme Court recognized the Central Elections Committee's power to disqualify a slate that "denied the integrity of the state of Israel and its existence," even though such authority was not explicitly granted by law.[28] In 1984 the court reaffirmed the *Yeredor* rule, but refused to expand it to enable the Committee to disqualify a racist party, or one that rejected the democratic or Jewish character of the state. The ruling prompted a public outcry, leading the Knesset to amend Basic Law: The Knesset by adding a new clause, 7a:

> A list of candidates shall not participate in elections to the Knesset, and a person shall not be a candidate in elections to the Knesset, should there explicitly or implicitly be in the goals or actions of the list, or the actions of the person, as the case may be, one of the following:
>
> (1) Negation of the existence of the state of Israel as the state of the Jewish people;
> (2) Negation of the democratic character of the state;
> (3) Incitement to racism.

The language of the law, as amended, indicates that the Knesset reached the conclusion that the general rule established by the Supreme Court in *Yeredor* was insufficient, and that the law needed to state explicitly that "destruction of the state" includes both its physical destruction and the destruction of its character as a Jewish state. But many in the Cabinet, Knesset, and Ministry of Justice felt uncomfortable with the use of the term "Jewish state" in a law addressing the disqualification of slates from contesting elections to the Knesset. They feared that the vague term might exacerbate tensions between Jews and non-Jews (by depicting Israel as a country for Jews alone) and among Jews (by defining Judaism as a national religion or culture).[29] Because of these concerns, the first draft of the amendment read: "negation of the existence of the state as contained in the Declaration of the Establishment of the State of Israel," which was the language that Chief Justice Agranat had used in *Yeredor*. In the end, the wording that

[27] EA 2/84 *Neiman v. Chairman of Elections for Eleventh Knesset*; EA 3/84 *Avneri v. Chairman of Central Elections Committee for Eleventh Knesset* [1985] IsrSC 39(2) 225; IsrSJ 8 83.

[28] EA 1/65 *Yeredor v. Knesset Elections Committee*, IsrSC 19 (3) 365.

[29] Minutes of the Knesset's Constitution, Law and Justice Committee, July 16, 1985, 17 (Minister of Justice Moshe Nissim).

was finally passed was "negation of the existence of Israel as the state of the Jewish people."[30]

It is doubtful whether a democratic country should deny the right to be elected of a group that seeks to change the character and culture of the state,[31] but that is not what interests me here. I want to show that when the Knesset decided to forbid, in a Basic Law, the participation in elections of a party that negates the existence of Israel as "the state of the Jewish people," it deliberately avoided using the expression "Jewish state" out of concern that such a charged and imprecise term could be more harmful than helpful. In 1985 many Israelis still felt that including the expression "Jewish state" in law, rather than reinforcing the state's Jewish identity, independence, and resilience, would actually set off misunderstandings and cultural struggles among Jewish groups and between Jews and non-Jews. Unfortunately, in 2002 the Knesset no longer had the concerns that bothered it in 1985. It passed an amendment rewording clause 7a from "negation of the existence of the state of Israel as the state of the Jewish people" to "negation of the existence of the state of Israel as a Jewish and democratic state."

But I have jumped ahead of myself. The expression "Jewish and democratic state" first appeared in Israeli legislation in 1992, in the deliberations surrounding Basic Law: Human Dignity and Liberty and Basic Law: Freedom of Occupation. The history of the expression "Jewish and democratic state" is reminiscent in some ways of that of the term "Israel's heritage." First, the Foundations of Law Act, as originally proposed, did not address the issue of Israeli society's identity; the same was true of the original versions of the Basic Laws of 1992. That fact was in keeping with the policy pursued by the Ministry of Justice since independence, which had been a fundamental tenet of Zionist policy since the movement's inception. The staff of the ministry's Legislative Department must certainly have remembered that one of the central reasons for enacting an Israeli constitution piecemeal was the desire to avoid having to write a formal preamble that would set off cultural conflict over how the Jewish state should be defined. For this reason, the Basic Laws enacted subsequently were designed to be dry and technical, setting out the structure of government and, now in the case of the 1992 laws, human rights. On top of this, in Basic Laws covering human rights there would seem to be even less of a need to refer to the society's national character, given that human and civil rights are universal by definition. (Even the rights to group culture or

30 Minutes of the Knesset's Constitution, Law and Justice Committee, July 16 and 23, 1985.

31 Kremnitzer, *Disqualification of Lists*, 39–54.

affiliation recognized in some constitutions are worded in universal terms.) Such was the position of Minister of Justice Dan Meridor and his staff when they drafted the government-sponsored bills. It was also that of Knesset Member Amnon Rubinstein, an opposition member of the Knesset and noted legal scholar, who ended up introducing Basic Law: Human Dignity and Liberty as a private member's bill. They believed that the proper place for the clause referring to the state's Jewish character – if such a text needed at all to be included in a constitution – would be in the formal preamble of the constitution that would, at some future date, be composed by aggregating the Basic Laws into a single document, not in the text of one of its articles. The proposed human rights laws thus began with a formal clause: "The basic human rights in Israel are based on the recognition of the value of the human being, the sanctity of his life, and his being a free person, and they shall be upheld in the spirit of the principles set forth in the Proclamation of the Establishment of the State of Israel."[32]

Second, as in the case of the Foundations of Law Act, during the legislative process involving the 1992 Basic Laws, some vague expressions were inserted into the bills as the result of political compromises in the Knesset. The expressions "Israel's heritage" and "Jewish state" are highly charged from a cultural, religious, and national point of view; as such, once they appear in one of the versions of the bills, it becomes nearly impossible to remove them without causing an outcry from the champions of Jewish culture, who charge that the Israeli legislature is denying its heritage. In both cases the Knesset was warned about the consequences of vague and emotionally charged provisions, but the legislators believed the cost was a reasonable one that was worth paying in order to achieve a desired result – in the first case, formally decoupling Israeli law from English law and declaring a new residual law; in the second, formally establishing human rights in Israeli law.

The enactment of the Basic Laws of 1992, along with other developments in Israeli constitutional law, were part of a global wave of "constitutionalization" at the end of the twentieth century. The trend was much influenced by the fall of the Soviet bloc and the end of the apartheid regime in South Africa, and was symptomatic of the rising power of the legal and economic elite as part of a trend toward privatization and society reorganization in the industrialized world. Countries all over the globe promulgated new or revamped constitutions, or amended existing ones. They established constitutional courts or greatly expanded the powers of existing courts, and bolstered the force of

[32] Karp, "Basic Law," 341; Rubinstein, "Story of," 83.

"constitutional values."[33] Similar changes occurred in Israeli law and society, in the form of the "judicialization" of the public sphere and the enhancement of the Supreme Court's authority, the increasing use of "constitutional values," the project of enacting a bill of rights (taking in the end the form of two Basic Laws), and in the end the advancement of a "constitutional revolution," meaning the assertion that Israel has a written constitution on the basis of which the Supreme Court can review legislation passed by the Knesset.

The first draft of the Basic Law: Fundamental Human Rights was written by the Ministry of Justice during the Seventh Knesset (1969–1974) and considered by the Cabinet and the Knesset. During the Twelfth Knesset (1988–1992) it was redrafted and, in April 1989, Minister of Justice Dan Meridor submitted it to the Ministerial Committee for Legislation. The Committee held seventeen meetings to discuss the proposal, held over the space of half a year, but was unable to move it forward for submission to the Knesset because of coalition pressures, mostly regarding issues of religion and state. In light of this, Knesset Member Amnon Rubinstein took the draft from the Justice Ministry and submitted it as a private member's bill in November 1989.[34] While the bill passed a preliminary vote, for political reasons it never came before the Constitution, Law and Justice Committee. The law's supporters did not give up. They understood that, despite political divisions, the winds of judicialization in Israel and the rest of the world offered a window of opportunity for the Knesset to legislate, even if in a limited form, Basic Laws regarding human rights. To ensure the passage of such laws, Rubinstein now took the Justice Ministry's draft apart and composed from its sections four bills on what he thought were uncontroversial matters: freedom of occupation, freedom of assembly, freedom of expression, and another general and inclusive law dealing with human dignity and liberty. Rubinstein hoped that, by dividing the Justice Ministry version into several narrower bills, he could avoid sparking a general debate over religion, culture, and the state, and avert a situation in which opposition to one or another provision of the law would halt the entire legislative process.[35]

As with other legal systems around the world, the Basic Law proposals in Israel were influenced by a constitutional model developed in Canada in the 1970s and 1980s and manifested in the Canadian Charter of Rights and

[33] Ackerman, "Rise of World Constitutionalism"; Hirschl, *Towards Juristocracy*; Law and Versteeg, "The Evolution and Ideology."

[34] Knesset Records, November 15, 1989, 412; Rubinstein, "Story of," 84.

[35] Karp, "Basic Law"; Rubinstein, "Story of."

Freedom of 1982 and rulings by the Canadian Supreme Court. A less rigid model than previous ones, it created a set of flexible arrangements that enabled a dialogue between different government authorities that was more appropriate for a late modern multicultural society.[36] Clause 7 of the proposed Basic Law: Human Dignity and Liberty was borrowed directly from the Canadian Charter's clause 1, with the addition of elements later added by the Canadian Supreme Court: "A person's fundamental rights are not to be denied or limited except by force of a legal provision appropriate for a democratic society and meant for an appropriate purpose and to an extent that does not exceed what is required."[37] The purpose of this provision was to empower the Knesset to place constraints on the rights enumerated in the Basic Law when that was deemed necessary, but to ensure that the limitations would be accomplished only by a proportionate law for an appropriate purpose, and only to the extent that the injury to human rights not be of a level that would seriously compromise Israel's democratic character. The wording was acceptable to the Ministerial Committee for Legislation and most of the members of the Knesset, because it enabled the proper operation of a law-based state. For example, it made it possible to enact laws that empowered the police to arrest lawbreakers under certain circumstances. Such a limitation of human freedom is acceptable under the limitations stated in this clause, and is therefore permissible. However, at a meeting of the Knesset's Constitution, Law and Justice Committee in July 1991, Yitzhak Levy of the National Religious Party raised an objection. He wanted to talk not about easy and clear cases of this type, but about problematic cases involving religious practices that were observed in Israel and even guaranteed by law, but are seen discriminatory by many Israelis.

> If the Marriage and Divorce Law is faced with this law, it will be possible to argue that it is not appropriate for a democratic state. [For example,] a man who is a *kohen* [a member of the priestly caste] may not marry a divorcee, and if I were a judge and I were not a believer, I would say that that is not appropriate for a democratic state. This matter will come before a bench of nine justices. It will undermine things that we see as foundations of the state of Israel, even though it is a secular state bound by the rule of law. We are walking a narrow plank. We have certain laws that are appropriate for a Jewish state and Israel is a democratic state. We are always moving along two

[36] For the influence of the Canadian Charter on Israeli constitutional history, see Segal, "Israel Ushers in"; Segal, "Israeli Constitutional."

[37] Clause 7 is based on the interpretation of the Canadian Supreme Court of Article 1 of the Charter in *The Queen v. Oakes*, [1986] 1 S.C.R. 103.

> axes, that of a Jewish state and that of a democratic state. One could add language to say "a law appropriate to a Jewish and democratic state." If my position is not accepted, I may submit this proposal as a reservation in advance of the second reading.[38]

Rubinstein, who introduced the bill in the Knesset, was concerned. "What will be disturbing in the addition [of "Jewish state"], in terms of the sound, not the content," he cautioned, "is that we are dealing with the rights of all inhabitants and all human beings in the country, and suddenly it looks as if it applies only to Jews."[39] But when he heard other proposals that were brought up for discussion, for example, to strike out the words "appropriate for a democratic society" or "for an appropriate purpose," he accepted Levy's suggestion as a compromise. "I can live with this addition," Rubinstein said. In the end, the committee decide to bring two different versions of the law before the plenum – the original draft and the draft with Levy's emendation. But that was not the end of the matter.

The polite exchange between Levy and Rubinstein was, of course, only the tip of the iceberg of a much broader political conflict between the religious parties and the secular majority. It was not in any way a cultural debate over defining Israel as a Jewish state. Rather, it was a fight over the division of political power between the state and the religious establishment (the state Rabbinate, the religious parties, and affiliated bodies). The Knesset representatives of the religious parties did not, in these debates, agonize over Israeli society's identity and culture. Rather, they were seeking to preserve the status quo ante of the relations between the state and the religious establishment, in particular the religious courts, which had authority over marriage, divorce, and other personal status issues. They wanted to ensure that the new Basic Law would not upset this balance. Their insistence on this point had stymied past initiatives to enact a Basic Law that would protect human rights. So as to allay the concerns of those who feared that the new law would upset the status quo ante, Rubinstein removed from the draft bill the clauses addressing equality, freedom of religion and belief, and even freedom of movement (which religious members of the Knesset feared would make it impossible to restrict traffic on the Sabbath in religious neighborhoods and communities) and the courts' powers of judicial review (which they thought might prevent religious legislation in the future). On top of that, he added a general statement about Israel's culture in the spirit of the declaration of

38 Minutes of the Knesset's Constitution, Law and Justice Committee, July 1, 1991, 15.

39 Minutes of the Knesset's Constitution, Law and Justice Committee, July 1, 1991, 17.

independence, and promised that previous laws would not be overridden.[40] But despite all these concessions by the advocates of an Israeli bill of rights, the legislative process remained stuck because of the close but inverse link that the religious parties had created between equality before the law and the country's Jewish nature. They were not prepared to accept the proposed wording of clause 7 ("A person's fundamental rights are not to be denied or limited except by force of a legal provision appropriate for a democratic society") without a qualification that would limit or even void the term "democratic" and explicitly exempt issues important to them from the purview of the Basic Law, in particular, the laws of marriage and divorce (like the exemption included in clause 5 of the Women's Equal Rights Law of 1951). But the law's sponsors were not prepared to accept such a gross curtailment of democracy and the rule of law, almost aborting this attempt to enact a Basic Law to protect individual rights. The solution that was found was to transfer the subject of the state's Jewish and democratic character from clause 7 to a declarative clause at the beginning of the law, clause 1, which stated that the purpose of the law was "to protect human dignity and liberty, in order to stipulate the values of the State of Israel as a Jewish and democratic state, in a Basic Law."[41] The religious Knesset members were willing to accept this version, because, beyond the assertion that Israel is a Jewish state, the word "equality" and the phrase "appropriate for a democratic society" had been stricken.[42] The supporters of the law were able to live with this formula because it made democracy a value and did not explicitly make the state's Jewish nature a limitation on democracy or equality before the law. Rubinstein later offered two other reasons for agreeing to the expression "Jewish and democratic state." First, the wording would ensure that the Law of Return could not be attacked on the grounds that it was unconstitutional; second, the expression was acceptable not just to the political right, but also to the left. The left had long opposed the annexation of the territories occupied in 1967, in part on the

[40] Karp, "Basic Law"; Rubinstein, "Story of."

[41] Clause 7 of the original version became clause 8, which stated that rights guaranteed by the law were not to be violated "save by means of a law that corresponds to the values of the state of Israel." In other words, it refers back to clause 1, the purpose of the law.

[42] The religious members knew, of course, that despite the omission of the phrase "appropriate for a democratic society," the vague formulation "Jewish and democratic state" would not prevent suits challenging the country's discriminatory marriage and divorce laws on the grounds that they violate human rights. After all, a Jewish state is not required to devolve responsibility for its marriage and divorce laws to religious institutions, and is not required to permit discrimination against women. For this reason, they were not satisfied with the formal declaration in clause 1, and demanded the status quo be entrenched explicitly by a provision that would assert that the Basic Law did not apply to laws passed prior to its enactment.

grounds that annexing millions of Arabs would be detrimental to Israel's character as a Jewish state, and would be a mockery of the Zionist idea.[43] Either way, the phrase, as indeterminate as it might be, seemed suitably solemn and appropriate for the first of Israel's Basic Laws to address human rights. In the opinion of many of its supporters, the law indeed brought about a constitutional revolution and inaugurated a new era in Israeli jurisprudence.

In short, the catchphrase "Jewish and democratic state" was born almost inadvertently. In contrast with the Hebrew law project, it came into the world not out of a desire to say something positive about the country's identity, but as a makeshift accommodation. It was ambiguous enough to serve as a political compromise regarding church and state relations, that is, between the state on the one side and the Rabbinate and religious parties on the other. Indeed, the last thing the members of the Twelfth Knesset, whether religious or not, wanted to do was to set off a culture war over the identity of the Jewish people's nation-state. Keeping the faith with the Zionist tradition of consensus democracy, they sought a solution to a political disagreement that was holding up the enactment of a partial Israeli bill of rights. Their ultimate success in passing such a Basic Law (even if it was truncated and fragmentary) concealed from many the fact that the Knesset had departed from its long-held policy and had defined the Israeli state's identity and values. The wording they arrived at, "Jewish and democratic state," was considered to be general and abstract enough that disparate elements of Israel's population could live in accord under it.

The formulation was seen as so successful at the time that it was also adopted in clause 5 of the Parties Law of 1992. Ten years later, as I have already noted, it was also included in clause 7a of the amended version of Basic Law: The Knesset. The original version of the Parties Law used a formulation identical to that used in the Non-Profit Associations Law of 1980: "A non-profit association shall not be registered if any of its objects negates the existence or democratic character of the State of Israel or if there are reasonable grounds for concluding that the non-profit association will be used as a cover for illegal activities." Recall that a similar formulation was originally used in clause 7a of Basic Law: The Knesset. In both cases, the Knesset finally decided that it would be more proper to forbid the existence of parties and slates that deny "the existence of the state of Israel as a Jewish and democratic state." In 2015, a proposal was tabled in the Knesset to amend the Non-Profit Associations Law in the same manner. The increasing number of

[43] Rubinstein, "Story of," 88.

laws using the language "Jewish and democratic state" indicated that it had become a key concept in political, legal, and public discourse in Israel.[44]

Unlike the Knesset, the courts were not eager to make any real use of the hazy expression. Their cool response was reminiscent of the debate over the term "Israel's heritage" in the Foundations of Law Act. At the end of the twentieth century, Israeli judges remained committed to the classic Zionist policy and did all they could to avoid addressing Israeli Jewish identity or making rules about how Jewish identity could best be expressed in state institutions and in the country's legal rules. Even the activist Supreme Court, which was much less reluctant to engage in lengthy deliberations and to express itself on controversial political and distributive issues, made a point of not taking up Israel's Jewish identity. The Foundations of Law Act had, as I have already noted, become a dead letter soon after its enactment, and judges hardly ever invoked it, even if they mentioned it here and there. Likewise, the expression "Jewish and democratic state," which every Israeli high school student knows, hardly ever appears in judicial rulings. True, the justices assert, in constitutional discussions, almost by rote, that Israel is indeed a Jewish and democratic state. As judges often do, they also make a point of quoting the declaration of independence and precedents that imply that Israel is a Jewish and democratic state (e.g., the justices frequently invoke Chief Justice Agranat's language in *Yeredor*). But the Supreme Court has never translated such declarations into concrete normative decisions, and they have, of course, never tried to define exactly how the state is Jewish. Israeli courts have never looked for a "Jewish" way to sign contracts, establish corporations, collect taxes, manage labor relations, treat criminals, or conduct a tender.

The Supreme Court's attitude toward the expression "Jewish state" is a faithful reflection of accepted intellectual discourse in Israel over the Jewish nature of the state. The Israeli discourse over the concept "Jewish state" is, in the vast majority of cases, guided by general principles from the fields of ethics and political thought, rather than from some specific Jewish nature that ostensibly dictates the Jewish nature and conduct of the state. The common intellectual discourse treats the Jewish state as a specific case of the universal modern phenomenon of the nation-state, and interprets and judges the state and its actions accordingly. In this view, policies in the areas of immigration, taxation, or punishment, for example, must be derived from general values that apply to every nation-state, not from an internal Jewish character that is

[44] I will survey the public debate over identity in the next chapter.

unique to Israel. That being the case, deciding such questions does not in any way require clarification and definition of what Judaism is.[45]

Even when the justices had no choice but to address issues connected to Israel being a Jewish democratic nation-state (e.g., with regard to discrimination against the Arab minority or elections to the Knesset), they did not discuss the nature of Judaism and how that impacts Israel. Instead, they limited their decisions to formal legal questions that can be clearly decided. For example, when the Supreme Court had to decide whether a party could be disqualified because its platform was opposed to Israel being a Jewish democratic state, the justices refrained from addressing the question of what a Jewish state is, and instead based their decision on general legal principles. In *Issacson v. Political Party Registrar*, Justice Mishael Cheshin wrote: "It would not be proper for us to concern ourselves here with the meaning of the expression 'Jewish state,' which we are not required to do."[46] All the justices consented to do in that case was to make a general statement that the value of being a "Jewish and democratic state" (the meaning of which is not clear) needs to be balanced against the freedom of citizens to band together to form a political party. This statement extricated them from the minefield of cultural and identity discourse to the solid and familiar ground of making a judicial determination between two clashing norms. In other words, they did not need to address the question of what a Jewish state is, but rather consider the procedural question of when the balance between two values is disrupted. The justices ruled, correctly, that for the purposes of determining the proper balance they did not need to decide what a Jewish state is, but only to determine whether the platform or actions of the party in question involved a serious infringement of the state's Jewish character. As one might expect, in all the cases considered by the Supreme Court, the justices never identified a threat that would, with near certainty, endanger the state's Jewish character. This ruling is just and reasonable because it is ridiculous to maintain that the platform of a small party could be a threat to the rich Jewish and Hebrew culture of six and a half million Jews, who constitute the national majority in Israel.

In *Issacson*, Justice Cheshin provided an unambiguous statement that another elusive phrase, "a state of all its citizens," can certainly not be taken

[45] Katz and Kedar, "Jewishness of"; Gavison, "Reflections"; Gans, *From Richard*. The discussion of the Jewish nature of the state is problematic principally because it is difficult to agree on the fundamental nature or basic characteristics that define Judaism (e.g., Is it spontaneous by nature? Pluralist? Reflective? Law-based?).

[46] CA 2316/96 *Issacson v. Political Party Registrar*, IsrSC 50(2) 529, 548; and see also LCA 7504/95 *Yasin v. Parties Registrar* [1996] IsrSC 50(2) 45.

to be a negation of Israel's standing as a Jewish state; in fact, he pointed out, the phrase is a meaningless tautology. Every country in the world is a "state of all its citizens," and that is certainly the case in every democracy that in practice enables the participation of the entire population in choosing the government and overseeing its actions. This is a consequence of the concept of the citizen (as opposed to the subject). The modern state is a political entity that, by definition, treats all its citizens equally and neutrally. At the same time, most, perhaps all, countries in the world are also nation-states that give preference to the symbols and culture of a group with ethnic, cultural-historical, linguistic, or religious characteristics, some of which are objective and some of which are subjective and imagined. In other words, there is no contradiction between Israel being a Jewish state and it being a state of all its citizens. The proper issue for discussion is not that of definitions and symbols but the policies that Israel actually pursues with regard to its citizens and others. Instead of arguing ad nauseum the pointless question of whether Israel is a Jewish state or a state of all its citizens, it makes more sense to devote those energies to, for example, considering the civil and ethical obligations of the Jewish state toward the members of minority groups living in its territory, and examining how to eradicate the systematic discrimination that these groups suffer from, and how to promote true equality and partnership in Israel. In any case, Justice Cheshin's opinion in *Issacson* did not address Israel's cultural identity; instead, it considered first concepts in political theory and sought to root out an unfortunate error that has gained traction in Israeli public discourse.

The only serving justice to address the concept of the Jewish state more substantively was Aharon Barak, but even he did so little, and sporadically, in lectures and scholarly writings, not in his judicial opinions.[47] Barak, of course, took care not to base his ideas on an intrinsic Jewish nature. In his view, Israel is a Jewish state because most of its inhabitants are Jews, and thus its public culture naturally expresses the culture and heritage of that Jewish majority. Nevertheless, Barak parted with his fellow justices inasmuch as he endeavored to explain what a Jewish state is. It is not at all obvious why he should have done so, given that Barak defined himself as a Herzlian Zionist, not an Ahad Ha'am Zionist whose primary interest was Jewish culture.[48] It may well be that

[47] Of course, the former deputy chief justice, Menachem Elon, frequently addressed the expression. But Elon retired in 1993, not long after the Basic Laws of 1992 and the Parties Law entered into force, and a large part of what he said on the issue was said as an emeritus judge and legal scholar. Elon saw the phrase as another manifestation of the Knesset's interest in restarting the Hebrew law project.

[48] Shavit, "Ex-Chief Justice."

he wrote on the subject because he felt a need to reply to the harsh attacks made on him by religious and right-wing groups, who argued that he was speaking for a small elite group that preferred universal Western culture to Zionism, Judaism, and Israeli culture. For example, in his book *Interpretation in Law* he wrote:

> The Jewish state is thus the state of the Jewish people ... a country which every Jew has the right to immigrate to, and for which the ingathering of the exiles is a fundamental value. A "Jewish state" is a state whose history is interwoven and intertwined with the history of the Jewish people, whose language is Hebrew, where the most important holidays reflect its national revival. The "Jewish state" is a state in which the Jewish settlement of its fields, cities, and farming communities is one of its major concerns. A "Jewish state" is a state that perpetuates the memory of the Jews who were slaughtered in the Holocaust.... A "Jewish state" is a state that fosters Jewish culture, Jewish education, and the love of the Jewish people. A "Jewish state" is a state whose values are those of freedom, justice, integrity, and peace that are to be found in Israel's heritage. A "Jewish state" is a state whose values are drawn from its religious tradition, of which the Bible is the most basic of its books, and the prophets of Israel are the foundation of its morality. A "Jewish state" is a state in which Hebrew law plays an important role, and in which the marriage and divorce of Jews are decided on the basis of Torah law. A "Jewish state" is a state in which the values of the Torah, of Jewish heritage, and the halakhah are basic values.[49]

This passage does not offer an in-depth discussion of modern Jewish identity or of the definition of Judaism and the Jewish state. Rather, it describes the sovereign state of Israel, in which Jews are free to maintain their culture. But even this general and neutral description was criticized by Ruth Gavison, another legal scholar, because it offers implicit support for the idea that the control of marriage and divorce by religious courts is an inevitable corollary of Israel being a Jewish state.[50] It goes without saying that such pronouncements did not appease Barak's religious and rightist critics. Despite the justices' efforts to refrain from defining Israeli identity and from entering into the cultural debate, these critics depicted the Supreme Court under Barak's leadership as a "Hellenizing" institution that gave preference to the democratic side of Israeli identity over the Jewish side.[51] Like it or not,

[49] Barak, *Interpretation in Law*, vol. 3, 332.
[50] Gavison, "Reflections" (Hebrew edition), 168–169.
[51] Cohen and Susser, *Israel and the Politics*, 85–91.

the courts and legal system as a whole found themselves being dragged into the cultural conflict.

The principal manifestation of the courts being drawn into the Israeli cultural debate, and thus being perceived as taking sides in what was seen as a cultural and political conflict between "Judaism" and "democracy," were proposed laws that sought to require judges to rule in accordance with Hebrew law (which I addressed above), and even more so to establish, in a Basic Law, Israel's identity as the nation-state of the Jewish people and to specify its Jewish symbols and characteristics.[52]

The first efforts to entrench the state's Jewish identity in a Basic Law or constitution were proposed at the beginning of the new millennium. In response to the constitutional innovations of the 1990s, and the public debate that these aroused, the Constitution, Law and Justice Committee of the Sixteenth Knesset (February 2003–April 2006) tried to draft what it termed "a constitution by broad consensus."[53] In the process, the committee consulted with a wide range of people and organizations – from the universities, the legal world, and the entire spectrum of Israeli society and politics. Moshe Koppel, a professor of computer science, head of the Israel Policy Center, and an Orthodox Jew identified with the political right, seems to have been the first to submit to the committee, in 2004, a proposal for a brief Basic Law of seven clauses that would constitutionally entrench the state's Jewish identity.[54] The "constitution by broad consensus" initiative never bore fruit in the end, but the idea that it was necessary to anchor the state's Jewish identity in law or a constitution did not die with it. It appeared thereafter in series of proposals and documents produced by right-wing organizations,[55] and gradually made its way into the Knesset. In August 2011, a group of legislators from the body's right-wing factions, led by Avi Dichter, submitted, for the first time, a draft of a Basic Law: Israel – The Nation-State of the Jewish People.[56] The bill declared: "The state of Israel is the national home of the Jewish people, in which they

[52] For the history of the Basic Law, see Rabinovitch, *Defining Israel*, 1–25.

[53] https://main.knesset.gov.il/Activity/Constitution/Pages/ConstProtocols.aspx.

[54] Rabinovitch, *Defining Israel*, 74–76.

[55] See, for example, the proposal of the Institute for Zionist Strategies (2006): www.knesset.gov.il/committees/heb/material/data/H18-12-2006_14-33-16_hukatmedinatisrael.pdf, and that of Moshe Koppel and Knesset Member Michael Eitan (2011): http://hukaeitankoppel.blogspot.com/ (both in Hebrew).

[56] 2011, P/18/3541, August 3, 2011. An identical bill was later resubmitted by Aryeh Eldad in the 18th Knesset (P/18/4096) and Ze'ev Elkin in the 19th Knesset (P/19/2502). See Rabinovitch, *Defining Israel*, 77–82.

realize their aspiration to self-determination in accordance with their cultural and historical heritage."

Likewise, the bill itemized the symbols of the state, such as its flag and seal, named Hebrew the country's official language, declared that all Jews have the right to immigrate to and settle in Israel, and made the Hebrew calendar official. It declared the Jewish Sabbath the official day of rest, and made Israel's Independence Day, Memorial Day for Fallen IDF Soldiers, and Holocaust and Heroism Day official public holidays. The draft also required the state to promote Jewish immigration to Israel and Jewish settlement in the territory of the state; to act in the interests of Diaspora Jews and to maintain relations with them; to foster Jewish heritage; to enable all Israel's inhabitants, both Jews and Arabs, to preserve their heritage; and to protect holy places. Finally, the bill declared that Israel is a democratic state, reiterated the provision of the Foundations of Law Act of 1980 that "the principles of Israel's heritage" were to serve as the state's residual law, and added to this that Jewish law should serve as a source of inspiration for the country's legislators. The bill submitted by Dichter and his co-sponsors was removed from the Knesset's agenda, but, during the two years that followed, other Knesset members from parties of the right submitted bills of similar wording.[57] In response, a group of opposition members introduced their own brief draft of a Nation-State Law, stating, "This Basic Law aims to secure and protect the values of the State of Israel as a Jewish and democratic state by giving the force of law to the basic principles stated in the Declaration of Independence, which is annexed verbatim to this law."[58] None of them was taken up and considered in depth.

These early versions of the Nation-State Law made no direct reference to the courts and their attitude toward (or disregard of) the expression "Jewish and democratic state." The supplementary material submitted with the drafts claimed that the purpose of the law was to resolve the anomaly between the Israeli public's broad understanding of Israel as a Jewish state and the fact that this understanding had no formal basis in law. According to the parliamentarians who submitted the bill, "The necessity of the Basic Law: Israel – The Nation-State of the Jewish People is particularly valid at a time when there are those who seek to abolish the right of the Jewish people to a national home in their land and the recognition of the State of Israel as the nation-state of the Jewish people."[59]

57 Rabinovitch, *Defining Israel*, 82–87.

58 2013, P/19/1539, July 22, 2013. For the English version, see Rabinovitch, *Defining Israel*, 87–93.

59 Rabinovitch, *Defining Israel*, 81.

The supplementary material did not state whether the reference to people who do not recognize the Jewish people's right to a national home in Israel signifies people in Israel or outside it. Neither did it explain to what extent, if at all, this constituted a concrete threat to Israel, nor how the legislation would solve the problem. It could be that Israeli Jews felt an urgency to entrench the state's identity in law in reaction to the rise of parallel nationalist sentiments among the country's Arab citizens that followed the signing of the Oslo agreements between Israel and the Palestinian Liberation Organization in the 1990s and the disturbances of October 2000, when police forces trying to quell demonstrations that broke out in Arab communities in Israel killed twelve protestors. Many Israeli Arabs then reached the conclusion that, to defend their rights, they needed to fashion a Palestinian-Israeli identity for themselves, distinct from other Arab identities but also from Israeli Jewish identity. A document entitled "The Future Vision of the Palestinian Arabs in Israel," drafted in 2006 by a group of Israeli Arab politicians and intellectuals, declared that civil equality between Jews and Arabs required recognition that the Arabs living in Israel had a right to national cultural and political autonomy, and to equality on both the individual and collective-cultural level:

> Defining the Israeli State as a Jewish State and exploiting democracy in the service of its Jewishness excludes us, and creates tension between us and the nature and essence of the State. Therefore, we call for a Consensual Democratic system that enables us to be fully active in the decision-making process and guarantee our individual and collective civil, historic, and national rights.[60]

The proposed Basic Law aroused much controversy in the Knesset. Realizing that the debate over the country's identity was deeply divisive and could lead to a culture war, Minister of Justice Tzipi Livni asked Ruth Gavison, a constitutional law scholar at the Hebrew University of Jerusalem, "to formulate a constitutional arrangement dealing with the nature of the state ... and anchor the components of its identity in a way that would integrate these values, the Jewish as well as the democratic."[61] Gavison submitted her report a year later, in November 2014. She chose not to offer model legislation. Instead, her report addressed the need to establish the vision of the state in law. First, she stated the importance of a common vision for Israel's citizens, and recommended carrying on with cultural and educational efforts to formulate

[60] Rinawie-Zoabi, "The Future Vision," 5.

[61] Letter from the Minister of Justice to Ruth Gavison, August 12, 2013 (www.justice.gov.il/StateIdentity/Documents/Livni.pdf).

and instill such a vision. But she also counseled that it would be best "to refrain, at this stage, from additional constitutional anchoring of the core vision through legislation, in part or as a whole." Given the danger inherent in the debate over identity, Gavison proposed that

> An attempt should be made to seek a law that will strengthen solidarity and not deepen rifts, so that the vision of the state will be strengthened and not weakened by the legislation. The legislation and the law should highlight civic solidarity in Israel; should enhance Jewish solidarity in Israel and abroad; and should manifest a fair, generous and inclusive attitude to the members of the Arab minority.[62]

But political events did not wait for Gavison's report. In May 2014, when a series of peace talks between Israel and the Palestinian Authority came to an impasse, Prime Minister Benjamin Netanyahu announced that he would further the Basic Law proposal. Subsequently, Knesset members from the coalition submitted private member bills based on Dichter's proposal. The war in the Gaza Strip in the summer of 2014 delayed debate on the proposals, but enthusiasm for the law in the political parties that were members of the government coalition remained high, and the government did not want to look as if it did not support the initiative to define Israel as a Jewish state. Four days after Gavison submitted her report, the cabinet announced, after a turbulent and difficult meeting, that it would further legislation of the Basic Law. It conditioned this, however, on the different versions of the law being united into a government bill under the supervision of the attorney general.[63] In response to the government's announcement, members of the opposition also resubmitted a more limited version of the bill based principally on the Declaration of Independence.[64]

The cabinet's declaration of support for the law, in November 2014, did not placate the coalition parties. In the end, opposition to the bill on the part of the Yesh Atid party, led by Minister of Finance Yair Lapid, and the Hatenua party, led by Minister of Justice Tzipi Livni, was a central factor in the coalition's breakup and the dissolution of the Knesset at the end of the year, just two years after the previous election.[65] When a new Knesset was elected at the beginning of 2015, there was reason to believe that the tumult surrounding the Nation-State Law would subside somewhat, given that the memory of the

[62] Gavison, "Constitutional Anchoring," 43–44.

[63] Announcement of the Cabinet Secretary, November 23, 2014. In Rabinovitch, *Defining Israel*, 95–99. See also Haviv-Rettig, "Nation-State Kerfuffle."

[64] 2014, P/19/2883, November 24, 2014. For the English version, see Rabinovitch, *Defining Israel*, 101–102.

[65] Rabinovich, *Defining Israel*, xv.

end of the previous Knesset was still fresh and opposition to the law crossed party lines and divided the coalition. For this reason, the coalition agreements granted some of the parties that joined it veto power over the wording of the law. That, however, did not stop the snowball that had begun rolling in 2011. In the summer of 2015, when the coalition supporters of the law saw that the Cabinet was dragging its legs and not submitting a government bill to the Knesset, they resubmitted a version of Dichter's original draft.[66]

But they made an important change. The supporters of Dichter's version no longer explained that the Jewish identity of the state had to be established by law as a response to anonymous elements who disputed the right of the Jewish people to national self-determination in a state of their own. A new justification for the law emerged – the desire to balance the democratic and Jewish components of the Israeli state's definition of itself, and in its Basic Laws. Uri Ariel, a cabinet minister for the right-wing religious party Jewish Home, said as much at a Cabinet meeting in November 2013: "The law is today a step in the right direction. There is ongoing erosion of the Jewish identity of the state of Israel. The law should be defined in a clear way so that the Supreme Court will not be able to interpret differently than the spirit of the legislators."[67] From this point onward, supporters of the law stressed that, in the absence of legislation that made the Jewish identity of the state explicit, the Supreme Court tended to focus on the principles of democracy and human rights rather than on national identity, to the chagrin of the Jewish majority. For example, the bill's supporters condemned Supreme Court rulings that placed limits, on human rights grounds, on the detention and expulsion without trial of asylum seekers and labor migrants who had entered the country illegally. The Court also angered the bill's supporters when it criticized legislation that denied residency rights to the spouses of Israeli citizens who entered the country from the Occupied Territories or enemy countries – even though the Court did not reject the policy itself. The justices, it was argued, should be required by law to rule on the basis of Jewish national interests.[68] The supporters of the law added a statement to this effect to the supplemental material to the law in 2015: "The purpose of this Basic Law is to protect in basic legislation Israel's status as the nation-state of the Jewish people in equal status to Israel's Basic

[66] 2015, P/20/1989, June 29, 2015. For the English version, see Rabinovitch, *Defining Israel*, 105–110. Prior to this, Binyamin Ze'ev Begin, a member of the Likud faction and son of Menachem Begin, submitted a shorter version of the bill similar to the version proposed in the past by the opposition. 2015, P/20/1587, June 29, 2015. For the English version, see Rabinovitch, *Defining Israel*, 103–104.

[67] Lis, "Netanyahu's Cabinet."

[68] Bakshi and Sapir, "Justifying the Nation."

Laws protecting human rights and the democratic character of the state."[69] In the public debate, this claim began to take precedence. The law, its supporters said, would end the Supreme Court's increasing bias, since the 1990s, in favor of human rights and democracy and against the states' Jewish identity.[70] The consequence was that the Court was dragged, to its detriment, into a polarizing political debate.

For two years, it looked as if disputes over the law within the coalition would prevent it from passing. But despite the fact that the Israeli public evinced little interest in the law, its supporters in the parties of the right, in the Knesset and outside it, continued to promote it. Under this pressure the Ministerial Committee on Legislation resolved in the summer of 2017 that the Cabinet would support the bill, which as a result came up for debate in the Knesset. The Knesset set up a subcommittee to determine the wording of the law, and negotiations over the final version commenced. In May 2018 the bill passed its first reading,[71] and after another long round of amendments and deletions, it was enacted on July 19, 2018. The final version that passed is largely declarative in nature and more moderately worded than the original versions.[72]

The public reaction to the law showed that a culture war was underway. The debate was polarized and combative. Supporters of the law claimed that its enactment was an important day in Israeli history, a day that fortified the country. Opponents of the law, in Israel and around the world, termed it a dark day for Israeli democracy, given that the law does not state that Israel is a democracy, does not include a statement of civil equality, and creates the impression that the Jewish character of the state takes precedence over democracy.[73] Israel's Arab citizens maintain that the law is racist, inasmuch as it entrenches Jewish legal, political, and cultural hegemony.[74] Supporters and opponents of the law staged stormy demonstrations, and petitions against it were submitted to the Supreme Court, which found itself at the center of a political polemic and a culture war.

In the next chapter, I will offer a broader account of the identity discourse and the law's place in the Israeli cultural debate.

69 Basic Law Proposal: Israel – The Nation-State of the Jewish People (2015, P/20/1989), July 29, 2015. For the English version, see Rabinovich, *Defining Israel*, 108.

70 See, for example, Bakshi, "Basic Law."

71 2018, P/20/1989, May 1, 2018.

72 See https://knesset.gov.il/laws/special/eng/BasicLawNationState.pdf (an unofficial translation of the law from the Knesset website); Lis, "Israel's Contentious."

73 See, for example, Green, "Israel's New."

74 See, for example, the opinion of Adalah: The Center for Arab Minority Rights in Israel, www.adalah.org/en/content/view/9569.

8

The Identity Turn and the Jewish and Democratic State

The new preoccupation with identity and culture in Israeli law at the end of the twentieth century was part of a larger worldwide trend. During the last third of the previous century, public discourse in the industrialized world shifted from the political-civil (the "rights discourse") and socioeconomic to questions of individual and group identity and their cultural corollaries.[1] These new questions were addressed in academic research, literature, and art, and were quickly translated into political and legal demands. At the turn of the century the wave reached its apex and inevitably affected Israeli jurisprudence. The identity discourse, as it was called, took two forms in the legal field. First, the new consideration of identity and culture make it necessary for the fields of politics and the law to recognize the need, and therefore the right, of each individual to affiliate with a cultural group. This in turn required legal defenses for collective-cultural human rights, such as language rights, the right to education according to a certain set of values, and the right to group affiliation. Furthermore, it demanded recognition of past and current discrimination in the distribution of rights and resources along gender and identity lines – in other words, that members of cultural minorities suffered from bias, and that it was systemic. Second, the identity discourse criticized the law for treating the individual primarily as a citizen with rights. This, the critics charged, distorted and trivialized what it is to be human, depriving the individual of important elements of her personality. The identity discourse thus became a central source of critique of modern law, demanding that it

[1] I use the word "culture" here in its broad sense as the sum total of a society's values, beliefs, and worldviews, and the ways of life that derive from this whole.

be supplemented, or enriched, so as to recognize and express the spiritual, emotional, and mental qualities of the human.[2]

Despite the identity discourse's critique of the rights discourse, it needs to be kept in mind that, historically, the new preoccupation with identity and culture emerged from the rights discourse. In fact, it was intellectually necessitated by it. In this sense, the identity discourse is actually the most recent (for now) wave of modernity. Since the Enlightenment, modern political life has been characterized by the demand, by different groups within society, for equal rights, opportunities, and socioeconomic conditions. For the last two and half centuries, women, members of disadvantaged economic and social classes, minorities, and immigrants have demanded equal political and legal rights. Later, they added to this a demand for welfare, proper living conditions, and a certain minimum threshold of equality in this regard. But even in democratic law-based societies, which were generally also welfare societies, many members of disadvantaged groups felt that they were still suffering from discrimination. The reason was that the same society that had granted them equal political rights, and sometimes a social safety net, was also demanding, explicitly or implicitly, that they adapt themselves to that society's cultural standard. In return for equality, they were expected to adopt the majority group's values, mores, and lifestyle. In the modern world, which has become more and more homogenous – with its universal citizenship, uniform and general law, bureaucracy, factories, and state schools – the original meaning of political equality has increasingly been forgotten. That meaning, the lack of discrimination, has been replaced by the idea of equality as a uniform standard. The result was that the rule of law diverged from society. The law of the land spoke in universal language, while society continued to discriminate against women and minority groups and treat them differently. Women found themselves in a position where they were expected to integrate into a world designed in accordance with male views and interest, ostensibly while enjoying formal legal equality. Ethnic, religious, and cultural minorities were expected to prove that they were equal, similar, or identical in all ways to their neighbors who were members of the majority group. This was the primary source of modern anti-Semitism, which emerged in the second half of the nineteenth century. While many countries emancipated their Jews and granted them equal rights, this came in tandem with the demand that the Jews demonstrate that they were entirely German, English, or French. In other words, they were expected to shed all aspects of their particular identity

[2] For a comprehensive theoretical discussion of the identity and cultural discourse and its Israeli incarnations, see Sagi, *Jewish-Israeli Voyage*.

and culture and to assimilate into the "real" society (and not just into the citizenry). In *The Origins of Totalitarianism*, Hannah Arendt argued that Nazi racial theory and the Holocaust were extreme and distorted versions of this anti-Semitism of equality. Even those Jews who converted to Christianity and changed their ways of life in order to gain an entry ticket into modern European society, which demanded conformity in exchange for equality, could not, catastrophically, divest themselves of what European society saw as their association with "Jewishness." Being Jewish, Arendt wrote, was seen as a pathological vice, and gradually came to be seen as an immutable racial property. In the end, this way of thinking proved deadly for the Jews.[3]

In the 1960s, disadvantaged groups began fighting against the gender and cultural standards they were expected to meet. Alongside liberal feminism, the feminism of equality, emerged cultural feminism, both moderate and radical, a feminism of difference. This later outlook demanded recognition of women's different identities, needs, and interests, and demanded that law, society, the economy, and the workplace change accordingly. Likewise, non-Western groups rejected the cultural hierarchy that Western culture promoted and called for multiculturalism, which would recognize their identities and cultures as worthy of respect, equal treatment, and protection. In the name of multiculturalism, they rejected conceptualizing equality as uniformity and demanded instead that it be seen as participation in a pluralist society and a lack of discrimination. Political and social changes that took place after World War I, and especially in the 1950s and 1960s, the era of decolonization and social conflict in the West, were fueled by these concepts, while at the same time accelerating their effect and bringing them into the center of public discourse. For example, the entry of large numbers of women into the workforce, higher education, and all other walks of life during World War I and again after World War II made it clear that the greatest obstacle to their true integration into society was the male standard according to which cultural, economic, and political systems operated. In much the same way, as members of ethnic and other minorities, such as natives and immigrants, gradually made their way into Western societies, they realized that they could not integrate on a true and equal basis into a non-pluralist world with no tolerance for the members of other cultures and no true willingness to incorporate them. This awareness led to a series of social and political

3 Arendt, *Origins of Totalitarianism*, 66, 84–87. Arendt devoted the first volume of this work to anti-Semitism, but argued that, despite the special aspects of Jewish history, modern anti-Semitism is in large measure one instance of a more general problem in the modern total and totalitarian world.

struggles. While these are remembered as a civil rights struggles, they were no longer efforts simply to gain individual legal, political, and social rights. They sought collective and cultural rights. The women who, in the 1950s, coined the term "gender" in its current sense no longer sought only equal civil rights; they demanded a change in the way society thought, and a reshaping of society so as to make it better fit the needs of both genders. Decolonization spurred this recognition. The defeat of the French army at Dien Bien Phu in Indochina in 1954, and the subsequent strategic reverse experienced by Great Britain and France in the Suez Crisis of 1956, brought home to the Europeans that their claim to cultural superiority over other peoples was not only morally outrageous but also baseless. Their cultural outlook had to change from a hierarchical to a multicultural egalitarian one that was more inclusive and cooperative. In the nature of cultural changes, the shift to a tolerant and pluralistic multicultural outlook occurred gradually and slowly, maturing only in the last quarter of the twentieth century. It then became the dominant form of identity and cultural discourse.

Late modernity's demand to recognize every human being's need to belong to a tradition and a culture, and to refrain from imposing a uniform cultural standard, translated into changes in all areas of life – gender relations, the structure of the family, labor relations, and the structure and identity of the political community. These changes were catalyzed by the technological revolutions of the twentieth century, most importantly the digital, information, and media revolutions. The internet, emerging in the 1990s, enabled every person not only to easily access large quantities of information but also to participate in its production, design, and dissemination. These new possibilities undermined hierarchies and established authority structures, from the authority of the teacher in schools and universities, through that of clergy and experts, to that of political leaders. The massive mobility of people, merchandise, and ideas, along with modern media and the internet, also challenged existing frameworks of identity and culture. Cultural-national labels (French, Jewish, Israeli) that were once perceived to be hard and fast grew more and more fuzzy. The world's great cities gradually became world cities, home to myriad people from around the globe, with "glocal" cultures, where the global and local live side by side. Cultural glocalism has slowly seeped out of the large cities, raising questions about the identity and culture of society as a whole. How should a given society's culture be delineated in light of the recognition that the society is composed of disparate identity groups undergoing ongoing change and intensive shaping through immigration and under the cultural influence of the economy, global media, and the internet? What should the institutions and law of such a society look like? How is the economic pie to be divided among its members? In the modern world, with its "assault of associations," Leon Wieseltier has written, "We are carrying too much. We are falling out of our hands. We need a basket. The name of the basket is identity."[4]

Questions of identity and culture have become more and more central in the academic and intellectual worlds as well, constituting what has been called the cultural turn in the human sciences. In the universities, this change has been manifested in the growth of modern cultural studies and hermeneutics. In *The Interpretation of Cultures*, the American anthropologist Clifford Geertz formulated the fundamental concept of this new scholarship. The important work of the human sciences, he maintained (following Max Weber), is to understand and interpret the webs of meaning, identity, and culture that people and societies have spun for themselves throughout history. Universities celebrated the cultural turn by offering courses, sponsoring research projects, and establishing cultural studies departments and programs. The issues of identity and culture have also taken a more central place in literature and art.

Likewise, a new identity politics has largely taken the place of the civil rights discourse and the discussion of social and economic questions. The new politics has been characterized by parties and organizations constructed on the basis of identity groups demanding recognition, political representation, and funding for their cultures. In Israel, this new way of thinking led to the establishment and success of ethnic parties (the Mizrahi-Haredi Shas party being the most notable one today), the fracturing of Israel's religious parties along cultural, religious, and ethnic lines (Hasidim, Lithuanians, Sephardim, and national-religious). Israel has also seen the emergence of Arab parties with cultural-nationalist or religious (largely Muslim) platforms. On the dangerous and ugly fringes, this phenomenon has produced racist hyper-nationalist parties, like Rabbi Meir Kahane's Kach.

The dominance of the identity and cultural discourse since the second half of the 1970s was also a response to comprehensive and deep processes that began during the last quarter of the twentieth century and which continue today. These led to the gradual collapse of the modern political and economic order put in place at the end of the nineteenth century. At the beginning of the 1970s, Western countries crafted a neo-liberal view of politics and economics that demanded an end, or a major curtailment, of government intervention in local and international commercial, labor, and capital

4 Wieseltier, "Against Identity."

markets. This involved the removal of restrictions on international commerce and capital transfers, large-scale and largely unregulated privatization of pubic assets and services, ongoing and mounting evisceration of welfare policy, repeal of labor protections, and growing economic disparity within and between countries. These changes led (and continue to lead) to a series of acute and wide-ranging economic crises that sent entire societies spiraling into poverty and social inequality. These crises began in Africa (which suffered from a long economic crisis beginning in the 1970s), then reached Latin America, East Asia, and finally hit the economies of the West and the world at large.

One of the most notable and influential changes that came with the new economic policy was that the so-called labor society, that stable social order in which most adults (more precisely, most men and increasing numbers of women) worked at steady jobs, frequently unionized ones, and their work paid for broad cradle-to-grave state-provided social services. This social model was gradually undercut by the new policies, a process which became especially salient throughout the industrialized world in the 1980s. Labor unions lost much of their power, unemployment rose to high levels, the number of working poor increased, and job security grew ever more tenuous. These phenomena affected both national and international labor markets. Sink-or-swim industrial policies caused a wave of factory and service closures in wealthy countries (where they were less efficient) and their transfer to places where production costs were lower. In the other direction, millions of desperate labor migrants abandoned poor countries and communities and followed the flow of capital and wealth while trying to get around the strict immigration policies practiced by wealthy countries. As organized labor lost its power, welfare programs contracted, privatization increased, and a huge amount of capital accumulated, which was not properly taxed and not fairly distributed.[5] The result was growing social and economic disparity that led to many feeling insecure about both the present and the future.

The devastation of the welfare state and labor society contributed to the rise of the identity and cultural discourse in three ways. First, privatization and the decline in welfare services eroded state power and shifted it to sectors of society. In Israel, for example, new ethnic and sectoral parties born in the 1980s gained power from privatization, which enabled them to establish their own sectoral educational and welfare services – Shas's school systems, welfare programs funded by West Bank settlers, and the social and educational

[5] Beck, *Brave New World*.

networks set up by the different arms of the Islamic movement. Privatization was thus the parallel of the cultural discourse in the social and economic sphere. Another product was a series of new middle-class political parties that combined national rhetoric with a sectoral identity. Despite their rhetoric, they operated in large measure as sectoral parties (beginning with the Democratic Movement for Change in the 1970s and continuing with today's Yesh Atid party).[6]

Second, the new economic forces, and the sectoral politics that came with them, encouraged the identity discourse because it not only gave voice to sectoralization and privatization, but also served as a smoke screen that obscured the dissolution of the welfare state, not to mention serious discrimination and violation of fundamental rights. For example, until the social protests of the summer of 2011, public debate in Israel and most of the industrialized world focused on questions of identity and culture, giving much less attention to economic inequality, labor and economic vulnerability, and fundamental social rights. In much the same way, the conversation between the Jewish majority and Arab minority in Israel has in recent years focused much more on issues of language and culture. It has largely disregarded the fact that Israeli Arabs are free to live their lives and educate their children in their own language and according to their own culture, yet suffer from severe discrimination and ongoing infringement of their civil-legal and social rights.

Third, the decline in job and economic security and the anxiety that it and the technological revolution and its accompanying cultural changes have created have contributed not only to the rise in the identity discourse but also to religious, national, and cultural self-isolation, throughout the world. Since the 1980s, Israeli society, and the Israeli legal system, have devoted much energy to Israeli identity and culture, often out of a feeling that these are menaced and under threat. Many are inclined to view the economic and cultural changes of the late twentieth century as "foreign," "universalist," or "globalist," engines of change coming from the outside and threatening local culture. The public discourse throughout the world is awash with polarities, such as "local-global," "particular-universal," "native-foreign," and of course "Jewish-democratic." This anxiety is also one of the explanations for the resurgence of religions and growing popularity of religious parties and organizations throughout the world, Israel included. The New Age search for spirituality is another manifestation of this process,[7] as is the redoubled piety of believers, and their greater adherence to local and particular customs.

6 Gutwein, "Identity vs. Class"; Gutwein, "Dialectics of Equality"; Yatziv, *Sectorial Society*.
7 Katz and Kedar, "Secular Israeli," 191–199; Katz, Ratzabi, and Yadgar, *Beyond Halacha*.

In Israel, this can be seen both among religious Jews of the modern Orthodox community, many of whom are becoming more Haredi in their lifestyles and beliefs, and among non-Jews, as manifested in increasing support for Islamic parties and a return to religion in the Druze community. Cultural isolation also takes the form of the establishment and growing strength of nationalist and even racist parties and organizations in many countries around the world, Israel included. These groups proclaim themselves the defenders of local and national culture and identity, and take a stand against immigration and foreign cultures that are inundating the state. They preach cultural purity and take action against labor and other migrants, or against cultural minorities. The struggle between Europe's Christian majority and Muslim immigrants is an example of a cultural struggle fed in large measure by a sense of fear, isolation, and cultural-religious extremism on both sides.

Cultural self-isolation extends beyond the areas of religion and nationalism. It has a wide range of cultural manifestations in all strata of society, including in the intellectual elite. Even though the members of this group do not like to admit it, anxiety about who they are and what practices and beliefs set them apart, along with fear of change, are what fuel their obsessive preoccupation with their culture and identity. Among social elites in Israel and around the world, especially their older or conservative members, this anxiety is linked to the common concern of intellectuals that their culture is in decline among the young – a phenomenon that appears in all societies and in all eras. Throughout history, adults have bewailed the younger generation, which is always accused of debasing language, culture, and spirit. But these voices seem to be louder now, with the vast and sweeping changes in all areas of life that have taken place since the end of the twentieth century, and the anxiety they express seems to be the moving force behind many cultural projects. Religious and secular study programs modeled on the traditional *yeshiva*, study festivals, Jewish identity and culture workshops, projects aimed at preserving and promoting "the riches of the Jewish bookshelf," and Jewish cultural festivals are just some of the programs that became popular in Israel at the end of the twentieth century and beginning of the twenty-first. These arise not just from the interest of the children and grandchildren of immigrants in their Jewish roots but also from a sense of urgency and concern that Jewish-Hebrew culture needs to be saved now, "just a moment before it vanishes." The same feeling has, for example, spurred "emergency programs" to instill "Israeli heritage" in the school system, from preschool up. It also lies behind the decision, in 1997, to mandate that the Israel Broadcast Authority's popular music station, Reshet Gimmel, play only songs in Hebrew (ironically, the music can be American, Arabic, Turkish, Greek, or French, as long as the words are in Hebrew). Likewise, it has spurred the new impetus, in the legal realm, for Jewish-Hebrew law and the legal definition of Israel as a Jewish and democratic state. The advocates of all these cultural projects are fired up by the same sense of mission, urgency, and cultural anxiety that lay behind Ahad Ha'am's cultural endeavor to collect and collate the treasures of Jewish culture in a form that could save them from the death of religious belief and make them accessible to modern Jews. The best known of these projects is *Sefer Ha'agadah* (*Book of Legends*), the collection of rabbinic stories and homilies that Hayim Nahman Bialik and Yehoshua Ravnitzky culled from the Talmud and midrashic works at the beginning of the twentieth century.[8]

Finally, cultural self-isolation has led to the judicialization of society. The law has become a prominent feature of politics and culture, and legal institutions have become more involved in shaping social policy. Traditional politics has proved unable to provide a response to the vast changes that have occurred in the labor society, economy, and culture, or to offer stability and certainty. The result has been increasing distrust of elected political institutions and contempt for politics as an instrument of social change. The prevailing capitalist state of mind, sectoral politics, and the identity discourse have together fostered the view that politics is corrupt, inefficient, petty, and dirty by its very nature. Elected officials are seen as status seekers who want only to advance their personal interests, or the interests of the sector that sent them into public life. In such a world, law seems like the final resort – it is a collection of basic rules of the game, the common denominator that makes social life possible, that can provide the predictability and stability that postmodern humankind seeks. The law's ostensible neutrality looked to many like an objective, clean, stable, and effective alternative to the corruption and ineptness of politics. Law has thus become a means of fashioning an alternative to politics, or itself an alternative.[9]

Cultural self-isolation has thus manifested itself in the increasing strength of both religion and the law. These two fields have, in recent years, developed a love-hate relationship that grows out of the tension between them and the theoretical and institutional struggle in which they are engaged. Yet the two fields have also worked together, as expressed by the religious discourse's penetration of the law, on the one hand,[10] and the judicialization of religion,

[8] Ahad Ha'am, "Treasure of Judaism"; Bialik and Ravnitzky, *Book of Legends*.

[9] Bareli and Kedar, *Israeli Republicanism*, 110–115.

[10] Ran Hirschl has noted the great similarity between the late modernist legal discourse and religious discourse, and also the alliance between religions and constitutional theory (and practice). See *Constitutional Theocracy*.

on the other hand. The latter is especially evident in law-based religions, such as Judaism and Islam, where the growing strength of religion has taken the form of stricter observance of religious law, at the expense of the non-legal elements of religion. As an expression of cultural self-isolation, the judicialization of society and religion is a patently modern phenomenon, quite different from the dynamic and pluralist nature of Jewish and Islamic law in previous generations.

This process of judicialization began in Israel in the 1960s,[11] and became especially visible in the 1980s. It could be seen primarily in the growing involvement of the courts, and the Supreme Court in particular, in areas that the judiciary had traditionally stayed away from, from family life to the shaping of public policy and intervention in matters of foreign and defense policy. Judicialization can also be seen in the growing importance of legal counsel in both civilian agencies and the military, as well as outside government. Moreover, these legal advisers have become more involved in politics, the economy, and culture, making the law a more salient presence in cultural and public life. In the media, columns and programs covering the courts have proliferated, and attorneys and judges have become familiar figures, and in some cases celebrities. The law's burgeoning importance has led to a huge rise in the number of law students. Law faculties at Israel's public universities have expanded and private law schools have opened.[12]

In Israel, the rise of the identity and cultural discourse has also been spurred by local factors, some of which are of course the products of the more general phenomena described above. The most important of these local factors is the decline of the labor movement and the metamorphosis of the Israeli political system from a consensus democracy based on a single dominant party (Mapai and its later incarnation, the Labor Party) into a polarized two-party system in constant crisis. This latter system prevailed from the end of the 1970s through the middle of the 2000s. There were two large rival parties of roughly equal strength, Likud and Labor, and a number of smaller sectoral parties – religious, ethnic-based, and national. The latter (except the Arab parties) served as the kingmakers; without their support neither of the large parties could form a government. As such, the small parties were able to wield power beyond their numbers, leading to the distribution of funds on a clearly sectoral basis. This sectoral politics was explained and justified largely by means of a

[11] Harris, "Spread of Law."

[12] On the judicialization of Israeli society, see Kedar, "Interpretive Revolution," 765–772; Almog, "Legal Revolution"; Gutwein, "Constitutional Revolution"; Mautner, *Law and the Culture*, 54–98.

new identity and cultural discourse that, for all intents and purposes, granted legitimacy to the undermining of the civil consensus in Israeli society. The identity discourse highlighted the political and other injustices that young Israeli society had inflicted on a variety of groups, such as Palestinian Arabs, Mizrahi Jews, and Holocaust survivors, and depicted the existing political order, and even the desire for social change, as the products of a discourse of aggression and arbitrary cultural conventions dictated by dominant social groups. Sectoral politics and the identity politics that fires and justifies it have ensconced in Israeli consciousness a view that society is a battlefield on which identity groups fight for advantage, thus underlining and even artificially inflating ethnic, religious, and national divides. In a feedback loop, this view has reinforced aggressive sectoral politics. In the 1970s, for example, the Black Panthers, a protest group of young Mizrahim, demanded an expansion of equality to truly include all parts of the population; the most potent Mizrahi political force since the 1990s, Shas, has demanded resources and used its political power to foster cultural uniqueness and exclusive identity that it claims to represent.

The decline of the labor movement is important not only because the structure of Israeli democracy has changed but also because of the decline of the hegemonic group that had controlled politics, social institutions, and also to a large extent Israeli culture since at least the 1930s. The decline of the labor movement as the dominant party that led governing coalitions and oversaw Israel's consensual democracy was but the political expression of this loss of hegemony. There were other manifestations as well. First, the Likud's rise to power marked and set in motion a process in which the labor movement and the organizations associated with it began to lose their hold over society and the economy. These included the Histadrut labor union and the economic concerns that the Histadrut controlled; Kupat Holim Clalit, the Histadrut's health service organization; youth movements; and, to a lesser extent, settlement movements. Second, the culture associated with the labor movement also suffered. The labor movement had, from its inception, seen itself not only as the engine of Zionism and Israeli culture, but also, in keeping with socialist tradition, as what Hegel called the "general class," that class whose interests and values reflect and largely coincide with society's general interests. This self-image of the labor movement percolated into Israeli culture and consciousness thanks to the movement's control of political, economic, and cultural institutions and, even more so, thanks to the movement's social-democratic and inclusive policies, and its long success in absorbing the country's myriad immigrants economically, culturally, and politically. When the labor movement began to decline, groups that had been on the margins of

Israeli society, or which had been overshadowed by the labor movement, began to move onto the center stage of politics and the social discourse and to vie for supremacy. In the absence of a hegemonic force, these groups engaged in a large-scale culture war, fought along the Israeli society's national, religious, ethnic, and economic fissures.[13] The cultural debate that arose following the decline of the labor hegemony was largely a replay of the cultural conflict that modern Jewish society had grappled with since the eighteenth century, as a result of secularization and modernization and the religious community's loss of its hegemony over governmental, economic, and cultural frameworks.[14]

Beyond political change and privatization, the identity and cultural polemic in Israel was spurred also by the huge demographic changes the country underwent in the 1990s – the large waves of immigration from the former Soviet Union and Ethiopia, and increasing labor migration. A million new immigrants and hundreds of thousands of labor migrants changed the face of Israeli society into something else entirely, requiring it to cope, for the first time, with phenomena such as large groups of immigrants who adopted a Jewish-Israeli lifestyle but who were not halakhically Jewish,[15] as well as immigrants and labor migrants who, because of their skin color, constituted a visible minority that suffered from severe and conspicuous discrimination. Finally, the intensification of Jewish settlement in the West Bank and Gaza Strip, the peace process of the early 1990s, the Palestinian uprisings, and Israel's disengagement from the Gaza Strip all required Israelis to grapple, once again, with the questions of the boundaries of their nation-state and majority-minority relations. All these also encouraged the rise of the identity and culture discourse in Israel.[16]

The cultural and identity discourse's intrusion into legislation and into legal and public discourse at the end of the twentieth century was part of a global trend, and thus not surprising in and of itself. In Israel, and in the world as a whole, these new cultural and socioeconomic developments produced two sorts of debate, constitutional and moral-political-social, that often critiqued the legal discourse on rights. In the legal-constitutional realm, it took the form of a demand for recognition of identity and culture as an additional, third form of human rights, alongside the two forms recognized by the law. The first of

[13] Mautner, *Law and the Culture*, 99–158; Kimmerling, *Invention and Decline*, 112–129; Kimmerling, *End of Askenazi Hegemony*.

[14] Mautner, *Law and the Culture*, 99–142, 181–192; Sagi, *Jewish-Israeli Voyage*, 175–179.

[15] Cohen, *Israeli Assimilation*.

[16] Cohen and Susser, *From Accommodation*, 71–170; Cohen and Susser, *Israel and the Politics*, 100–126.

these was civil-legal rights, such as the freedoms of speech and assembly, to vote and be elected, and free access to courts. The second was social rights, such as the right to health and welfare. Now the law was expected to recognize collective-cultural rights as legal and even "constitutional." The right to one's language, to education according to specific values, to affiliation with a religion or recognition of a certain lifestyle were gradually recognized by courts and legislatures as bearing legal force. Furthermore, the constitutional identity discourse demanded that human, civil, and social rights be coupled with identity because, in reality, rights and resources are often distributed in accordance with affiliation with a specific gender or identity group.

At the same time, recognition of the importance of identity and culture became part of the extra-legal discussion that sought to supplement the legal rights discourse with a broader social and moral one that sees human beings as more than just creatures with rights. It could be seen in channels of communication outside the law, such as those that were put in place in Rwanda after the genocide of the mid-1990s, the Truth and Reconciliation Commissions established in South Africa after the fall of apartheid, and the dialogue, mediation, and conflict resolution processes that have become accepted all over the world. The identity discourse in its fullest sense is, in fact, an extra-legal one almost by definition. It is a dynamic dialogue among people and groups who unendingly examine and interpret their traditions and values in light of a heterogeneous, complex, and constantly changing reality, and in light of the cultures and values of other groups. Law cannot really address identity itself, its dilemmas, and the relation between commitment to a given tradition and the constant need for change, because the law must reach decisions. It can only speak "legalese," that is, in terms of rights, duties, responsibilities, and immunities. As such, it must translate the "full" identity discourse into the language of the legal discourse of rights. The law does not really address the identity discourse, only the rights that derive from identity.[17] The legal discourse focuses on compromises and balances between cultural rights and the rights and interests of others, such as freedom of movement, or public safety. That explains why the new identity discourse served, in the last third of the twentieth century, as a principal source of critique of the limited rights discourse that portrays human beings as one-dimensional, and calls for the legal discourse to be complemented by wider practices and dialogues.

[17] Sagi, *Jewish-Israeli Voyage*, 147. Sagi argues persuasively that the rights discourse is the foundation for the identity discourse, as it assumes the abstract universal identity of human beings while also recognizing the particular identity of each one.

In the previous chapter, I showed that jurists did not encourage the identity discourse's incursion into the law. Most of the top figures in the Justice Ministry opposed the inclusion of the expressions "Israel's heritage" and "Jewish and democratic state" in legislation, and judges avoided, to every extent they could, addressing questions of identity and culture.[18] The cultural debate was fanned largely, on the one hand, by the sectoralized political system and, on the other, by intellectuals and educators. Despite this, and despite the fact that most jurists were uncomfortable with it, the law has played a central role in the turbulent debate that has been going on since the 1980s over the question of Israel's Jewish identity and culture. Not only have many jurists taken part in the debate,[19] but its very title – the Jewish and democratic state debate – is taken from the language of the law, and it has been defined and conducted as a conflict between the state's Jewish and democratic attributes. Despite the courts' neutral rhetoric, and despite their refusal to define Jewish identity, they too have contributed to the debate over identity and culture by agreeing to be the central arena where groups and sectors of Israeli society battle out their conflicts.[20] The expression "Jewish and democratic state" has thus become the central axis of the constitutional debates conducted by the Knesset, civics lessons in schools, education programs in the Israel Defense Forces, and discussions in civil and social bodies of various types. The central question in all these is how to translate the nebulous expression "Jewish and democratic state" into concrete constitutional-legal and social arrangements. In other words, how can the state's Jewish identity, and the Jewish identity of its legal system, institutions, educational system, and cultural activities, be maintained?[21]

The law has, for example, affected the substance and form of public discourse. Sectoral politics, along with economic, social, and cultural changes in Israel, have impelled intellectuals, academics, rabbis, educators, and public figures to launch numerous projects to brake what they see as the centrifugal forces threatening to tear Israeli society apart. Among other things, they have sought to encourage dialogue between the different groups to create

[18] I have addressed this issue at length in Chapter 7.

[19] See, among many examples, Elon, "Constitution by Legislation"; Barak, *Interpretation in Law*, 328–347; Barak, "Values of Israel"; Gavison, "Democracy and Judaism"; Gavison, *Can Israel*; Margolin, *State of Israel*; David, *State of Israel*; Rubinstein and Yakobson, *Israel and the Family of Nations*. A special issue of *Tel Aviv University Law Review* 19, no. 3 (1995) was dedicated to debate on Jewish and democratic state.

[20] Gutwein, "Constitutional Revolution."

[21] For example, the central textbook for civics classes in Israel has the title *Being Citizens in Israel: In a Jewish and Democratic State*. See Addan, Ashkenazi, and Alperson, *Being Citizens*.

sociopolitical cooperation and find Israeli society a common denominator of culture and values that can counteract the explosive forces. At the same time, the Israel Democracy Institute and other bodies have led an initiative to enact what they call a "constitution by consensus." As its name implies, it seeks to be an inclusive document that also expresses the identities of the varied groups in Israel's democratic society.[22] Law has played a central role in these initiatives. First, the meetings organized to draft a model constitution were conducted in the form of legislative debates or discussions of public policy. Their goal was not only to enable those involves to ponder, talk, and clarify issues together, but also to make it possible to find practical solutions to conflicts that need to be resolved. Problems of concern to Israeli society, such as education, immigration, and employment, were raised, and the participants tried to solve them in a practical way that could gain the consent of the different groups they claimed to represent. The results of these meetings were summed up in documents of a legal character, such as "compacts" and legislative proposals.[23] Furthermore, many of the meetings were convened under the Jewish and democratic state rubric, taken from the Basic Law.

While these "encounters" and "compacts" sought to give voice to the identity and culture discourse, they actually have been couched in the legal rights discourse. The participants did not maintain a long-term open dialogue examining their identities in relation to other identities. Rather, as in political negotiations or a legal discussion of limited time, they stated their rights, interests, and needs along with their identities, and were prepared to compromise, but not to truly change. Indeed, the goal of the encounters was largely practical – to find balances and compromises between different concepts of identity in Israeli society and ensconce these compromises in legal documents such as compacts or a proposed constitution.[24]

At first glance, these dialogue encounters did not extend beyond the format of similar meetings that have taken place since the dawn of Zionism, and which were meant to find a way toward common political action in keeping with the Zionist movement's tradition of consensus democracy. The most that could be said against them was that they lacked authority and were politically pointless because most of the participants were intellectuals who claimed to speak in the name of publics that had not chosen them as their voices. But, unlike previous eras, the encounters that took place at the end of the twentieth century were conducted as part of the awakening identity and culture

[22] Shamgar et al., *Constitution by Consensus*.

[23] See, for example, Gavison and Medan, *Gavison–Medan Covenant*; Dromi, *Brethren Dwelling*.

[24] Sagi, *Jewish-Israeli Voyage*, 152–153, 178.

discourse, and the explicit major goal of most of them was to fashion a common Israeli identity. Intellectuals, academics, rabbis, educators, and artists demanded that Israelis "boldly confront" who they are, and at the same time fashion a common Jewish-Israeli identity and ways that it could be expressed in their private and public lives. To that end, they sponsored thousands of seminars, conferences, dialogue encounters, study groups, and Jewish identity workshops. In all this, the recent Israeli discussion of these issues has gone beyond the traditions of the Zionist movement and Israeli society, which made a clear separation between political and legal discourse and cultural encounters, and which deliberately avoided any attempt to delineate a Jewish-Israeli identity. The legal nature of the cultural debate grew even stronger in 2011, when the draft of the Basic Law: Israel – The Nation-State of the Jewish People (called the Jewish Nation-State Law for short) was introduced in the Knesset. The purpose of the proposed law was to secure the state's Jewish identity as a constitutional requirement. At the beginning of the new millennium, the law became the central axis of a vehement debate over identity and culture, the central arena of the conflict. The bill went through eight different incarnations and was the subject of considerable political, religious, and cultural controversy, to the point that it helped bring down Israel's two-year-old government at the end of 2014, leading to new elections early the following year. It was finally enacted in the summer of 2018, despite the impassioned opposition of both Jews and non-Jews in Israel and around the world.[25]

A comparison between the constitutional debate in Israel since 2000 and the brief one that followed the establishment of the state is instructive. In both cases, the participants were not all that interested in questions of governance and human rights; their major concern was matters of identity. In the country's early period, the issue at hand was the wording of the preamble to a constitution; since the turn of the century, the heart of the constitutional debate has been the meaning of the phrase "Jewish and democratic state." The fruitless Knesset debate of the early 1950s led Israel's parliament to refrain from defining Israeli identity in its constitution, and instead to enact a constitution piece by piece, without a preamble defining the Israeli demos. Likewise, when the Knesset took up the issue of how to inculcate Jewish consciousness through the schools, the debate ended with general and equivocal declarations rather than operative decisions and budgetary outlays;[26] debates over culture in meetings of the early Zionist Congresses had ended

[25] Rabinovich, *Defining Israel*, xv.

[26] Minutes of the Knesset Education Committee, November 19 and 26, December 3, 1957; June 2 and 6, 1959; Knesset records, June 9, 10, and 15, 1959.

in much the same way. The Israeli political leadership, like the Zionist leadership before it, sought in every way possible to temper the heat of the identity debate, lest it turn into a culture war that could do great harm to the fragile state. "There are at present much more urgent matters before us, and they must be solved before this *kulturkampf* takes place in our midst," Prime Minister Ben-Gurion told the Provisional State Council in 1948.[27]

In contrast, at the beginning of the twenty-first century, it was the government and ruling party that sought, for all intents and purposes, to legislate the missing preamble to the constitution, in the form of the Nation-State Law, and to transform the cultural polemic into a constitutional struggle in the Knesset, courts, and public. It was a real revolution in Zionist thinking, a post-Zionist step that backtracked from the semi-official policy of Hovevei Zion, Herzl, religious Zionist leader Rabbi Yitzchak Yaacov Reines, Jabotinsky, and Ben-Gurion, all of whom sought to avoid cultural conflict. In their view, cultural questions should be dealt with in separate cultural and educational arenas and kept out of legislation and legal discourse. We have come a long way since 1899, when Hovevei Zion leader Moshe Leib Lilienblum declared: "If the good of our people is precious to you, if you are true Zionists, advocate Zion alone ... do not destroy our unity, let no person demand of his compatriot what he will not give up under any circumstances."[28]

Presumably the members of the Knesset, cabinet ministers, and intellectuals involved in today's public debate indeed wish to shape an inclusive politics and reinforce solidarity in Israeli society. The Basic Laws enacted in 1992 did not use language that made Judaism a limit on democracy and equality before the law. This may have raised hopes that the expression "Jewish and democratic state" would be understood as a term calling for inclusion, solidarity, and commonality, not as one that placed "Jewish" against "democratic" and which would set off a large-scale polemic about Israeli identity. At the time those Basic Laws were enacted, perhaps, it was still possible to hope that the law would be wiser than its legislator, that society would interpret the laws in a way that would neutralize their "cultural sting." Unfortunately, the opposite happened. Soon after it first appeared in law, the coinage was not read as a uniting and inclusive constitutional declaration, but as constitutional recognition of the deep fault running through Israeli society, and as a symbol of the stormy and sometimes violent cultural debate that has roiled Israeli society ever since.

[27] Minutes of the Provisional State Council, December 16, 1948, 24–25, ISA.

[28] Lilienblum, "Symbol of Jealousy," 266.

The phrase "Jewish and democratic state" was painted in the colors of an identity and culture war principally because of the severe political disputes bound up in the enactment of the two Basic Laws of 1992. The poisonous atmosphere of the 1990s reached its tragic apogee with the assassination of Prime Minister Yitzhak Rabin in 1995. Then, when sectoral politics and the shrill identity discourse were at their height, Basic Laws laying out human rights became, immediately after their enactment, the center of religious and cultural dissension.[29] The *Mitral* case of 1993 made it clear that even Basic Law: Freedom of Occupation could set off a conflict between religious and secular Jews. The case involved a series of suits filed by a meat importer who claimed that his right to freedom of occupation prevented the government from restricting, for religious reasons, the importation of non-kosher meat. The initial suit set off a furor in the Knesset and Cabinet, which reached its height when Shas threatened to bolt from Yitzhak Rabin's government if no solution was found – which would have aborted the peace process the government was pursuing. The end result was that the Basic Law was amended by adding an override clause that empowered the Knesset to pass, under certain conditions, a time-limited law that would override the provisions of the Basic Law.[30]

But for many Israelis (both religious and non-religious), the Basic Laws of 1992 had by this time become fixed in their minds as threats to the Jewish character (religious or national) of the state. The Supreme Court's use of the Basic Laws to constrain legislative initiatives regarding kashrut, conversion to Judaism, conscription into the army, and other controversial issues on which the secular majority and religious minority differed cast the Court into the maelstrom of the identity and culture debate and early on painted the legal discourse and public debate in the black-and-white terms of an (imagined) tension between Judaism and democracy.[31] Later, the supporters of the Jewish Nation-State Law would claim that its purpose was to anchor the Jewish identity of the state in a Basic Law on the grounds that there had been, over the previous twenty years, a dramatic erosion in the weight the Supreme

[29] Cohen and Susser, *Israel and the Politics*, 73–126; Sapir, *The Israeli Constitution*, 31–74; Mautner, *Law and the Culture*, 44–53.

[30] HCJ 3872/93 *Mitral Ltd. v. Prime Minister and Minister of Religious Affairs* [2003] IsrSC 57 (5) 485.

[31] On the claim that the Supreme Court in fact took the secular-liberal side in the culture debate, see Mautner, *Law and the Culture*, 143–158. Ran Hirschl has shown that, like other Supreme Courts around the world, the Israeli Court took a liberal point of view by stressing in particular the civil-legal discourse of negative rights. See Hirschl, "Negative Rights."

Court ascribed to Israel's Jewish character.[32] According to the explanatory notes appended to the July 2015 version of the bill, "The purpose of this Basic Law is to protect in basic legislation Israel's status as the nation-state of the Jewish people in equal status to Israel's Basic Laws protecting human rights and the democratic character of the state."[33] The hope that the Basic Laws of 1992 would articulate a fundamental and accepted definition of Israeli identity was dashed. The cultural war that Lilienblum, Herzl, Jabotinsky, and Ben-Gurion had feared was now a reality.

It is ironic, or perhaps tragic, that the "Jewish and democratic state" debate actually distorts the image of Judaism, Zionism, and Israeli society. It distorts Judaism by disregarding its dynamic nature and pluralist history, reducing it to a conservative and hermetic cult that adheres to its ancient rules and refuses to recognize the winds of change that modernity has brought. It distorts Zionism in that it denies the fundamental Zionist view that Judaism is a broad national cultural position that bridges over modern Jews' differences of religion and culture, and because it turns its back on the Zionist movement's great success in establishing a functioning, democratic, law-based, open, and pluralist state in which Jews of diverse kinds are free to live full Jewish lives.[34]

The accepted interpretation of the phrase "Jewish and democratic state" also misrepresents the nature of Israeli society. An entire Israeli generation, born and educated after the enactment of the Basic Laws of 1992, believes that there is a contradiction, or at least painful tension, between the terms "Jewish" and "democratic," seeing them as two values that represent different worlds. Even if they do not contradict each other, in this view, they are in conflict, and it is thus necessary to balance them and compromise between them. Even more seriously, this generation sees the expression "Jewish and democratic state" not just as a definition of the state of Israel but rather as a faithful *representation* of Israel's polarized society, and even legal acknowledgment of that reality. In this warped depiction, Israeli society consists of two camps, each bearing its single banner – Jews versus democrats, religious Jews versus secular Jews, advocates of "authentic" Jewish culture versus modern "Hellenizers" who prefer universal values of foreign origin, such as citizenship and democracy. That, of course, is a lamentable error. There is no tension at all between "Jewish" and "democratic." Millions of Jews, religious and non-religious, live as citizens of democratic, law-based countries, and happily it

[32] See, for example, Bakshi, "Basic Law."

[33] Basic Law Proposal: Israel – The Nation-State of the Jewish People (2015, P/20/1989), July 29, 2015. For the English version, see Rabinovich, *Defining Israel*, 108.

[34] Kedar, "On the Danger"; Kedar, *Should Jewish Identity*.

causes no agonized and painful tension for their identities. The counterfeit tension between being a Jew and being a citizen of a democratic country never bothered the Zionist movement; it arose only in the wake of the enactment of the Basic Laws of 1992 and was exacerbated by sectoral politics and a belligerent and vulgar version of the identity discourse in Israel.

The problem is that this baseless view shapes a polarized and dangerous social reality. The expression "Jewish and democratic state" may have been meant (so hoped its formulators) to reinforce the civic unity of society and to delineate a fundamental Israeli identity, but in the quarter-century since the phrase entered the law books sectoral ghettoization and isolation has reached new heights. This ghettoization can be seen not only in sectarian political parties, schools, and other institutions, but first and foremost in geographical segregation.[35] Haredi, national-religious, and secular Jews, all of whom live in the "Jewish and democratic state," largely live in separate communities or neighborhoods and, more recently, may even serve in separate army units. The same is true of different Arab groups, and lately of refugees and labor migrants. They also attend different schools. They can live full lives without ever engaging in deep conversation with someone from a different group, much less having to live as neighbors and civic partners, or to display solidarity in any practical way. Even though everyone lauds the identity discourse, and despite the call to respect and even include the other, Israelis are increasingly closing themselves off in separate, homogeneous communities. They have no real experience of living alongside others who live their lives and view the world in different ways, and they do not engage in any real open and tolerant dialogue about identity with those others. Huge socioeconomic, political, and sectoral disparities, and the intolerance of the Israeli identity and culture debate, are manifestations of this segregation at the same time that they reinforce it.

Finally, the insistence that Israel's Jewish identity find expression in laws and judicial rulings is a danger to the law and weakens the rule of law and Israel's democratic character. Law is not an appropriate arena for fleshing out sensitive questions of identity, as identity is an evasive, dynamic, and changing thing that cannot be defined in a clear, consensual, and stable way, whereas the principal job of the law is to decide social conflicts and direct behavior. The demand that judges take part in the cultural polemic sidetracks them from their important task of resolving disputes and is detrimental to an important social institution. It also requires judges to take sides in an identity

[35] Yacobi and Cohen, *Separation*.

conflict that cannot, in fact, be decided, and thus undermines the legitimacy of the courts and the rule of law, which depend on the law being seen as fair, impersonal, and objective.

The identity and culture discourse has made an important contribution to society. It has given a voice to silenced groups and contributed to the creation of a more egalitarian, open, accepting, and pluralist society engaged in constant examination and updating of its identity (even if it does not acknowledge explicitly that it is doing so). A legal system that recognizes that society's voices are many and varied is an important means by which we can express our new multicultural sensitivity. We use law to uproot unacceptable phenomena of discrimination and exclusion, and to create a fairer and more equal division of social goods. But the key thing to remember is that a true identity discourse is one of uncertainty; it is ongoing and never-ending, a dialogue that goes back and forth between tradition and change, between the cultures and values that require us, like it or not, to reinterpret our identities. The law is not the right place for such a discussion. Inserting vague formulas of identity, such as "Israel's heritage" and "Jewish and democratic state," or "protect[ing] Israel's status as the nation-state of the Jewish people" in the legalese of a Basic Law has not bolstered Israel's Jewish identity. On the contrary, it has set off cultural conflict that threatens to tear Israeli society apart. This cultural debate has corroded the civic unity of Israeli society, and as part of that the legitimacy of the law itself. It has done damage to democracy, and has even dealt a heavy blow to the concepts of Judaism and Zionism that tie Jews and Israelis together. Because of the enormous danger involved in bringing the culture and identity debate into the law, it behooves us to compare the current situation to the long history of failures to found Israeli law on Jewish-Hebrew content and declarations of identity. We also need to keep in mind Israeli society's impressive success in constituting an advanced and independent Israeli cultural and legal system while avoiding a penetrating, courageous, and deep discussion of the Jewish-Hebrew content of the law. The comparison shows that it would be best to curb the demand to express the Israeli character of Israeli law by basing it on Jewish content and highlight other ways of constituting Israeli culture and Israeli law. That will be the subject of this book's final part.

PART III

Zionism, Democracy, Law, and Culture

9

Zionism

Making and Preserving Hebrew Culture

This book's two previous parts show that the Israeli character of Israeli law cannot be based on Jewish content (or style) in the law. The history of the last century is replete with failed attempts to imbue Israeli law with Jewish-Hebrew substance. Even the inclusion of a general declaration in Israel's Basic Laws stating that the country is a "Jewish and democratic state," that its residual law would be "the principles of freedom, justice, equity and peace of Hebrew Law and Israel's heritage" or that Israel is the nation-state of the Jewish people, turned out to be ineffectual, causing more damage than good. Must we regretfully conclude, then, that Israeli law is not really Israeli? Not at all. The Jewish state has indeed produced its own Israeli laws and legal system, often displaying originality, drawing from and perpetuating Jewish heritage. In this final part of my book I will reexamine Zionist history and again juxtapose it with the history of Israeli law. I will show that Zionism is closely bound up with Jewish culture and that it has played a major role in sustaining and reinforcing it. The same can be said for Israeli law and the Jewish legal tradition. In the present chapter I will address the relationship between Zionism and Jewish culture, and in the next I will consider Israeli law as the most important instrument for founding and maintaining Jewish culture and law.

The plaint that Israeli law lacks Jewish-Hebrew content is, in fact, a reflection of an analogous hoary and familiar charge made against the Zionist movement. The imputation that Zionism had severed all ties to Judaism was voiced already in the infancy of Jewish nationalism, both by the movement's opponents and by its own cultural faction. Zionism's opponents claimed that it could not make any claim to be a manifestation of Judaism, which was a religion or civilization that could not be reduced to the formalism of a state or laws. The eighteenth-century philosopher Salomon (Shlomo) Maimon, for example, argued that Jewish integration into the life of a civil state required the utter termination of the Jewish people as a separate collective entity.[1] This view would eventually metamorphose into the anti-Zionist position that favored "spiritual" Jewish life in the Diaspora over non-natural attempts to consummate Jewish life in a Jewish nation-state. Many Jewish intellectuals, both religious and non-religious, took this position in the nineteenth and twentieth centuries, among them the historians Simon Dubnow and Salo Baron, philosophers Franz Rosenzweig and Hermann Cohen, and the poet and polemicist David Frishman. Baron, for example, viewed Jewish history as a process of ongoing liberation from the state and from territory. Dubnow, for his part, described Jewish national life as "uprooted from its political soil," displaying itself "on intellectual fields exclusively."[2] In his essay "On Judaism," Frischmann wrote that "a nation without a land was not and is not just possible in my view, but it is for me the singular goal to which the spirit of history aspires. An eternal people is a people without a state."[3] Similar anti-Zionist arguments have been made in the twentieth century by thinkers such as George Steiner, Noam Chomsky, Bernard-Henri Lévy, and Daniel Boyarin, who have set Jewish spiritual universalism against the political aggression that is the nature of the state, and which, in their view, is clearly evident in Israel's actions.[4]

In contrast with the anti-Zionists, the cultural Zionists, both inside and outside the World Zionist Organization, believed not only that Zionism could indeed be an expression of Judaism, but that it was in fact the most authentic manifestation of modern Jewish culture. Their objection was that the Zionist movement was sidestepping the issue of Jewish identity inasmuch as it disregarded the dilemmas of identity and culture that millions of Jews were grappling with, and doing nothing to offer solutions.

From Zionism's birth, the movement's intellectuals have complained bitterly that it was turning a blind eye to culture and identity. They lamented what they saw as Zionism's detachment from the Jewish spirit and Jewish culture, and warned that a national movement that turned its back on its heritage would be a tepid one that would be unable to found a proper and durable society and state. This critique reached its height in the Zionist cultural debate at the turn of the nineteenth century. While it died down after World War I, when it looked as if the admonishments of Ahad Ha'am,

1 Belfer, *Split Identity*, 57–77, and the many sources there; Katz and Kedar, "Jewishness of the Jewish," 443–450.
2 Dubnow, "Content of Jewish," 262; and see also Baron, *Social and Religious*, vol. 1, 16–25; Rosenzweig, *Briefe*, 238.
3 Frischmann, "On Judaism," 24.
4 Belfer, *Split Identity*, 68–72, and the many sources there.

Berdyczewski, and the Democratic Faction had come to an end, it reemerged on the eve of independence. Intellectuals and jurists then began again to demand that the future state put questions of spirit and culture front and center. One of the most prominent figures who took this position during the first several months of independence was Martin Buber, who had in his younger years been a member of the Democratic Faction. Buber criticized the young state of Israel for, he charged, making a break between the nation and the principle of its existence.[5] His critique merged with the general pessimism voiced by Israeli intellectuals, who bewailed the enervation of Jewish culture in general and that of Israel's population in particular, in the wake of independence and the enormous wave of immigration.[6] In short, intellectuals and writers have always attacked the Zionist movement and the state of Israel for indifference to the Jewish spirit and Jewish culture.

But that accusation is false. Yes, the Zionist movement consistently demurred, from its very inception, from taking part in the polemics over Jewish culture. The movement adhered to this semi-official policy until the establishment of the state, and it continued under the state. But that does not mean that Zionism ever ignored questions of identity and culture. It hardly could, and certainly did not want to, first of all because of the fact that no culture comes from nowhere. All cultures undergo gradual change and are largely based on traditions and a cultural inventory. Even if it is clear to us that the Zionists sought to construct a new Hebrew culture, they could do so only by making massive use of old Jewish building blocks and familiar cultural molds, into which they poured new content.[7]

Zionism is awash in Jewish culture simply by virtue of being the Jewish national movement. All that is necessary to grasp this is to take another look at the other solutions that Europe's Jews considered as they faced their economic, political, and cultural problems. Until the appearance of Jewish nationalism, meaning Zionism, the only two options available were assimilation into European society or emigration. These two options shared two characteristics. First, they faced outward, outside the European Jewish community, whether to the surrounding society or to a "new country." Second, they were by their very nature individual solutions. They could solve the problems faced by a single person, family, or at most a certain professional group. But most Jews could not or did not want either to emigrate or to

[5] Buber, "Judaism and Culture," 233; and see also Ratzabi, "The Jewish State"; Shavit, "Messianism, Utopianism."

[6] Kedar, *Mamlakhtiyut*, 92–103.

[7] Even-Zohar, "Emergence of a Native Hebrew," 179–184.

assimilate, whether because they lacked the financial resources that emigration required, because the surrounding society refused to accept them as legitimate members, or because the cultural or religious price that assimilation often demanded pained them. These difficulties made it urgent to find a collective solution. During the last third of the nineteenth century it became eminently clear that the problems faced by individual Jews were part of a larger Jewish problem. A huge Jewish collective was ensnared in a thicket of political, legal, economic, and cultural difficulties. The solution needed to be a collective, national one. Unlike emigration or individual assimilation, Zionism did not offer itself as a solution to any specific Jew; rather, it was a collective solution to the dilemmas faced by European (and later world) Jewry as a whole.[8] It was Jewish, inasmuch as it was directed at that group of people who saw themselves (or were seen by others) as Jews. Zionism's objects and subjects were, by definition, Jews, not just anyone seeking a more secure future. That was the important difference between Zionism and the attempts by many European Jews to assimilate and become German, English, French, Hungarian, or Russian, but of the "Mosaic persuasion." Zionism did not demand that Jews give up their culture and identity as the price, as Heinrich Heine put it, of "the ticket of admission to European culture." Instead, it offered them a way to continue to live as a distinct public with its own culture. The need to preserve Jewish culture thus lies at the very foundation of Zionism. It is its motivating force and, in large measure, also its goal. To this end, it hardly matters that it is not clear exactly what that Jewish culture constitutes. The Jewish people's desire to continue to live in the modern world as a collective with a distinct culture (even if the nature of that culture is disputed by the members of the collective) is what propelled Zionism and made the national idea into the reigning view, first in Eastern Europe, and later in the rest of the world.

Zionism's strong connection to Jewish culture grew not only out of it being a national-collective solution to the Jewish problem, but also out of the substance of the national solution that it offered. Zionism told a story that was accepted by most Jews. Three currents that offered national solutions to their plight vied for the hearts of the Jews of Europe at the cusp of the nineteenth and twentieth centuries. All offered collective solutions that began with the assumption that the Jews were a distinct public with its own culture and other national characteristics, facing a specific set of problems. One was autonomism, as advocated by Simon Dubnow in one form and the

8 See, for example, Lilienblum, "Guardianship and Supervising."

socialist-Yiddishist Bund movement in another. It took form in parallel with Zionism and demanded equal civil rights along national, but not territorial, cultural autonomy in the countries in which Jews lived.[9] Another national current, one that grew out of Zionism at the beginning of the twentieth century, was territorialism, which called for the establishment of a Jewish national entity on a territory elsewhere than Palestine.[10] While autonomism was more popular (especially among Jewish intellectuals), and even though at times the territorialist option looked as if it were more realistic, Zionism retained its claim to primacy.[11] It was the first of these solutions to appear. Proto-Zionists were already writing, preaching their doctrine, and in some cases even settling in Palestine in the 1860s, and the Hovevei Zion movement, which advocated and furthered settlement in Palestine, took form in the 1880s. Zionism also had the greatest symbolic power, with the greatest ability to serve as a mobilizing ideology. By evoking collective Jewish symbols from the liturgy and Jewish culture (first and foremost the symbol of the Land of Israel), and basing itself on Jewish history and the eschatology of the prophets, it was able to find its way into the hearts of the Jewish populace. They accepted it as a framework for thinking about the Jewish nation, even if they did not intend to move to Palestine.

It is best to distinguish between Zionism as a national ideological framework and the Zionist solution itself, which was the establishment of an independent Jewish state in Palestine. Zionism's problem was not its national ideological scaffolding – not the frame story that it told. Its story was the same one told by many modern Jews, and gradually became accepted by all, if in different versions. Zionism's problem was the specific solution it proposed. It became increasingly clear that the Zionist project faced huge difficulties – transferring millions of Jews to Palestine, obtaining the consent of the land's foreign overlords, coping with the local Arabs, the country's difficult physical conditions, and international diplomacy. As such, a sovereign entity in Palestine could not remedy the ills of most of the world's Jews, neither their political-civil and economic problems nor their dilemmas of identity and culture. Until the 1920s, actual Zionist settlement in Palestine was indeed slow and unimpressive, especially given the huge pressures the Jews were under in Europe, and in comparison to the huge dimensions of Jewish emigration within and beyond Europe to America and elsewhere. At the end of fifty years of immigration and settlement, the Jewish community in

9 See Rabinovitch, *Jewish Rights*.

10 See Rovner, *In the Shadow*; Elroey, *Homeland Seekers*.

11 See Smith, "Zionism and Diaspora"; Stanislawski, *Zionism*.

Palestine remained small and undeveloped, without economic independence and unable to defend itself. Palestine did not attract Europe's Jewish masses, nor could the Zionist movement say how it planned to move millions of Jews from Europe to Palestine and how the Jewish national home would actually help the Jews who lived in Palestine and those who would remain in the rest of the world. The Zionist inability to respond to the plight of most of the world's Jews and its limited success in settling Jews in Palestine were the source of the principal critiques leveled at the movement. It was for these reasons that the Congress of Russian Zionists in 1906 resolved that, in addition to building a national home in Palestine, the movement needed to take action to help Diaspora communities and to achieve equal civil rights and cultural autonomy for the Jews of Europe. Even fervent Zionists like Ben-Gurion acknowledged that, while furthering settlement in Palestine, Zionism needed "to fight for national rights and national self-determination in the Diaspora."[12]

While the Zionist project proceeded only by fits and starts until at least the end of the 1920s, the Zionist idea was a great success already at the end of the nineteenth century. Its success went beyond its dissemination of the idea of establishing an independent Jewish state; it also, perhaps even more importantly, came to serve as the first framework for thinking that expressed and inculcated the concept that modern Jews are a nation and that the solution to the dilemma of modern Jewry had to be a collective and national one. Zionism was able to serve as the organizing ideology that shaped that modern Jewish collective's symbols of identity and culture (such as the Jewish historical narrative), and put it into action both in the Diaspora communities, new and old, and in Palestine.[13] At least since the period between the two world wars, the national paradigm shaped by the Jews has been accepted by most of the world's Jews – in Eastern Europe, the Islamic world, and even in the West. Many of the Jews of Germany and Western Europe had no choice, when faced with the rise of Zionism, but to shed their liberal-integrationist positions and adopt a national one (even if, in most cases, not Zionism).[14] Even many American Jews saw themselves in collective-national terms, although they disputed the Zionist position that privileged national Jewish life in Palestine. Organizations such as the World Jewish Congress, founded in 1936, and the American Joint Distribution Committee, founded in 1914, operate to this day as *national* Jewish organizations, not simply religious and philanthropic ones, even if their take on nationalism is broader and different from that of Zionism.

[12] Ben-Gurion, *From Class to Nation*, 13.

[13] Mintz, "Jewish Nation"; Mintz, "Upbuilding of Eretz-Israel."

[14] Miron, *The Waning of the Emancipation*.

They recognize the importance of Zionism and the Jewish state in Palestine, but nevertheless view the Jews as a dispersed nation, as Dubnow did, a nation that has always had a number of geographical centers. (Today the two major ones are in Israel and North America.) Even most Jewish opponents of Zionism act and speak within the collective-national framework.

The cultural symbols at the foundation of Zionism are the source of its strength and its advantage over other Jewish collective and national concepts. First, Zionism successfully, in the end, won out over the foundation myths and concepts of the collective that sought to portray the Jews as a religious-cultural minority that was an integral part of the cultural space in which it lived. That view sought to constitute a number of Jewries – Russian, French, German, and American, to name a few.[15] Second, Zionism also won out over other concepts of Jewish nationalism that emerged subsequently – autonomism and territorialism. These other versions of Jewish nationalism failed not only for external reasons, namely, the refusal of other countries to grant the Jews a territory on which to found a state, or the refusal of the countries of Eastern and Central Europe to grant their Jews broad cultural autonomy. They also fell short for intra-Jewish reasons. In final analysis, they lacked the drawing power of Zionism because these two other approaches sacrificed important Jewish cultural features. Autonomism's problem was the extent of Jewish identity that it sought. There was no reason to believe that European countries would grant their Jewish minorities true cultural autonomy of a kind that would make it possible to maintain an independent, comprehensive, and flourishing culture in the long term, and to impart it to the next generation. The territorialists had the opposite problem. An independent Jewish territory was meant to guarantee the independence of the new Jewish culture, but its price was giving up one of the principal Jewish cultural symbols, the Land of Israel. That was the reason why Zionism was, for the Jewish masses, the principal Jewish national movement and the meta-narrative that organized their identity. This was the case even if on the individual level those Jews had no intention of settling in Palestine, but rather sought a better life in Europe or elsewhere. The more Zionism came to be accepted as an idea, the more it became central to Jewish culture and a platform for Jewish cultural renewal. Itamar Even-Zohar has remarked that Zionism's success in becoming the Jewish world's most important framework of thought made it easier to create a new Hebrew culture that was Jewish, but unique and

[15] Nathans, *Beyond the Pale*. On the attempts to establish a Russian (or other) Jewry, see Miron, "Modernization, Assimilation"; Moss, "At Home," and the many sources there.

different from the Jewish cultures of the older religious community in Palestine and of Jewish communities in other countries.[16]

Zionism was thus entirely permeated with Jewish culture. It was born out of the drive to find a response to the problems Jews faced as a distinct collective, and its solution was based on defining the Jewish people as a nation with distinctive cultural characteristics. As such, Zionism (as opposed to other Jewish national movements and, of course, anti-Zionism) always stressed the distinguishing features of Jewish culture, first and foremost its historical narrative, the vision of the prophets, and the nation's indissoluble ties to the territory of its birth. It was for this reason that the movement rejected the British proposal to settle Jews in East Africa and unswervingly opposed territorialism. It was also the reason why the World Zionist Organization ultimately recognized (in decisions made at the Congresses of 1901 and 1911, and of course at the congress of Russian Zionists at Helsingfors in 1906) that the Zionist movement needed to devote some of its energies to the "work of the present" – educational work within existing Jewish communities – not just to achieving its ultimate goal of a state in Palestine. For the same reason, the Zionist movement, and later the state of Israel, always insisted that they were part of the history of the Jewish nation, with its cultural and religious heritage. In other words, Israel never thought to do as Mustafa Kemal Atatürk did when he compelled his new Turkey to sever its ties to Islam and to Turkish society's central symbols of culture, identity, and history, such as its distinctive dress, its traditional capital, and its use of the Arabic alphabet. While Zionism was fundamentally a modernist, dynamic, revolutionary, and secular movement, it recognized the cultural importance of religion and Jewish heritage in its broad sense for Jewish nationalism. That is, it recognized the Jewish faith and Jewish history as the source of its formative stories and national cultural symbols, which were adopted by secular Zionism. The Zionists understood that severing the nation from its Jewish cultural sources would not only offend millions of Jews, but deprive the movement of the emotional energy the nation needed to achieve its goals. When the state was founded, it was also obvious that alienation from Jewish heritage and culture would be detrimental to the effort to build a unified society.[17] Prime Minister David Ben-Gurion spoke to this issue in response to a proposal that the identity cards that all Israeli citizens were required to bear simply identify them as being Israeli,

[16] Even-Zohar, "Emergence of a Native Hebrew," 177–180.

[17] Shapira, "Ben-Gurion and the Bible"; Ohana, *Messianism and Mamlachtiut*; Kedar, "We Need the Messiah."

rather than including, as they did, a line identifying their national identity – Jewish, in the case of Jews:

> There are Jews in this country who have a theory and are preaching it. According to the theory, an Israeli nation has come into being here, to which Jews do not belong, and the Jews of the world are a religion rather than a nationality.... A new generation has been born here that is mostly not religious, and it would be dangerous if it [were to see itself as] Israeli and not Jewish. It needs to know that it is Jewish.... We need to instill in [the people's] hearts the recognition that we are first and foremost Jews, part of the Jewish people.... For this reason, we cannot allow only "Israeli" to be written on people's identity cards, they must state "Jewish."[18]

Thus, Zionism never entirely suppressed the cultural issue; rather, it adopted a moderate stance that manifested itself in several ways. First, the Zionist movement kept the cultural Zionists on a low burner. At the Second and Third Zionist Congresses, for example, several long hours were given over to (futile) debates on cultural issues. But the movement nevertheless consistently refrained from including any binding language on the subject in its official documents, from allocating any large sums to the cultural Zionists' schemes (much to their chagrin), or from taking any other operative measures. The reason was not just the leadership's disinclination to do so, but also the fact that, despite the intensity of the debate, the participants proved unable to achieve any real agreement on how to put their ideas into action. Even if the movement had wanted to allot funds or carry out the Congresses' amorphous decisions about Jewish culture, it was not clear what it should fund or what specific policy it should carry out.[19] Despite this, however, writers and intellectuals were always given places of respect and honor in the movement and its leadership. Despite the intense opposition to Ahad Ha'am's cultural Zionism on the part of most of the movement's leaders, they addressed issues of culture and identity and believed that it was their duty to shape a virtuous society in the future Jewish state. Zionism's towering figures, the most known of whom would be Herzl, Jabotinsky, and later Ben-Gurion, were not just important political leaders but also writers and intellectuals who sought to shape society and culture.

Second, Zionism spoke in a collective national language and saw itself as speaking for and representing the entire Jewish people, and voicing all its problems and needs. It did not speak just for one segment of the nation.

[18] Meeting of Mapai Knesset faction with the party secretariat, July 13, 1958, 7, BGA.
[19] Holtzman, "Born Culture," 25–29.

It always stressed the national-collective aspect of Judaism, the people's shared history, its common hopes and difficulties, and that emigration and individual assimilation were not appropriate for most Jews and in any case did not solve the problem of the Jews as a national-cultural collective. That is how the Zionist movement spoke, and that is also how it acted. Externally, it presented itself as the Jewish democratic national movement, representing (even when it enjoyed the support of only a minority of Jews) all the Jews of the world. No less importantly, on the intra-Jewish side, it was a democratic movement that not only claimed to represent and express the will of all Jews, but also did so in practice. Both the Hovevei Zion movement and the Zionist movement that followed were characterized by a potent ethos of unity and mediation. The Zionist movement saw itself as a bridge over the things that separated different Jewish groups. Hence the unrelenting efforts of Hovevei Zion, Sokolow, Herzl, and even Ahad Ha'am (although less so in his case) to reach accommodations with the Haredi Jews of Eastern Europe. This ethos was also the source of the movement's distaste for factionalism and parties (which in the end arose primarily in the wake of the cultural polemic), and the deep-seated sense of national unity and civil-republicanism that would be a central feature of the Israeli state.

Third, Zionism did all it could to translate its ethos of unity into democratic procedure. Participation in Zionist Congresses and the movement's other institutions was based on free and direct elections in which all dues-paying members could vote – women and men. Furthermore, the political system of the movement, and later of the Yishuv in Palestine, took the form of consensual democratic government by coalition, with an emphasis on the representation and expression of all opinions. These coalitions were based on a multiparty system in which different groups received representation through political parties that expressed their positions. Proportional elections ensured that all groups were represented and had a say, and created a flexible fabric of interparty agreements.[20] The Zionist and later the Israeli national proportional electoral system lacked procedural checks, such as a high minimum threshold of votes needed to gain representation, or the division of the country into electoral districts and a requirement that, to receive representation, a party

[20] The other model of democracy, which the Zionist movement rejected, was the majoritarian option. As its name implies, in such a system the majority rules, and the stress is on governance by a ruling majority. Political power is concentrated in the hands of the majority that wins the elections, which generally does not require coalition partners. In practical terms, majoritarian democracy is generally a two-party system, and the government is formed by the winning party only. The losing party sits in opposition in parliament, but not in the cabinet.

must cross a threshold of votes in a minimum number of districts.[21] The proportional system has many disadvantages – it exacerbates political differences, gives minority groups extortionary power, encourages the multiplication of parties, and makes it difficult to form a stable and functional government. Nevertheless, the Zionists realized from the start that this system would serve as the best defense against cultural warfare and the movement's dissolution, because it gave widely varied kinds of Jews a way they could express their affiliation with the general national collective and participate in the movement's leadership institutions despite their differences.

Zionism's treatment of the questions of religion and culture is a classic example of consensus politics. The movement refrained from making any sort of binary choice on questions of culture and identity, and went so far as to try to avoid debates on these issues. Instead, it sought to resolve conflict in the areas of religion and culture by placing the emphasis on the broad common denominator (what I call the "moderate cultural option") and by adopting flexible political compromises.

Since not all differences could be entirely suppressed or resolved with flexible and ad hoc arrangements, Zionist leaders had to agree, despite their aspiration for united national and civic action, to the establishment of semi-independent religious-Zionist political and educational frameworks. While they at first hoped that it would be possible to avoid party politics and that the differences over education would fade on their own, the cultural conflict at the beginning of the twentieth century and the many disputes over education in Europe and Palestine made it clear that consensual politics and national unity had their limits.[22] Herzl reached agreements with the religious leadership of Russian Jewry, and the writer and Zionist leader Nahum Sokolow with Haredi rabbis.[23] Ahad Ha'am accepted, at the second conference of Russian Zionists in Minsk in 1902, that a separate semi-independent religious school system would be necessary.[24] And this continued as part of Israel's policies in the form of the establishment of a state-sponsored religious school system, the recognition of separate Haredi schools. Since the establishment of the Zionist-religious Mizrahi movement at the beginning of the twentieth century, Zionist policy did not aim to prevent the establishment of religious parties but rather to bring these parties into the consensual coalitions that governed the Zionist movement, the Yishuv, and independent

[21] Rahat, "Israeli Electoral System"; Kedar, "Israeli Early Voting System."
[22] On the disputes over education, see Luz, *Parallels Meet*, 98–104, 128–133.
[23] Sokolow, *To Our Teachers*, 69. And see generally Anish Stiftel, *The Mediator*.
[24] Ahad Ha'am, "Spiritual Revival," especially 301–305.

Israel, "so that religious Judaism will bear civic responsibility," in Ben-Gurion's words.[25]

Fourth, the Zionist movement took upon itself to operate in a way that would facilitate civil cooperation and good neighborliness. For example, it respected the need for kosher food and Sabbath and holiday observance at Zionist gatherings, and later in the state's institutions. This made it possible for Jews from different backgrounds to live together and maintain a civil society and common public space. Such arrangements were put into writing in the "status quo agreements" that the leaders of the Jewish Agency drafted and sent to the leaders of Agudat Israel in 1947.[26] Beyond these basic compacts, the Zionist movement did its best to keep conflict over culture and religion on a low flame. This muting policy was an important element of Zionist consensus democracy. The movement's refusal to get involved in the polemics surrounding the questions of who is a Jew, what Judaism is, what constitutes Jewish culture, what makes a state Jewish, and what is Jewish law were all meant to enable Jews from different groups to work together within the Zionist movement.

Fifth, the Zionist movement made a point of stressing the cultural symbols common to and accepted by most Jews. The most important of these is the Jewish historical narrative, told as a national history. It is the story of a nation united by a common religion, language, and culture, shaped in the Land of Israel and then, exiled from its homeland, scattered all over the world. Planting Zionism in Jewish history was a huge source of strength for it as a national movement, because all Jews knew the story from the liturgy, and it was a central component of their identity. It hardly makes a difference whether this chronicle of an ancient dispersed people now undergoing a national awakening was accurate, or whether some parts of it were invented. All that mattered was that millions of modern Jews knew the story as their own and that it was part of their collective memory. The historical account that Zionism offered dealt not just with the past; it was the foundation of the Jews' sense of sharing a common present and future as well. The story was the source of Jewish hopes and the prophetic eschatology that promised a redemption in the Land of Israel combined with the salvation of humanity as a whole. The historical-eschatological narrative is important because the view that Judaism is a culture that formulated and sanctified the humanistic

25 Knesset Records, November 3, 1952 (Ben-Gurion in the Knesset during the debate over Agudat Israel's resignation from the coalition over the issue of national service for religious girls).

26 Friedman, "Chronicle of the Status-Quo."

political-moral values expressed in the Bible and other Jewish texts was the one thing that all the contending sides in the cultural polemic agreed on. It united Ahad Ha'am and Berdyczewski, the cultural Zionists and the political Zionists, secular Zionists and religious Zionists (even if the latter did not view it as a sufficient definition of Judaism).[27]

Another symbol at the heart of the Zionist idea and its realization was, of course, the Land of Israel – Zion – both physical and symbolical. Giving its name to the movement, it was this symbol that set Zionism apart from territorialist nationalism, which sought principally a haven for persecuted Jews. It imbued the Zionist project of immigration to Palestine and construction of a society and nation there with profound cultural and ethical significance. Immigration to Palestine was not just moving from one country to another. It was an ascent (the literal meaning of the word *aliyah*, which also denotes immigration to Israel), a return to the land of the Jewish people's forebears, and an ingathering of the Jewish exiles. No less importantly, Zion was a symbol also for those millions of Jews who had no interest in settling in Palestine. Zionism's moderate cultural policy was also expressed in its attitude to the Land of Israel: even though the land was a central and extremely important symbol for the movement, Zionism did not seek to define that land's boundaries and did not sanctify any particular map. On the contrary, for the central current of Zionist thought, Zion as a symbol was always more important than the physical Zion. The Land of Israel was not seen as the movement's final goal; it was an instrument for reaching the symbolic Zion, which meant creating an exemplary Jewish society.[28]

Another common symbol that the Zionist movement stressed was the Hebrew language. The principle that Hebrew is the Jewish national language (even if not the Jews' spoken language) was accepted by most Jews (many of had some notion of it, as it was the language of Jewish liturgy), even if most of them did not speak it and did not try to learn it. In fact, the attitude of the Jewish masses to Hebrew was much like their attitude to the Land of Israel and Zionism as a whole – they adopted the symbols as important elements of their collective identity, even though most of them had no intention of putting the idea into practice. The revival of the Hebrew language was important not only as a prominent cultural symbol but also as a major instrument of the Jewish national revival. Zionism did a good job of taking advantage of the energy produced by the "Jewish revolution," the huge cultural and literary awakening, in Hebrew and Yiddish, among the Jews of Eastern and Central

27 Katz and Kedar, "Secular Israeli," 172–174.
28 Dothan, *Land in the Balance*.

Europe at the beginning of the twentieth century.[29] Hebrew language and literature became means of disseminating the national idea among the Jewish masses.

Finally, the Zionist movement made national secular use of Jewish religious symbols. The movement's flag, which became Israel's flag, was designed to represent the traditional *tallit*, the Jewish prayer shawl, and the seven-branched lamp that was one of the sacred objects in the Temple, the *menorah*, was chosen as the national seal.

The Zionist movement's moderate cultural policy could also be seen in its consistent support for the establishment of a Jewish university. Since it had already been clear back in the Haskalah period that elementary education aroused a great deal of dissension and conflict between religious Jews of different streams and secular Jews, the Zionist movement devoted little of its energies to primary education, leaving it to the different groups within the Jewish collective and to local communities. In other words, the muting policy was applied to this subject. Instead, the movement stressed the need for a Jewish national academy. Establishing a Hebrew university in Palestine became one of the Zionist Organization's goals. While the project did not proceed without conflict (e.g., some thought it should be solely a research institution; others insisted it also had to be a teaching university), the university became a national symbol that channeled the desire for a national-cultural revival that would also be modernist and progressive.[30]

Zionism thus did not dismiss the identity and cultural problems of modern Jews, but it believed that the best way to solve them was by means of national self-determination realized in a Jewish state in the Land of Israel. It is this same concept that guides Israeli law.

[29] Harshav, *Theses*.

[30] Katz and Heyd, *Hebrew University*.

10

Israeli Law as a *Lieu de Mémoire* of National Identity and Culture

Like Zionism, Israeli law is not indifferent to its cultural dimension. The Israeli character of Israeli law is not expressed in any uniquely Jewish-Hebrew content, as there is no agreement about what, specifically, such content should be, and no one knows how to translate it into the legal norms of a modern state. Repeated waves of attempts to fashion law that is "truly" Jewish have crashed on the sandbars of these simple facts. In this chapter I will show how the attempts to imbue the country's laws with Jewish-Hebrew content were not the only ones to aim to constitute a specifically Israeli system of law. Israel has in fact developed an independent and advanced system of law, one that plays a major role in maintaining the Jewish legal tradition and making it accessible to the public at large. This accomplishment is a prime example of how Zionism has succeeded in maintaining a living and dynamic Jewish culture in the modern world.

A discussion of the Israeliness of Israeli law cannot, as Hebrew law promoters and cultural Zionists often do, disregard the fact that Israeli law is Jewish and Hebrew simply on the formal grounds that it is the law of the state of Israel, that is the Jewish people's nation-state, and that those who craft and use it are Israelis who are the citizens of a sovereign state of Jewish culture. The Israeli nature of Israel's law ensures, first and foremost, that Israelis are free to shape it as they wish in accordance with their values, needs, and interests. Such was, in fact, the fundamental claim of Zionism: that the best guarantee that Jewish culture (and therefore law as well) could thrive was the establishment of an independent Jewish state with a Jewish majority.

If that is the case, the Israeli character of Israeli law is determined, first of all, by the fact that it is the law of the state of Israel. The determining factor in this case is not the substance of the law, but its formal affiliation to a particular independent state. To give one example, we distinguish between Belgian and Dutch law not because they are different in substance but because, formally, they belong to two different countries. When Belgium and Holland were, from 1815 to 1830, both parts of the United Kingdom of the Netherlands, the law of that state was unitary, and distinct from other legal systems, such as French and English law. Again, what counted was formal affiliation, not the content of the law or the culture from which it derived. It was the law of the United Kingdom of the Netherlands, even though its actual substance was profoundly influenced by French law, and it was the law of a *United Kingdom*, despite the significant cultural, linguistic, and religious tensions between its northern and southern regions. Israeli law is Israeli by the very fact of it being the law of an independent Israeli state. That is no small thing.

In a much deeper way, beyond this formal fact, the Israeli nature of the country's law derives from the fact that Israel's citizens are at liberty to shape, interpret, and apply their laws independently, in keeping with their culture, values, and needs. Irrelevant in this context is the important sociological question of which of the country's social groups is dominant in the process of creating the law: Do legislative institutions and judges create the law from above, or are particular elites imposing their worldviews, or does society produce law from the grassroots? The essential point is that the Israeli character of the law is inherent in the fact that it is Israelis who produce and apply it.

Like Zionism, which turned its back on cultural conflict and focused on creating a sovereign civic polity in which Jews were a majority, the Israeli legal system has kept its distance from attempts to base Israeli law on "substantive Jewish content," instead putting the stress on the law's formal independence. The Israeli legal system insisted from the start that it would not be subordinate to a foreign legal system, and that Israelis would formulate, interpret, and apply the country's laws independently of external dictates.[1] An examination that focuses on the formal-institutional independence of Israeli law, rather than on demands that it be based on Jewish-Hebrew content, shows that it is one of the world's most independent and fascinating legal systems. The insistence on independence has two sides – a positive, creative one and a negative, disengaging one.

On the one side, legal independence is a creative act. The Israeli governmental and legal systems from the start insisted that Israeli law would not be copied or imported from any given foreign legal system. Rather, laws would be enacted by Israelis and would suit the country's circumstances, not transplanted from a country responding to other conditions. This is not to be taken for granted. In fact, almost no other legal system in the world has

[1] Likhovski, "The Time."

done this. Most countries, even large and mighty ones with glorious histories and intense national pride, have copied entire laws, or at least large sections of laws, almost verbatim, even when these laws did not accord with their own cultures. For example, most European countries copied – rather than took inspiration from – the French Napoleonic Code, and later the German, Italian, or Swiss codes (the last two of which were themselves heavily influenced by those of France, Austria, and Germany). In the early twentieth century, even great powers, such as China, Japan, and Turkey, copied large swathes of important European codes, with only minor revisions. Most countries that emerged from the process of decolonization incorporated major parts of European and American legislation. Following the fall of Communism, the countries of Eastern Europe, Central Asia, and the Far East imported much of the important European codes and promulgated constitutions modeled closely on those of the United States, Canada, or Western Europe. It is no accident that most of the world's countries have taken their laws from elsewhere, in particular from just a few countries whose legal systems are seen as the exemplars of modern, effective, and well-thought-out law. Since stability, efficiency, functionality, and predictability are essential to the proper functioning of a legal system and its acceptance by the citizenry, it made sense for new countries to carry over large parts of the laws imposed and enacted by their erstwhile colonial overlords. Any attempt to start from scratch risked social and legal chaos. It was best, then, to adopt familiar models of legislation, procedure, and legal theory, even if this meant transplanting a foreign system that impinged on the local culture. In these cases just a handful of minor adjustments were made to paper over the cultural gap and the potential for friction between the foreign code and local mores.[2] When Israel was founded, its leaders and senior legal figures shared this concern about destabilizing their society, but nevertheless did not take the easy path of simply copying foreign legal methods. Legislating independently is complex, lengthy, and relatively expensive, from both economic and cultural standpoints, as it opens up debates on the identity of the drafters of the law that are liable to turn into political crises.

I do not mean to say that Israeli law has not been influenced by other legal systems. First, not to do so would have invited chaos and created a legal

[2] Zweigert and Kötz, *Introduction to Comparative Law*, 154–156, 178–179, 218–237 (discussion of the civil codes of France, Germany, and Switzerland and on legislation and legal thinking elsewhere in the world); Kanamori, "German Influences"; Han, "Snapshot of Chinese"; Örücü, "Infusion of the Diffusion"; Örücü, "Impact of European"; Kedar, "Law, Culture," 184–186.

vacuum. On its founding, Israel continued to use, wholesale, the laws of the British Mandate (just as the Mandate administration took over the Ottoman system that preceded it). But it was clear that this was done only for the sake of stability and security, and that the new country would act quickly to replace the Mandate code with its own modern laws wherever that was necessary. In the 1950s the Ministry of Justice embarked on drafting new laws covering all areas of life. The result, in the 1960s and 1970s, was a massive wave of new legislation that reshaped nearly all of the country's civil law (inheritance, obligations, and property law, and parts of family law). At the same time, the Knesset passed a number of basic laws, a broad web of social and criminal legislation, and much else. It was a huge task, barely imaginable in its extent and the resources expended on it. Yet even during this difficult and pressured period, Israel did not do what most other countries had done. True, Israeli laws frequently adopted solutions borrowed from elsewhere, but these were not copied word for word or clause for clause, but were rather reformulated in light of Israeli society's needs, values, and interests. Furthermore, Israeli legislators examined different sources rather than limiting themselves to just one model. They plumbed Anglo-Saxon, European, and other systems from around the world, as well as the Jewish legal tradition. The deciding criterion was the present needs of Israeli society. On occasion it transpired, during or after the drafting process, that the Israeli solution had a precedent in a foreign system or in Jewish law, but these were provisions that were arrived at independently and not taken from those sources.[3]

Second, Israeli legislators and judges frequently referred to, learned from, and took inspiration from other modern legal systems, as they continue to do today. During the country's early years, its Ministry of Justice participated in a project sponsored by Harvard Law School, in which they consulted with senior American legal scholars in the drafting of progressive laws. This project, in which some of the finest scholars of American private law participated, operated until 1961, when the Harry and Michael Sacher Institute for Legislative Research and Comparative Law (established in 1959), at the Hebrew University, became fully operational.[4] Obviously, the legal arrangements established in Israeli legislation and jurisprudence are not hugely different from their counterparts in other developed countries. In the final analysis, human and social problems are much the same all over the world, and the

[3] Yadin, "Custodian Law."

[4] Cohn, *Personal Introduction*, 222–224; Likhovski, "Argonauts of the Eastern"; Radzyner, "Inheritance from Uncle Sam."

spectrum of available solutions is not a broad one. Nevertheless, Israel never copied or transplanted entire laws or provisions *en masse* from other places.

As the subject here is the creative aspect of legislation, it is important to note that, from its inception, the Israeli system has hewed the two prime markers of legal independence in modern culture by producing its own constitution and civil code. These are the two fundamental texts of modern Western law. Both types of documents emerged out of the same political, intellectual, and cultural milieu of the eighteenth century; both express the fundamental ideas of modern law; and both bear profound symbolic meaning that is not attached to other legal norms or institutions, as symbols of legal and national progress and independence. In Israel, the two documents share a similar history. It was clear to the first Israelis that, on gaining independence, the country had to enact a constitution and a civil code. It turned out, however, that this was a delicate and dangerous task, given the complex circumstances surrounding the establishment of the state and the building of Israeli society. Legislators feared that the promulgation of such central documents would set off a cultural and ideological war and lead to a dangerous political struggle. The Knesset decided to postpone these tasks, but they were only put off, not abandoned. Rather, the decision was to write them section by section – the constitution as a series of basic laws and the civil code as a series of smaller laws – to be combined, at the end, into two large documents.[5]

Some thought that, in doing this, Israel was evading the writing of a constitution and civil code, but in fact the plan was followed systematically. To date, the Knesset has enacted thirteen basic laws, and, between the beginning of the 1960s and the beginning of the 1980s, it passed twenty-four laws as part of the project of creating a new civil code. Throughout this period, the legal system and the Knesset made it clear that this was a two-stage process; at some point in the future the full constitution and code would be completed.[6] At the end of the 1970s, after the passage of a new criminal code, the Ministry of Justice formed a Codification Committee charged with uniting

5 I have discussed the issue at length in Chapter 6.

6 The amalgamation of the Basic Laws into a constitution was foreseen in the original decision of July 13, 1950 (the Harari decision) to legislate a series of Basic Laws rather than a constitution: "The First Knesset charges the Constitution, Law and Justice Committee with preparing a draft constitution for the country. The constitution will be constructed chapter by chapter in a way that each one will constitute a Basic Law on its own. The chapters will be brought before the Knesset . . . and all the chapters will be combined into the constitution of the state of Israel." Knesset Records, July 13, 1950. Uri Yadin, head of the Justice Ministry's Legislation Department, argued that the same applied to civil law, which would be legislated over a period of time and eventually be amalgamated into a complete code. Yadin, "Custodian Law," 494.

the civil legislation into a single, well-structured, and advanced code.[7] After thirty years of work, it produced a draft code in 2004. After further discussions in the ministry, the government submitted a revised draft to the Knesset, which commenced deliberations.[8] Likewise, the enactment, in 1992, of two basic laws addressing human rights prompted a number of jurists, scholars, and politicians to claim that Israel's constitution-writing process had reached its end, as the basic laws now covered the two basic subjects addressed by constitutions – the structure of government and individual rights. The process that began with the Knesset decision of July 1950 was now at its end; the basic laws together formed a constitution. This claim was reinforced by the fact that these two final basic laws stipulated that Israel is a "Jewish and democratic state," a grand statement that sought, for the first time, to provide a definition of the Israeli demos and identity. The enactment of the Basic Law: Israel – The Nation-State of the Jewish People, further reinforced this position. In 1995, the Supreme Court ruled, in *United Mizrahi Bank v. Migdal*, that the constitution-making process had reached an advanced enough stage that the court could declare that the country indeed had a constitution, even if it had not yet been completed.[9] I do not mean to rule on the question of whether or not Israel has a written constitution. Rather, I simply mean to say that the ongoing deliberation over the constitution and civil code shows that the country was indeed committed to enacting these two constitutive documents, of important national import and symbols of progress and independence. It is an excellent example of Israel's moderate cultural policy. The Israeli legal and political elite did not disavow legal symbols of independence, namely, a constitution and a civil code, but rather postponed enacting them as single documents, eschewed the formal and symbolic preambles that are usually attached to such instruments, and divided them into separate articles so as to avoid the cultural conflict that would have been involved in enacting such important legal texts.

It should be no surprise that the person most identified with the claim that Israel in fact possesses a constitution (the "constitutional revolution" claim) is also the person most identified with the codification of the country's civil code – Aharon Barak. Barak was a specialist in civil law and a student of Gad Tedeschi, the person who, more than anyone else, represented the European

[7] Kedar, "Law, Culture," 192.

[8] The bill was submitted to the Knesset in 2011. The deliberations of the Constitution, Law and Justice Committee have been delayed because of a lack of agreement on the code's general principles and purposes, enumerated in articles 1 and 2.

[9] CA 6821/93 *United Mizrahi Bank v. Migdal Cooperative Village*, IsrSC 49(4) 221.

legal tradition in Israel and who was one of the great advocates of the systematic codification of civil law.[10] As such, Barak helped draft part of the new civil legislation and to inculcate the idea that this body of civil legislation is a coherent legal entity representing a single Israeli theory of law. As attorney general, Barak, along with Uri Yadin, head of the Justice Ministry's Legislative Department, set in motion the process of codifying Israel's civil law. At his request, Yadin produced an initial draft of a civil code, and Barak set up and headed a Codification Committee.[11] In the end, as a Supreme Court justice and later chief justice, Barak declared that not just one but two legal revolutions had taken place in Israel: a constitutional revolution and a "codification" revolution in civil law. "From the establishment of the State until the present day," he wrote, "two quiet 'revolutions' have occurred in Israeli law – the first in the area of public law, and the second in the area of private law. In public law we have witnessed the incorporation of a functional constitution.... In private law we have witnessed the coalescing of a civil codification."[12]

Israel's courts also produced an original Israeli jurisprudence. During the country's initial years, judges referred frequently to English law, with which they were familiar and to which Israeli law was very similar. In certain cases, which I will examine below, they were even required by law to refer to English law. But in time, English law ceased, for all practical purposes, to serve as a binding standard, and subsequently and gradually ceased also to be the principal source of inspiration for Israeli jurists.[13] Today, Israeli judges still often reference foreign, largely Anglo-Saxon, court decisions, for the purposes of inspiration, comparison, and study. But they do not see themselves as obligated to foreign law. Neither do they consider themselves required to refer to one particular system over all others. Studies have shown that, while Israeli judges frequently compare Israeli law with that of other countries, they generally base their rulings on Israeli rather than foreign precedents.[14]

The history of Israel's court system shows that the independence displayed by Israeli judges, and their success in producing original Israeli law and jurisprudence, is even more impressive than that displayed by the country's legislators. Unlike the latter, who were sovereign a priori, empowered to enact

[10] On Tedeschi, see Likhovski, "Czernowitz, Lincoln," 652–656.

[11] On the history of the Israeli Civil Code, see the supplementary material submitted with the bill: www.knesset.gov.il/committees/heb/material/data/H06-07-2011_11-33-01_595.pdf; see also Barak, "Interpretation of the Civil Code," 160–161.

[12] Barak, "The Codification" (1990), 628.

[13] Shachar, Harris, and Gross, "Citation Practices"; Shachar, "Reference Practices"; Radzyner, "Halakha, Mishpat Ivri."

[14] See note 13 and compare Markesinis and Fedtke, "Judge as Comparatist," 106–108.

original Israeli law as they saw fit, the country's judges were bound by law to defer, in certain matters, to English law. As I have already noted, when Israel was established, it left Mandate law in place, with small revisions, so as to maintain social and legal stability. Under Mandate law, English law flowed into Palestine through three channels. The first was precedents – English court rulings were binding on Mandate judges. The second channel was interpretation – most Mandate laws included clauses that referred judges to English law for the purposes of interpretation. The third channel was residual law. Section 46 of the Palestine Order in Council made English law the residual law in Palestine, meaning that judges were to refer to English law when they found no solutions in Mandate or Palestinian legislation or judicial rulings. These channels were part of the Mandate law that Israel adopted after independence, and thus formally bound Israeli judges.

Here is where we also see the disengaging aspect of the process. Israeli jurists were well aware of Israeli law's subordination (in these three aspects) to English law, although it rankled them. It should hardly be surprising, then, that on the eve of independence some of them advocated severing those connections. But stopping the flow in those channels was not a simple matter, as the connection to English law was critical to the law's stability and ongoing development. In any case, the common opinion among the Israeli jurists was that the requirement to refer to English law could be ended only by formal procedure, that is, by legislative act, or at the very least a judicial determination.

The first of the channels to be severed was that of the binding precedent. This was done relatively quickly, for two reasons. First, subordinating Israel's courts to those of England constituted a gross violation of Israeli sovereignty. As such, Israel repealed the recourse of appealing judicial rulings to Britain's Judicial Committee of the Privy Council immediately on declaring independence.[15] It was clear, then, that it would not be long before the binding precedent rule would be ended. The second reason for the relative alacrity with which this rule was canceled was that it was relatively easy to do. Since the subordination to English precedents had been created in the first place by rulings of the Mandate courts, it could be ended by judicial fiat, without requiring action by the Knesset. So, in 1957, Israel's Supreme Court declared explicitly, in *Kochavi v. Becker*, that judges were not obligated to follow British precedents established after the establishment of the state.[16] The reason that nearly a decade nevertheless passed before this step was taken was that many

[15] It is understandable from Clause 12 of the Law and Administration Ordinance, 1948.

[16] CA 81/55 *Kochavi v. Becker* [1957] IsrSC 225.

Israeli attorneys thought that, despite the infringement of Israeli sovereignty and national pride, the requirement to refer to British precedents provided stability. As Israel's own courts had not yet had a chance to create a body of rulings in many areas, many attorneys thought it best to set aside national pride and make use of an advanced legal system with a wealth of experience that had created norms in a swath of important fields. While the spine of stability that British rulings granted Israeli law was certainly not to be taken lightly, the Supreme Court ruled that a corollary of the fact of Israel's independence was that Israel's independent legal system was not subordinate to any foreign law. The court ruled that British precedents created after independence were no longer binding in Israel.

It took longer to do away with the other two channels, those of interpretation and residual law. The reasons were that jurists largely agreed that these would require legislation, and that the questions of interpretation and residual law had been at the center of several theoretical legal debates that did not touch on Israeli law specifically. These controversies had to do with the question of whether voiding English law's standing as residual law would be tantamount to vacating the English law that Israeli courts had already incorporated under its authority. In other words, the question was whether canceling section 46 would apply from that moment onward, or whether it was like cutting down a tree at the trunk, meaning the death of all the branches that had previously sprung from it. Another question was: When does a law that is unenforced become obsolete, that is, when does custom trump law (desuetude)? There were also other questions regarding interpretation, the filling-in of lacunas, and judicial creativity.[17]

Even though judges in Israel referenced English law largely in search of inspiration and for comparative purposes, rather than out of obligation, and even though many Justice Ministry officials, led by the head of the Legislative Department, thought that there was no need for a formal revocation of the obligation to refer to English law for interpretation,[18] they decided to do so anyway, for the sake of legal stability and clarity. In 1972, the Knesset amended clause 15 of the Law and Administration Ordinance, 1948, to read: "All instructions in law according to which it or expressions in it are to be

[17] See Tedeschi, "Abrogation of Article 46."

[18] Yadin, "Custodian Law," 494: "One who surveys Israeli judgments as a whole will see that we have freed ourselves, thanks to the spirit of independence beating in the hearts of our judges, from being subject to English law. We have freed ourselves not only with regard to innovations produced by English courts [in the wake of the *Kochavi* affair] . . . but also in matters in which the explicit interpretation clauses in laws from the Mandate period explicitly refer to English law." And see the sources Yadin cites there.

interpreted according to English law or according to the legal interpretation principles accepted in England will no longer be binding." The application of the requirement to refer to English law as residual law was also gradually restricted over the years because, as part of its emphasis on the independence of Israeli law, the Knesset included in some of the important civil statues enacted then (on inheritance, land, and contracts) clauses stating that section 46, the residual law provision, did not apply to them. In other words, in all matters relating to these laws judges were not required to refer to English law in the case of lacunas.[19] But while the residual law provision had been limited, it was still in force. For that reason, throughout the 1970s debates raged over eliminating it. In the end, this happened only when the Foundations of Law Act was enacted in 1980.

The ostensibly technical argument of the legal debate over annulling section 46 is important because it was in fact a vehement debate on the independence of Israeli law and the Israeli nature of the country's legal system. That is why jurists referred to it as the "debate over the law's independence." They took three distinct positions. One was that of Uri Yadin, head of the Legislative Department, which in practice was expressed as the ministry's semi-official opinion. It argued that Israeli law was independent both formally (as the law of the sovereign state of Israel) and in practice, as thirty years of Israeli independence had created a reality in which statutory provisions requiring reference to English law had become obsolete and void for all intents and purposes. Yadin's first argument in this regard was a formal legal one – once Israel liberated itself from the British yoke, the laws that required Mandate judges to refer to the law of the mother country were no longer binding. "This fundamental change, which we achieved gradually, is one of the 'changes deriving from the establishment of the state and its agencies' (in the words of clause 11 of the Law and Administration Ordinance). Just as the country became independent in terms of government, language, economy, education, and so on, so the country's law has become an independent law."[20] Yadin supplemented this formal claim with a practical one. During its years of independence, he argued, Israelis had taken the opportunity to create an advanced state-of-the-art legal system that met the needs of Israeli society – modern legislation, a rich body of judicial rulings, and sophisticated academic

[19] In the legal argot of the time, these laws were called the "independent statutes." Here are the independence clauses in each of those laws: Clause 150, Succession Law, 1965; Clause 160, Land Law, 1969; Clause 24, Contracts Law (Remedies for Breach of Contract), 1970; and Clause 63, Contracts Law (General Part), 1973.

[20] Yadin, "Custodian Law," 494.

legal writing. That being the case, "Israeli law as it is emerging . . . does not need a complementary legal method, neither English law nor Hebrew law."[21] Furthermore, even though the requirement to refer to English law remained on the law books, in the real world Israeli judges and jurists no longer turn to English law to fill out lacunas. Instead, they use the plethora of legal sources available to them in Israeli law. In practice, Yadin concluded, section 46 was obsolete and moot. The independence clauses included in the lands, contract, and inheritance laws were no more than declarative; there was no real need for them.[22] Later, Yadin argued that it was better to allow section 46 to die a natural death, as any formal legislative voiding of it would set off a debate over what residual law should replace English law. There was no good reason to instigate pointless cultural and ideological dissension over a legal concept that was in any case controversial.[23]

The second position might be termed that of the "Tel Aviv school." Its most notable spokesman is Daniel Friedmann. In this view, as long as a requirement to refer to the English system exists in law, it cannot be disregarded on the grounds that the provision is obsolete and no longer appropriate for life in an independent country. Furthermore, Friedmann argued at the time that, as long as section 46 of the Palestine Order in Council was in force, the independence clauses in the inheritance, lands, and contracts statues had no real significance, as they were but islands of ostensible independence in a legal ocean that was still subject to English law. Friedmann's position, like those of Yadin, above, and Barak, below, was grounded in a specific school of legal theory. In Friedmann's case, it is that of the positivists, who maintain that the law is a set of clear norms with identifiable sources of authority, meaning authors. On this account, section 46 was legally binding as long as the Knesset had not formally repealed it. Friedmann most likely would agree that, from a national point of view, it would be best to see section 46 as obsolete and moot, but his legal-theoretical position was that the law operates principally in accordance with clear positive norms. Therefore, Israelis proud of their national independence should formally annul section 46.

Friedmann's view on residual law was consistent with his general approach to the new civil legislation project. According to the project's enthusiasts, Barak and Yadin, the new legislation was evidence of Israeli law's

21 Yadin, "Custodian Law," 495.

22 Yadin, "Custodian Law."

23 Barak, "Foundations of Law Act," 280–283. This is an appendix to an article in which Barak relates the history of the enactment of the Foundations of Law Act. He presents there at length Yadin's categorical opposition to the law and to the idea of residual law.

independence and originality, constituting a further link in the glorious chain of Jewish law. Friedmann took a much more cautious view. He argued that care should be taken not to see either the period that had transpired since the establishment of the state nor the civil law project as clear proof that Israeli law had become original and independent. Despite the pride that Israeli jurists took in the new legislation project, the new laws had no particularly Jewish substance or form. In fact, modern forms of legislation (abstract laws and codes) are foreign to Jewish tradition. Furthermore, the substance of the new Israeli laws was not generally taken from Jewish tradition. Friedmann's position was that, since it was difficult to speak of manifestly Jewish-Hebrew-Israeli legal content, the debate over the Israeliness of Israeli law in fact revolves around the issue of the law's independence, and that independence was not complete as long as Israeli law was formally subordinate to English law with regard to filling in lacunas. This subordination could be corrected, Friedmann argued, only by enacting a special law voiding section 46 and replacing it with another provision for addressing lacunas. It could not happen simply by persuading everyone that section 46 had been rendered moot by the simple fact that a well-developed independent Israeli system of law had come into existence.[24]

The third position was that of what has been called the Jerusalem school, led by Hebrew University civil law expert Gad Tedeschi and his student Aharon Barak, who was even more adamant than his teacher. It was a middle position that was essentially close to Yadin's, while formally acknowledging that section 46 required judges to refer to English law in those rare cases in which they happened on a lacuna. He thus agreed with Friedmann that, in the end, there would be no recourse but to enact a law voiding section 46. Barak did not go so far as to accept the claim that in independent Israel the requirement to refer to English law had been rendered moot, but he maintained that, given that Israeli law was independent and advanced, there would almost never be a lacuna that would require judges to do so. Barak's position derives not only from a nationalist view insisting on the independence of Israeli law but also from a jurisprudential position that claims that legal lacunas are extremely rare, and may well not exist in a theoretical sense.[25] In debates conducted during the 1970s and 1980s, Barak was prepared to

[24] See Friedmann, "Another Note," 470. And see also Friedmann, "Provision Concerning"; "Independent Development"; and "Interpretation of Modern."

[25] The claim that denies the existence of lacunas derives from the view that law is a normative system that includes not just written rules but also other types of norms. These include unwritten rules (such as customs), values, and principles and rules of interpretation and judicial creation. On this view, there can be no lacunas in the law, only a need to interpret and

entertain that there might nevertheless be rare cases of lacunas, meaning cases in which it would not be possible to find an answer in positive law, and as such he recognized, in opposition to Yadin, that section 46 was in force and that it needed to be formally repealed.[26] But he stressed that most cases that were considered lacunas were in fact ordinary problems of interpretation (requiring a decision between two norms or two logical and legitimate interpretations of a specific norm).[27] Finally, Barak added that it would also be proper to pass a law revoking section 46 because some of the new Israeli legislation included language exempting them from section 46, creating incoherence among Israeli laws and public uncertainty about the section's application.

When he was appointed attorney general, Barak decided, as I have already noted, to put an end to this academic debate by formally severing the connection between Israeli and English law. He promoted a law repealing section 46, which would ensure that Israeli law would be independent formally and not just in practice. It was a move consistent with the other nationalist initiatives he took in the legal field, as the moving force behind the efforts to enact a constitution and Israeli civil code. It was also consistent with his academic work, in which he sought to develop an original Israeli jurisprudence. Neither was he afraid to address questions of Jewish identity and culture.[28] The Ministry of Justice thus prepared a bill to revoke section 46 and name another set of laws, rather than England's, as Israel's residual law. As anticipated, it set off a turbulent debate between the Justice Ministry and the Knesset about what residual law the Jewish state ought to have. This was the origin of the Foundations of Law Act, 1980, which I addressed at length in Chapter 7.

The enactment of the Foundations of Law Act was part of a general policy of disengagement. A positive Israeli legislation process was not sufficient; the policy was to revoke, via formal legislation, outmoded laws created by the foreign overlord that had ruled the country before the establishment of the state. The goal was to sever Israeli law from any subordination to foreign law. As such, following the enactment of the Foundations of Law Act, and in parallel with commencing work on an Israeli civil code (*dinei mamonot* in Hebrew), the Knesset enacted two laws in 1984 that accomplished just this. The first was the Repeal of the Mejelle Law, 1984 (the Mejelle was a civil and

decide between different sorts of legal norms (e.g., between a written rule and an unwritten legal principle such as "a transgressor should accrue no benefit"). See Dworkin, *Law's Empire*.

[26] See, for example, Tedeschi, "Abrogation of Article 46"; Barak, "The Independence"; "The Codification of the Civil Law" (1973); "Provision Concerning."

[27] Compare Tedeschi, "Lacunae in the Law."

[28] Kedar, "Aharon Barak."

procedural code enacted at the end of the Ottoman period and thereafter formed the central part of that regime's legal system), and the second the Obsolete Legislation (Repeal) Law, 1984.[29]

The story of how the channels of interpretation and residual law were severed is of interest because it shows just how central the issue of the independence of Israeli law was to the Israeli legal discourse. The advocates of Hebrew law and cultural Zionism generally portray the debate over the Israeliness of Israeli law as one between two camps. On the one side are the "authentic Jews" who are unashamed of their national culture and national law and want to base the substance of Israeli law on their national heritage. On the other are the "Hellenizers" who look to the world outside, forsaking their own culture, law, and national pride. But the debate over severing the channels that connected Israeli law to English law show that the actual facts differed in two ways from this simplistic, misleading, but commonly accepted account. First, there were never really two separate camps. People like Haim Cohn and Aharon Barak, often portrayed as the greatest opponents of Jewish law and of giving Jewish culture expression in Israeli law, were in fact the greatest fashioners of Israeli national law. In every position they served in – as attorneys general, judges, and legal scholars – they fought to make Israeli law independent. Second, the debate over the requirement to refer to English law shows that the Israeliness of Israeli law is not limited to the content of the law but is also expressed in the law's form and language, as well as in other formal and institutional characteristics. Focusing the debate on Jewish-Hebrew content thus distorts the character of Israeli law.

In addition to insisting on formal independence, Israeli law (like the Zionist movement) adopted a moderate cultural policy that, while refusing to base Israeli law on manifestly Jewish material (largely for the reason that it was not clear what Jewish content was), also adopted symbols, expressions, values, and norms from Jewish heritage to the extent that these did not exacerbate cultural divisions and as long as they could be adapted to modern life. By far the most important of these symbols was the Hebrew language. During the pre-state period, the fruitless effort to create a Hebrew law based on traditional Jewish sources was superseded by what Assaf Likhovsky has called a struggle for "law in Hebrew." Jewish lawyers insisted on speaking Hebrew in court and in contacts with British institutions of government. This effort continued just before and after independence. The Legal Council of the preparatory Situation Committee for Israeli independence established a special body to draw

[29] In fact, this was the second Obsolete Legislation (Repeal) Law. A first law was passed in 1967, together with the new civil legislation.

up Hebrew legal and governing terminology, and the Justice Ministry and courts later continued to translate legal terms from foreign languages into Hebrew.[30] It should be stressed that the effort to coin Hebrew legal terms grew out of more than a practical need to create a professional terminology. In fact, lawyers love to use foreign terms. It was unambiguously a project that grew out of nationalist commitment, a desire to express the connection between the new Israeli culture and its Jewish heritage. The new Hebrew legal language deliberately drew on earlier strata of the Hebrew language, from the Hebrew of the Bible, the Mishnah, and medieval literature, to demonstrate the continuity of the language from the time of the ancient Hebrews to the present day.

Here are just two examples. The first comes from civil law. At the beginning of the 1950s, Supreme Court Justice Shneor Zalman Cheshin taught a course in unlawful enrichment at the Hebrew University. Justice Cheshin chose not to translate the term literally from English or from another modern language into modern Hebrew. Instead, he took a phrase from a verse from the book of Jeremiah (17:11) and called this area of law *asiyat osher velo bemishpat*, "one who amasses wealth by unjust means." What is important to know in the context of this book is that Israeli jurists adopted and used this biblical expression, and it became the name of the law governing unjust enrichment that the Knesset passed in 1979. The law's name ties it to Jewish tradition, even though by and large its actual provisions are not drawn from the halakhah, but rather derive from a modern Western economic and legal worldview.[31]

The second example comes from criminal law. In the late 1970s, the Ministry of Justice took up the task of relegislating large portions of the country's criminal law. This included drafting new versions of the Penal Code (published in 1977), the Criminal Procedure Law, and the Crime Register Law (the latter two published in the early 1980s). When the latter law was reformulated, the Justice Ministry and the Knesset wanted to emphasize the right to rehabilitation. Here, too, the Justice Ministry eschewed a foreign title, one that simply, for example, transliterated the word "rehabilitation" into Hebrew. Neither did it simply make up a modern Hebrew name. Instead it turned to the Mishnah, taking from that compendium's Gittin (Bills of Divorce) tractate an expression not commonly used in modern Hebrew, *takanat hashavim*, which literally means "the correction of returners" and

[30] Cohn, *Personal Introduction*, 224–225.
[31] See Lifshitz, "One Derives."

refers there to the return of stolen property, to indicate the concept of rehabilitation.[32] The legal system's insistence on using Hebrew legal terms and highlighting the connection to ancient and medieval Hebrew accords with the Zionist movement's moderate cultural policy. While the movement took care not to get caught up in a divisive cultural debate, in the end it made Hebrew its language and a central and agreed-on symbol of the Jewish-Zionist national revival.

Israeli law did not suppress Jewish law (or Jewish heritage in its broadest sense). On the contrary, it serves as a *lieu de mémoire* that preserves it, on several levels, in public and cultural consciousness.[33] I have already shown that, in the formal sense, the very existence of Israeli law enables the existence of a law that is created, interpreted, carried out, and enforced by Jews. But I argue more than this. Just as the state of Israel enables the continuation and flourishing of all Jewish cultures, so Israeli law enables the continuation of Jewish law on several levels.

First, Israeli law formally conserves the norms of Jewish law. The state of Israel is the only country in the world in which the positive law at times gives expression to Jewish law's point of view, whether by directly referencing it, as in parts of family law, where Jewish religious law applies, or by the direct absorption of norms, values, and concepts integrated into binding legal provisions, judicial decisions, or at the very least in guiding obiter dicta, memoranda, and academic legal writing.[34] Some advocates of the Hebrew law project are displeased with the small number of norms that have been taken from Jewish religious law into Israeli law, but the formal presence of legal language, terminology, and guiding principles derived from the Jewish religious legal tradition is not a matter of little import, in particular given the fact that there is no consensus regarding the content of Jewish law and heritage, the ways in which they might be translated into legal norms, and the way they could or should be recast to fit modern life.

Second, and even more importantly, the laws of the state give Jewish law a symbolic presence in Israeli legal and cultural discourse. This happens in several ways. One, already noted, is the integration of Jewish legal principles

[32] Crime Register and Rehabilitation of Offenders Law, 1981. The passage from the Mishnah, Gittin 5:5, reads "about a stolen beam that was built into a castle, [the owner] collects its monetary [value], due to the correction of returners." It rules that a thief may retain a beam he stole and used in building his house, and instead pay damages to the owner, so as not to require the thief to demolish his house in order to return the beam itself. The logic of the ruling is that it will make it easier for the thief to repent his transgression.

[33] Nora, *Lieux de mémoire*.

[34] Elon, *Jewish Law*, vol. 4, 1624–1729.

and rules in legal norms of various types. Another is the incorporation into Israeli law of terms and idioms taken from the lexicon of Jewish law – in the titles of laws, fundamental concepts, and principles of jurisprudence. The advocates of cultural Zionism and Hebrew law are dismissive of these and see them as mere lip service and attempts to buy off the promoters of Hebrew law with symbols that lack any grounding. But these terms and idioms are of great cultural significance, because, de facto, they maintain the presence of Jewish heritage in the contemporary Hebrew language, Israeli culture, and Israeli law, even at a time when most Israelis are ignorant of their source in traditional texts. Terms like *takanat hashavim* (correction of returners) and *'asyat osher* (unjust enrichment), as well as many others, are not attempts to mute or numb religious Jews and cultural Zionists with empty symbols. Rather, Israeli law takes these norms and idioms from halakhic texts and brings them into the central squares of Israeli cities, thus resuscitating them and making them part of the lively Jewish legal and cultural milieu of Israel. It turns Jewish law from a dead letter into a living moral system for a large, dynamic, and variegated Jewish (and non-Jewish) public. Formal Israeli law and the public and academic debate around it do for Jewish law what Zionist education did for the Hebrew language – it revives it, transforming it from a sacred code that was alien even to most religious Jews and known only to a few scholars, all of them men,[35] into a living and developing organ of Israeli society's common law, as expressed in the language of many Israelis, both men and women. Israeli intellectuals lament nostalgically about the Jews' lost heritage, but they are blind to the fact that this heritage was impenetrable to most of the Jewish public. They also disregard the many and rich new possibilities that the sovereign Jewish state and its laws open before Jewish law, including the exciting potential it offers for the development of Jewish culture.

Furthermore, even if not all that many norms, values, and expressions have been borrowed from Jewish law, they nevertheless serve as windows into the worlds of Jewish culture. They constitute a link to those other worlds, and are on exhibit in Israeli law's "display window," directing the reader or listener to it. They preserve Jewish law in the Israeli collective memory and invite Israelis to investigate it. At the same time, these contents are imbued with new cultural and legal meanings, and constitute a living bridge between Jewish heritage and today's vibrant Israeli culture.

[35] In fact, throughout history, Jews have lived not only according to the halakhah. The halakhah has been principally the object of study, whereas social life was conducted according to a wide range of coexisting norms, halakhic, non-halakhic, and of course non-Jewish ones coming from the countries in which and societies among which Jews lived.

The Israeli legal system has also put in place institutions that preserve Jewish law. For example, it has been customary since the founding of the state for one of the seats on the Israeli Supreme Court to be held by an expert in Jewish law who can integrate its values and rules in his opinions, even if only as non-binding obiter dicta. (Some charge that the "Jewish law seat" is simply a euphemism for a seat reserved for a religiously observant judge.) In 2018, the Supreme Court was provided with a senior law clerk for Jewish law, charged with helping justices who seek to express Jewish law in their opinions. But, beyond this, judges at all levels routinely integrate the halakhic point of view into their rulings.[36] The Ministry of Justice and the Knesset also have small Jewish Law Departments, responsible for providing legislative and Knesset committees, the courts, and government ministries and agencies with briefs summarizing the halakhic position on issues they address. Another task performed by the Ministry of Justice's Jewish Law Department is the maintenance of an edition of the laws of the state in which they are paralleled with the provisions of Jewish law. This makes it easy to reference relevant halakhic passages. The department also conducts seminars for judges and state attorneys. On top of that, all the country's law schools require their students to take at least one course in Jewish law.

In this case, too, the advocates of the Hebrew law project often dismiss the "Jewish law justices," the Justice Ministry and Knesset departments, the senior law clerk for Jewish law at the Supreme Court, and the law school course requirement as sops meant to silence them and avert any real and serious attempt to imbue Israeli law with Jewish law. But this is a major error. First, it misconstrues Israeli society. The very existence of these institutions and customs makes an important cultural statement. It is not to be taken for granted, given that it comes with a not insignificant economic and political price tag. Israeli society's willingness to maintain and fund this system testifies to its desire to maintain a connection with Jewish tradition. In fact, every attempt to grapple with the issue of identity at a more "meaningful" or "true" level must necessarily and quickly deteriorate into cultural and religious conflict. On top of that, it is a historical error. This book proves that there is not, and never has been, any feasible way of compelling more profound compliance with Jewish law in Israel (or in any other modern country). What is at issue is not a lack of goodwill, but the impossibility of agreeing on a definition of Jewish culture and Jewish law, and how to integrate them into Israeli law.

36 www.justice.gov.il/Units/MishpatIvri/MishpatIvriBapsika/Pages/MishpatIvriBapsika.aspx [Hebrew].

The presence of Jewish law and culture in Israeli law must thus always be, by definition, symbolic. The belief that it is possible to force Israeli law to base itself on Jewish heritage of religious law is morally unacceptable and operatively impractical. It is morally objectionable because it would not be proper to impose on a society behavioral norms that it perceives as alien and outside its realm of consensus. It cannot work operationally because Israeli law must always accommodate itself to present needs. For example, Israeli laws addressing unjust enrichment correspond to modern conceptions of economics and society rather than to traditional Jewish law, even though the Hebrew term for the concept has its origin in the Bible. But even if Israeli law were to adopt formally not only the Hebrew term but also some of the arrangements stipulated in Jewish law for addressing this issue, Israeli society and courts would presumably interpret and apply those provisions in ways that match current needs and experience, rather than in the ways customary in the Talmud or Middle Ages. In that case, Jewish law would remain anyway merely a symbol rather than a guide for practice. Culture and law are dynamic because human thought is not frozen. *Homo sapiens*, the wise human, is indeed *Homo faber*, the human maker who constantly alters her conscious, cultural, and physical surroundings. The nostalgic wish to freeze culture, language, religion, and law is psychologically and socially understandable, but unfounded practically and unacceptable morally.

The debate over Israel's law of inheritance is a case in point. To repeat, the draft of the Succession Law authored by Haim Cohn explicitly departed from the halakhah on several points. For example, it mandated inheritance by daughters, gave equal standing to female and male heirs, and did away with provisions that give the eldest son a larger portion. Rabbi Shlomo Goren, the Israeli Defense Forces' chief military rabbi, opposed the draft categorically because of its deviation from Jewish religious law, even though he recognized that, in the modern context, it would be impossible and improper to act in accordance with the halakhah's inequitable provisions. He proposed that the law formally adhere to the halakhah, but that in practice *takanot* (rabbinic edicts), procedural rules, and legal fictions could be used to provide for equality under the law in practice. Rabbi Goren's suggestion was actually about symbols – he wanted the law to retain the vestiges of the Jewish religious tradition, for example, the rule discriminating against women in inheritance, even though the actual legal reality would be entirely different. He knew very well that most Israelis, including most religious Jews, would not agree to live under a discriminatory inheritance regime. Whatever the letter of the Succession Law, society would find ways to adapt it to its current way of life – that is, to get around the written provisions of the law and institute an egalitarian system of inheritance.

Clearly, then, the debate over Jewish law and Jewish tradition is not a polarized one between the "authentic" Jewish camp and the universal "Hellenizing" camp, with the latter willing to grant at most a symbolic, rarefied, and limited place to Jewish culture. Even if the debate is formulated in this binary way, the issue of the Israeliness of Israeli law is, in the end, a debate over a cultural position. One side, a minority composed of intellectuals from all currents in Israeli society, sees Jewish cultural symbols and heritage as static and elemental and seeks to grant them a central and even coercive position. This group seeks to express the Israeliness of Israeli law largely by imbuing it with Jewish-Hebrew norms and symbols. The other side, the majority, sees Jewish cultural symbols as being dynamic in nature, constantly changing and evolving. This group seeks to express and change them in accordance with the values and needs of the people here and now, abjuring debate over the nature of Judaism and the content of Jewish law. Instead, it seeks to imbue Israeli law with cultural symbols and Jewish heritage only on condition that they are uncontroversial and appropriate for a modern dynamic society.

The meta-cultural debate over whether or not to wage a culture war in the field of law has been personified in the figures of Menachem Elon, who died in 2013, and Aharon Barak, two men with very similar biographies, despite the fact that Elon was Barak's senior by thirteen years. Before appointment to the Supreme Court, both were professors of law who were seen as major authorities in their specializations, and both received the Israel Prize for their scholarly work, Elon in the field of Jewish law and Barak in civil law. Both served as senior officials in the Ministry of Justice, Elon as senior adviser to the attorney general and the ministry's first adviser on Jewish law, Barak as attorney general. Yet, despite these similarities, they disagreed on the question of just how Israeli law was and should be Israeli.

Elon insisted that the Israeli-Jewish nature of Israeli law should be ensured by imbuing it with Jewish content. He was religiously observant and identified Hebrew law with Jewish religious law. However, he recognized the religious and political barriers to simply taking the halakhah and making it the law of a modern state. He thus saw the Hebrew law project as largely a national-cultural one, even if his work cannot be separated from messianic hope that imbuing Israeli law with norms from religious law would in the end bolster the Jewish religion. Elon was one of the last advocates of the Hebrew law project in the spirit of Ahad Ha'am and the Hebrew Law Society founded in Moscow by Eisenstadt and Dickstein. It was at the Tel Aviv School of Law and Economics, founded by these two, that Elon received his legal education. His academic project was the study of the history and foundations of Jewish law, and the ways it could be assimilated into Israeli law. Elon believed to his dying day that Israeli law could be based on values, rules, and legal institutions drawn from Jewish law.

Barak is no less of an enthusiastic Zionist jurist than Elon was. But he sought to make Israeli law Israeli largely by developing an independent Israeli jurisprudence and by stressing cultural symbols and the independence of Israeli law by, for example, drafting an Israeli constitution and civil code. As a Zionist, Barak recognized the importance of Jewish symbols in Israeli law and culture, but preferred Herzl's political-civic vision and a moderate cultural policy. In a newspaper interview after his retirement from the Supreme Court, he said: "I can say of myself that I am a Zionist in every bone and fiber of my body, and not an Ahad Ha'am Zionist. A Herzlian Zionist. A Zionist who believes in a Jewish nation-state that is meant to solve the Jewish question."[37]

Elon's and Barak's differing versions of Zionism reached their height in the 1980s in a debate over the purview of the Foundations of Law Act, which I described at length in Chapter 7. It is generally portrayed as a cultural polemic between the religious Elon and the secular Barak, between Elon, advocate of Jewish culture, and Barak, advocate of Western culture. But the truth is that the debate between them was an all-in-the-family one between two approaches to Zionism that both aimed to base Israeli law on the substance of Hebrew law. Elon identified Hebrew law with the halakhah in its broadest sense, whereas Barak offered a dynamic Herzlian approach that placed the emphasis on independent Israeli legal creativity, symbols of independence, and a moderate cultural policy.[38] Elon believed that Jewish heritage obligated Israeli jurists. In contrast, Barak stressed that, while judges were rooted, simply by being Jews, in the Jewish heritage, they could not be subordinate to it, no matter how culturally valuable that tradition is.

The Israeli nature of Israeli law thus derives, first and foremost, from its status as the law of the sovereign state of Israel and its civil society, just as the French nature of French law derives from its being the law of the sovereign French state. This may seem like a rather meager and emaciated definition, a skeleton lacking both flesh and spirit, but in fact it allows modern Jews to shape their laws as they see fit in their sovereign state. A quick overview of Israeli law shows that this is precisely what Israelis have done and continue to

[37] Shavit, "Ex-Chief Justice."

[38] See, for example, FH 13/80 *Handles v. Bank Kupat Am*, IsrSC 35(2) 785, 798 (Barak J.): "Only in this way [by means of free creativity] can we create for ourselves, through a painstaking and fundamental 'legal struggle,' a legal method, jurisprudence, and basic concepts appropriate for our country's modern needs." Barak was probably referring to Rudolf von Jhering's well-known work, *The Struggle for Law* (1872).

do. The country's modern, democratic, and dynamic law, into which many symbols taken from Jewish heritage are interwoven, exactly fits the needs of Israel's modern, dynamic, and secular (in the cultural and political and, for most Israelis, also religious sense) society. It is a society that preserves Jewish cultural symbols, even as it interprets them in constantly changing fresh (religious and non-religious) ways. Some purists see this as a dismal and shallow muddle that does not properly address Jewish identity and the obligation to pass on a rich and firmly rooted culture to the generations that follow. But most Israelis do not have an issue with their dynamic Jewish culture. They justifiably disregard the static purist approach. History shows that they are right to do so. Israel has developed a varied and lively culture and legal system that are based on the traditions of the past but also look clearly into the future.

Conclusion

Zionism and the question of identity are fundamentally in tension. On the one hand, the Zionist movement came into being as a response to the anxiety felt by European Jews regarding their identity and culture in the face of secularization and modernization. If Judaism was merely a religion, then non-believing and non-observant Jews ostensibly had no cause to think of themselves as Jews anymore. If it was simply an ethnic culture, it seemed to many poor and backward compared with the cultures around them. Zionism told the Jews that they were a nation, on a par with all the other awakening nations of Europe, and thus supplied them with a new, common, and inclusive identity shared by all Jews no matter what their religious beliefs and practices and despite their cultural diversity. Furthermore, Zionism's fundamental claim, that the Jews are a nation with a common history, common fate, a shared connection to an ancestral land, and other collective cultural traits, was the source of Zionism's strength as an idea and as a practical program, as it offered a national narrative that was accepted, almost intuitively, by the Jewish masses in Europe and around the world.

On the other hand, Zionism did not limit itself to portraying the Jews as a nation. It also demanded the actualization of Jewish nationalism in a sovereign state in Palestine, on the grounds that only a sovereign entity could enable the perpetuation of a free and flourishing Jewish culture over time. Given the heated debates among Jews over the nature of Jewish culture and identity, the bulk of the Zionist leadership concluded that such cultural polemics were detrimental to the realization of Zionism's goal. Early on, these leaders realized that a unifying national framework (i.e., the idea of Zionism and the Zionist movement) would do little to lower the flames of controversy. In light of this, the movement adopted a moderate cultural policy, emphasizing the aspects of national identity that were accepted by the majority, while muting disputes over identity and culture (e.g., the question of defining what Judaism is). The movement's official documents and operations studiously omitted any reference to these issues. The policy was reinforced by a flexible system of coalition agreements that enabled cooperation despite disagreements. Zionist policy in the cultural field required careful and tactful conduct that would, on the one hand, maintain the cultural narrative that was the source of Zionism's strength and provided most of the energy for the work on its program, and, on the other hand, take precautions against turning ideological-cultural fervor into a mania that would consume the Zionist project.

This policy was censured by intellectuals, both religious and not, but the fact is that, remarkably, Zionism achieved its goals. It succeeded in leading a profound process of secularization and modernization, as well as a broad political, economic, and cultural revolution in the lives of contemporary Jews, without a culture war and without violent cultural coercion. It managed to fashion an open, dynamic, democratic, and ultimately pluralistic society. Furthermore, as a republican democracy characterized by civic unity and common purpose – the Zionist-Israeli term is *mamlakhti* – Zionism has enabled the flourishing of a vibrant and varied Israeli Jewish culture or, rather, a spectrum of Jewish cultures: religious and secular, high and popular, Eastern and Western. Nearly seven million Israeli Jews participate in it. They, speak, read, and write in Hebrew, and conduct a rich artistic and literary life. It would be no exaggeration to say that we live in a golden age of Jewish culture of unprecedented range. A hundred or so Hebrew books are published in Israel each week, nonfiction and fiction, and poetry, both sacred and secular. Never in the history of the Jewish people has there been a cultural flowering of such impressive scope and variety as there is today in Israel. Pace the plaints of intellectuals and rabbis, Jewish religious culture thrives in Israel as never before in Jewish history. Never before have so many Jews had access to the Jewish canonical bookshelf. In the past, in most communities, women did not read and write at all, and most men had only a limited and general education in their heritage. Furthermore, the Jews never before had at their disposal as efficient a cultural distribution agent as a modern state, with its educational, cultural, and communications networks. This cultural creativity can be seen in the law as well. In the seven decades since independence, Israel has produced a body of legislation, court rulings, and law literature impressive in its depth and independence of thought.

In short, the news of the death of Jewish culture and law has been greatly exaggerated. They are alive and kicking and developing in new and fascinating ways. While Israelis do not agree on a definition of their identity, and while the debate over this issue continues to agitate Israeli society, that in no way impinges on its dynamic and vigorous culture. Zionism's success in Israel is so impressive that Ahad Ha'am's vision has actually come to be: Israel serves as a Jewish cultural lighthouse that sends its cultural rays out to the entire Jewish world, and to non-Jews as well. Of course, Israel is not the only Jewish lighthouse. There are vibrant centers of Jewish life elsewhere in the world, especially in North America and Europe, that maintain intellectual and spiritual links with Israel. But in none of these other places can Jews live a free, varied, and full Jewish culture, as both individuals and a collective, as they can in Israel. Israeli culture is so creative and intense that it is now exported. The tens of thousands of Israelis who live today in Berlin, New York, and other large cities around the world have created an Israeli cultural diaspora. These lively and creative communities produce Israeli culture, literature, art, and scholarship on a high level, nourished by both their Israeli roots and their local milieus.[1] An independent and democratic Israel is important today not only for the maintenance of Israeli culture but also for the flourishing of Jewish culture, both Israeli and non-Israeli, all over the world.

Jewish culture in Israel is, to make an understatement, not so bad at all. The anxiety of intellectuals has been the major force behind the fruitless cultural debate in Israel. Intellectuals, scholars, rabbis, educators, and artists have made common cause to persuade Israelis that they are sinning against themselves and their children by their failure to clearly define their identity and to imbue their culture, law, and state with Jewish significance. But these critics simply disregard the fact that Israeli society does not – in fact, cannot – ignore their culture and identity. The Zionist movement is awash with Jewish culture, the rich and exciting culture that has developed in Israel.

The problematic idea that Jewish law (or Hebrew law) can be assimilated into (or imposed on) Israeli law remains very powerful among religious Zionism's rabbinic and political leadership:

> In general, the key national-religious ... (and to a certain extent, Haredi) rabbinic and political figures believe that the assimilation option is an ideal that should be adhered to. While some of them agree that it has not produced sufficient gains from a religious point of view, they do not attribute this to problems inherent in the option but rather to real-world obstacles and difficulties. On their account, they must, as leaders, grapple with those difficulties tenaciously and resolutely until they successfully inculcate the halakhah into the common law as broadly as possible. The chrysalis, they believe, will eventually emerge as a stunningly colorful butterfly. Behind the scenes, they foster hopes of demographic salvation, meaning that the

[1] Oz-Salzberger, *Israelis in Berlin.*

> religious community's higher rate of natural increase will bring the advocates of assimilation greater political power and make it possible to carry out the program more vigorously in the future. Have no doubt – the religious intuition of many years, which fosters assimilation, is alive and kicking. It continues to nurture the vision that leads religious Zionism's concept of how Judaism is to be expressed in the state of Israel.[2]

These words apply just as well to secular intellectuals who proclaim themselves advocates of cultural Zionism or defenders of Hebrew culture. The longing for an Israeli legal system based on Hebrew-Jewish content grows out of a utopian hope that Israeli society will be able to contend "bravely" with its identity and fashion for itself a proud and glorious culture that combines the best of Jewish heritage with the best of modern culture (as if the two are completely separate). This almost messianic view insists on disregarding the hurdles that stand in the way of the Hebrew law project and render it unworkable. In particular, it ignores the lack of consensus among Jews about the definitions of Judaism, Jewish culture, and Jewish law.

Most of those who fear for the fate of Jewish culture are in fact apprehensive about the future of a particular form of religion or culture that they know and believe in. Even if they understand in theory that culture, language, religion, and law are always and inevitably evolving, they have trouble accepting that dynamism and how far it leads away from the model and tradition that they know and love. They interpret this natural evolution as enervation of the spirit and generational decline. Their laments are nostalgic elegies of decline and *Weltschmerz*, the sorrows of the world. They bemoan the world of yesteryear that will never return, and the slow death of the Jewish culture they once knew (or hoped to see). Their sorrow blinds them to the Jewish-Hebrew cultural flowering in Israel and around the word. The sense of cultural alarm and anxiety voiced by rabbis, intellectuals, and educators in fact has no basis in reality; to a great extent it grows out of conservatism and fashionable pessimism.

Israel's democratic, secular, and dynamic culture cannot be compelled to accept one particular version of Jewish-Hebrew norms in the name of religious or cultural heritage, nor a static, essentialist conception of law and culture. Cultural coercion is wrong, both morally and religiously; moreover, it is impossible, because culture, like language, religion, and law, never stands in place but rather undergoes evolutionary change and development. Parts of Jewish culture are neglected, but many other parts of the past and of Jewish

2 Stern, "What Is Jewish," 18–19.

heritage are very much present in today's culture, or are being reconceptualized and reinvented. To offer one example, ancient Hebrew is a component of modern Hebrew, even if the spoken language of today's Israel differs from biblical and Mishnaic Hebrew to an extent that a modern Hebrew-speaker has trouble understanding those texts. And another: the music Jews played and sang in past generations is present in Israeli music. Sometimes it is easy enough to make out ancient melodies quoted in Israeli music, but most of the influence comes in the form of structural, rhythmic, and harmonic motifs below the surface. The Jewish legal heritage has a similarly complex position in Israeli law. In their law and in their culture, today's Israelis use symbols from Jewish heritage in accordance with their needs and their views. Israel's legal system and academic legal studies promote the presence of a variety of Jewish symbols in the law and use them in legislation, court rulings, legal memorandums, and legal studies. In fact, Israeli law as it stands is today the most important preserve of and monument to Jewish law. It has moved Jewish religious law out of the study hall, changing it from a dead letter familiar only to a few thousand *yeshivah* students to a living norm that serves millions of Israelis – men and women – or is at least available to them as an important symbol of their heritage and an open and inviting window into Jewish culture.

This claim is not, however, accepted by some intellectuals and jurists. They argue that Jewish heritage and Jewish law have only a minimal and pathetic presence in Israeli law, and that it can and should be given a more honorable place in Israel's legal system. This could be done, they claim, if the Israeli public simply displayed a bit more goodwill and put out a little more effort. The grievances of contemporary Israeli intellectuals are no different from plaints of Jewish intellectuals of previous generations. The last two centuries have seen a *meta-cultural* debate between a small number of thinkers who have advocated giving priority to cultural action and the great majority of Jews and their leadership who have placed practical action first. The debate dates back to the Haskalah, the Jewish enlightenment of the eighteenth century, when many Jews were in practice synthesizing their traditions with modern culture. Against them, the advocates of the Haskalah, the Maskilim, stridently protested what they saw as false enlightenment, by which they meant the adoption of modern culture without thought about the change in values that needed to accompany that acceptance.[3] As I have related, a similar meta-cultural debate marked the early days of Zionism, between the advocates of cultural Zionism and the Zionist majority that focused on Jewish settlement in

3 Feiner, "Pseudo-Enlightenment."

Palestine and sought a political solution to the Jewish problem. During the British Mandate there was similar conflict between a small group of jurists and intellectuals who sought to revitalize Hebrew law, and the Jews living in Palestine, who supported the ideas behind the Hebrew law project, but in practice preferred to use the effective and fair Mandate legal system.

Other than the artificial and coercive nature of cultural revival and invention projects, the culturalists turn a blind eye to the fact that, even if Jewish law had a larger presence in Israeli law, it would nevertheless be no more than a symbolic presence. Jewish and Zionist-Israeli history, as related in this book, shows that the Hebrew law project was doomed to fail. Outside the fantasies of a small number of jurists, intellectuals, and rabbis, there was no real *commonly agreed-on* way to institute an effective and functional Jewish-Hebrew legal system appropriate for a modern mass democracy. In fact, the advocates of Hebrew law and cultural Zionism never really sought a purely Jewish alternative to modern Israeli law. Their writings have remained on the academic-theoretical level, where it never had to cope with the responsibility for the proper running of a democratic society and complex and developed economy. At most, then, the halakhah could serve as a font of symbols, inspiration, and ethical and legal critique.[4] But that is precisely the function it has today. Perhaps it would be possible to enlarge this critical function. Whatever the case, it is practically impossible and would be morally improper to inculcate – that is, impose – the halakhah (or Jewish heritage) in a deeper way in Israeli law.

History shows that the romantic (in both senses of the word) attempts to ground the law of any given society largely on its particular culture and history have proved to be clumsy and artificial, and have always failed in the end. That was, for example, the fate of the German historical school of law founded by Friedrich Carl von Savigny. Savigny, who lived in the nineteenth century, wanted to shape German law in accordance with German legal heritage. He believed that he and his students could, through historical and ethnographic study, unearth an authentic German legal culture molded by the nation's history, and that this could serve to construct a modern German legal system. Savigny was, of course, correct in his claim that a society's laws need to accord with its cultural conventions, but he failed utterly in his attempt to find or invent a German cultural-legal heritage that could serve as a basis for modern German law. He and his disciples searched vainly for such authentic pan-German legal foundations rooted in the nation's history.

[4] Stern, "What Is Jewish," 44–58. Stern proposes there that the fundamental humanist values with which Jewish law and heritage are imbued serve as ethical criteria for Israeli law.

In the end, his students, who were among the shapers of the law in united Germany, had no choice but to base the Reich's law code on the Roman model, those parts of it that were shared by the united country's different components, and on general principles of legislation and interpretation. The laws fashioned by these German jurists, known as the Pandectists, were indeed German laws, and in many senses actually original German law, but not because it was based on authentic German content, but rather because it was fashioned by Germans in accordance with the values and needs of late nineteenth-century German society. The same thing happened with other historical-cultural movements that emerged in Europe at that time, and to the Hebrew law project, which was very much influenced by the views of Savigny and his students. It is hard to believe that the artificial attempt to revive the Hebrew law project could have succeeded where the projects that inspired it all failed.

The Israeli character of Israeli law is manifested not only in the Jewish symbols with which it is imbued (values, specific norms, terms, and concepts), but also by means of the meticulousness with which its independence is preserved. Israeli law is Israeli and Jewish-Hebrew by nature because it is the law of sovereign, autonomous Israelis who legislate for themselves, by themselves, in their own language, and in accordance with their own needs, interests, and values. Israeli law has placed exceptional emphasis on its independence from the very start. There are two aspects to this independence, one of disengagement and one of creation. First, Israeli law severed its connections rather quickly from formal subordination to formal law (subordination to English law was repealed, and outdated laws inherited from the Ottoman and Mandate regimes were gradually replaced). It also ensured that its legal thinking not be subjugated to foreign legal thinking. Second, Israeli law has been notable for its impressive creativity, in independent legislation and judicial rulings. Finally, the independence of Israeli law is manifested in symbols of independence, from the use of the Hebrew language and Hebrew terms, to the ongoing effort to enact the symbols of legal independence accepted in modern law – a constitution and a civil code.

All this shows that Israeli law does in fact express an independent Jewish-Israeli identity that grows out of a long Zionist policy. Nevertheless, the Knesset decided, in the 1980s, to insert into legislation explicit phrases such as "Israel's heritage" and "Jewish and democratic state," and in 2018 to declare, in a constitutional Basic Law, that Israel is the nation-state of the Jewish people. This was a momentous deviation from the policy of muting cultural controversy and from the consensual form of democracy pursued by the Zionist movement and the state of Israel up to that time, and it threatens to throw off the delicate balance that Zionism maintained with the issue of identity. Indeed, these formal declarations, along with the intensive public preoccupation with their meaning, has not done a thing to bolster Israeli society's Jewish identity or to cause Israeli law to be more Jewish (or Hebrew). Israel has not become more Jewish since the words "Jewish and democratic state" were added to its laws, or since judges were commanded to refer to the principles of Hebrew law or "Israel's heritage" when they find no answer to a question in legislation or precedent. The formal declarations of Israel's Jewish nature and the values of Israel's heritage have not even done anything to inculcate humanistic-Jewish values into Israeli law. On the contrary, they seem to have reinforced nationalist chauvinist elements in Israeli society. In contrast, the cultural-legal controversy awakened by this new legislation has brought to the fore, and even artificially bolstered, dissension over identity and culture in Israeli society, both among Jewish Israelis and between them and the country's non-Jewish citizens, in particular, the large native Arab minority.

Despite the good intentions of the legislators and humanistic intellectuals who supported these changes, the expression "Jewish and democratic state" has largely been appropriated by extremist nationalist Jewish groups that not only disseminate a distorted account of supposed tension between "Jewish" and "democratic" values, but do so from within a worldview that for all practical purposes gives their narrow conception of Judaism, as a religion and a nation, precedence over democracy. Basic Law: Israel – The Nation-State of the Jewish People enacted in 2018 testifies to this dangerous view, which ignores the profound democratic-civic (*mamlahti*) nature of the Zionist movement and Israeli society, not to mention the danger of a culture war and cultural coercion.

It would thus be best to refrain from declarations making Jewish law, Hebrew law, or Israel's heritage into Israel's residual law, into a principle that "must" obligate the legislative process or judicial interpretation. Such proclamations do much more damage than good, even if they remain dead letters. Such a legal requirement brings with it a constant threat of dangerous cultural dissension detrimental to democracy, civil unity, and the rule of law. The real discourse of identity is an ongoing, endless one, full of doubts, conducted on both the private and public levels. It is a dialogue between tradition and change, a conversation between values and the different cultural components that make up our ever-changing system of identities. The law is not the appropriate arena for deciding between different takes on identity or views of Jewish culture. If judges accede to the requirement imposed that they decide what the heritage of Israel is, or what Israel's values as a Jewish state are, they cannot avoid taking on a particular cultural-political hue, which impinges on the legitimacy of the courts as neutral and objective institutions. Some Israelis see courts' refusal to make use of Jewish law and heritage, or to get into the definition of a Jewish state, as an unacceptable political act by judges who have "forgotten what it is to be Jews." It is thus best to refrain from such legislation altogether. What is important to realize is that Jewish and Hebrew culture would not have suffered even if the Knesset had not ensconced the country's Jewish identity in law. Even in the absence of such laws, Israel will be the (Jewish) state of nearly seven million free Jews who live a variegated and vigorous Jewish culture. Neither the law alone, nor political and academic discourse, constitute Jewish culture. It exists and develops by virtue of the fact of the lives of Jews who are free to fashion it themselves. During the cultural controversy of the early twentieth century, Moshe Leib Lilienblum castigated Ahad Ha'am and his disciples:

> "The people of Israel live and want to live!" That is the entire teaching of [Hovevei] Zion and Zionism. Answers to the question: "Why does it want to live?" or "What does it need life for?" are entirely superfluous, because the question itself is of unparalleled ignorance, and if we were to pose that question to another nation, we would be answered with a laugh of revulsion.[5]

This position was and remains the cornerstone of Zionism. Some ten months after Israel came into being, Prime Minister David Ben-Gurion invited, not for the first time, a number of intellectuals to a meeting about Israeli society and the ways to raise up the nation. The discussion once again highlighted the differences between the dynamic-democratic political Zionism represented by the prime minister and the static cultural approaches to which some of his intellectual and scholarly guests subscribed. When the philosopher Hugo Bergmann wondered (in a tone worthy of Ahad Ha'am) what the state of Israel's humanistic goal was, and what it would offer the Jews of the world, Ben Gurion replied in Lilienblum's spirit:

> The construction of the state is both material (economic) and spiritual (moral-social). I do not believe that our most pressing question is what we will offer Scandinavian Jewry. They can come here and with us create the new substance of our lives. That is the "humanistic" substance required of us. If we make the lives of Jews here – full, productive, secure, and independent lives – that is of great human substance.[6]

[5] Lilienblum, "Guardianship and Supervising," 332.

[6] Minutes of a meeting of the Prime Minister with authors, March 27, 1949, BGA: Minutes of Meetings.

It is not just Hovevei Zion and Herzl who resonate in Ben-Gurion's words. Voltaire is also part of the mix. In the final scene of *Candide*, the two protagonists, Candide and the philosopher Pangloss, have a conversation. Pangloss recalls their adventures, weaving them into a fabric with transcendental meaning. Candide's response is simple. "That is well put," he says. "But we must cultivate our garden."[7] Israeli jurists should take a lesson from Voltaire's hero, as well as from Lilienblum, Herzl, Jabotinsky, and Ben-Gurion. It is better to leave the discussion of culture, for all its importance, to writers and poets and editorialists, and to focus on fashioning an independent, effective, democratic, and fair Israeli legal system consistent with fundamental humanistic Jewish-universal values. It is best to work to solve the problems of Israeli society and improve the quality of life of all its citizens and inhabitants. Those who fear that the law produced in Israel is not sufficiently Jewish should rest easy. Haim Nahman Bialik, often called Israel's national poet, once wrote: "Everything that is being created in Palestine by Jews . . . is also a part of Judaism, and is pervaded by the spirit of Judaism. That is the concept of culture that is growing here in the Land of Israel."[8]

7 Voltaire, *Candide*, 88.
8 Bialik, "Hebrew Culture," 174.

List of Legal Cases

ISRAELI CASES

Dawikat v. Government of Israel, HCJ 390/79, IsrSC 34(1)1.
Handles v. Bank Kupat Am, FH 13/80, IsrSC 35(2) 785.
Horev v. Minister of Transport, HCJ 5016/96, IsrSC 51(4) 1; IsrLR 149. [1997]
Issacson v. Political Party Registrar, CA 2316/96, IsrSC 50(2) 529.
Jerzhevski v. Prime Minister, HCJ 1635/90, IsrSC 45(1) 749.
Kenig v. Cohen, FH 40/80, IsrSC 36(3) 701. [1982]
Kochavi v. Becker, CA 81/55, IsrSC 225. [1957]
Leon v. Acting District Commissioner of Tel-Aviv, HCJ 5/48, IsrSC 1 58. [1948]
Mitral Ltd. v. Prime Minister and Minister of Religious Affairs, HCJ 3872/93, IsrSC 57 (5) 485. [2003]
Neiman v. Chairman of Elections for Eleventh Knesset; EA 2/84; *Avneri v. Chairman of Central Elections Committee for Eleventh Knesset*, EA 3/84, IsrSC 39(2) 225; IsrSJ 8 83. [1985]
Ornan v. Minister of the Interior, OM 6092/07 *(Jerusalem)*, Nevo July 15, 2008.
Ornan v. Minister of the Interior, CA 8573/08, Nevo October 2, 2013.
Rufeisen v. Minister of the Interior, HCJ 72/62, IsrSC 16 2428. [1962]
Shalit v. Minister of the Interior, HCJ 58/68, IsrSC 23(2) 477. [1970]
United Mizrahi Bank v. Migdal Cooperative Village, CA 6821/93, IsrSC 49(4) 221. [1995]
Yasin v. Parties Registrar, LCA 7504/95, IsrSC 50(2) 45. [1996]
Yeredor v. Knesset Elections Committee, EA 1/65, IsrSC 19 (3) 365.

FOREIGN CASE

The Queen v. Oakes, 1 S.C.R. 103 (Canada Supreme Court). [1986]

Legislation

ISRAELI LEGISLATION

Agency Law, 5725–1965
Basic Law: Freedom of Occupation
Basic Law: Human Dignity and Liberty
Basic Law: Israel – The Nation State of the Jewish People
Basic Law: The Knesset
Civil Code Bill, 5771–2011
Contracts Law (General Part), 5733–1973
Contracts Law (Remedies for Breach of Contract), 5730–1970
Crime Register and Rehabilitation of Offenders Law, 5741–1981
Criminal Procedure Law (consolidated version), 5742–1982
Custodian Law, 5727–1967
Festival of Matzot (Prohibition of Leaven) Law, 5746–1986
Foundations of Law, 5740–1980
Land Law, 5729–1969
Law and Administration Ordinance, 5708–1948
Law of Return, 5710-1950
Non-Profit Associations (*Amutot*) Law, 5740–1980
Obsolete Legislation (Repeal) Law, 5744–1984
Parties Law, 5752–1992
Penal Law, 5737–1977
Pig-Raising Prohibition Law, 5722–1962
Repeal of *mejelle* Law, 5744–1984
Succession Law, 5725–1965
Unjust Enrichment Law, 5739–1979

NON-ISRAELI LEGISLATION

Canadian Charter of Rights and Freedoms (1982)
French Civil Code (1803)
Mejelle (1869–1876)
Palestine Order in Council (1922)
Swiss Civil Code (1907)

Bibliography

Ackerman, Bruce. "The Rise of World Constitutionalism." *Virginia Law Review* 83, no. 4 (May 1997): 771–797.

Addan, Hana, Varda Ashkenazi, and Bilha Alperson. *Being Citizens in Israel*. Tel Aviv: Ma'alot Press, 2001. [Hebrew]

Ahad Ha'am (Asher Ginsberg). "At the Crossroads." In *The Complete Writings of Ahad Ha'am*, edited by Leon Roth: 1–437. Tel Aviv and Jerusalem: Dvir Press and Hotzaa Ivrit Press, 1965. [Hebrew]

(Asher Ginsberg). "The Jewish State and the Jewish Problem." In *Nationalism and the Jewish Ethic: Basic Writings of Ahad Ha'am*, edited by Hans Kohn: 66–89. New York: Schocken Books, 1962.

(Asher Ginsberg). "Old New Land (Altneuland)." In *The Complete Writings of Ahad Ha'am*, edited by Leon Roth: 313–320. Tel Aviv and Jerusalem: Dvir Press and Hotzaa Ivrit Press, 1965. [Hebrew]

(Asher Ginsberg). "The Spiritual Revival." In *Selected Essays by Ahad Ha'am*, translated by Leon Simon: 253–305. Philadelphia: Jewish Publication Society of America, 1912.

(Asher Ginsberg). "This Is Not the Path." In *The Complete Writings of Ahad Ha'am*, edited by Leon Roth: 11–16. Tel Aviv and Jerusalem: Dvir Press and Hotzaa Ivrit Press, 1965. [Hebrew]

(Asher Ginsberg). "The Treasure of Judaism in the Hebrew Language." In *The Complete Writings of Ahad Ha'am*, edited by Leon Roth: 104–114. Tel Aviv and Jerusalem: Dvir Press and Hotzaa Ivrit Press, 1965. [Hebrew]

Almog, Oz. "The Legal Revolution and Its Cultural Meaning." *Alpayim* 18, no. 2 (1999): 77–132. [Hebrew]

Almog, Shmuel. *Zionism and History: The Rise of a New Jewish Consciousness*. New York: St. Martin's Press, 1987.

Anish Stiftel, Shoshana. *The Mediator: Nahum Sokolow's Leadership between Tradition and Zionism*. Jerusalem: Zionist Library Press, 2012. [Hebrew]

Arendt, Hannah. *The Origins of Totalitarianism* (new edition with added prefaces). New York: Harcourt Brace Jovanovich, 1973.

Bakshi, Aviad. "Basic Law: Israel – The Nation-State of the Jewish People: The Legal Necessity." The Institute for Zionist Strategies, November 25, 2016: http://izs.org.il/papers/aviadbakshifinal4.pdf. [Hebrew]

Bakshi, Aviad, and Gideon Sapir. "Justifying the Nation State: On the Lack of Nation State Considerations in Judicial Rulings on the Citizenship and Entry into Israel (Temporary Order) Law (5763-2003)." *Tel Aviv University Law Review* 36, nos. 1–2 (2013): 509–534. [Hebrew]

Barak, Aharon. "The Codification of the Civil Law in Israel." *Tel Aviv University Law Review* 3, no. 1 (May 1973): 5–26. [Hebrew]

"The Codification of Civil Law and the Law of Torts." *Israel Law Review* 24, nos. 3–4 (1990): 628–650.

"The Foundations of Law Act, 1980 and Jewish Heritage (*Moreshet Israel*)." *Shenaton Ha-Mishpat Ha-Ivri: Annual of the Institute for Research in Jewish Law* 13, no. 1 (1988): 265–284. [Hebrew]

"The Independence of the New Civil Codification; Risks and Prospects." *Hebrew University Law Review* 7, no. 1 (June 1976): 15–33. [Hebrew]

"Interpretation of the Civil Code 'Israeli Style.'" In *Essays in Memory of Professor Guido Tedeschi: A Collection of Essays on Jurisprudence and Civil Law*, edited by Izhak Englard, Aharon Barak, Alfredo Mordechai Rabello, and Gabriela Shalev, 115–162. Jerusalem: Nevo Press, 1995. [Hebrew]

Interpretation in Law, vol. 3: Constitutional Interpretation. Jerusalem: Nevo Press, 1994. [Hebrew]

"The Provision Concerning 'the Independence of the Law' in the New Israeli Legislation: A Reply to Professor Friedmann." *Hebrew University Law Review* 5, no. 1 (September 1973): 99–104. [Hebrew]

"The Values of Israel as Jewish and Democratic State." In *Aharon Barak's Selected Essays*, vol. 1, edited by Haim H. Cohn and Yitzhak Zamir, 445–453. Srigim: Nevo Press, 2000. [Hebrew]

Bareli, Avi, and Nir Kedar. *Israeli Republicanism*. Jerusalem: Israel Democracy Institute (2011). [Hebrew]

Baron, Salo Wittmayer. *A Social and Religious History of the Jews, vol. 1: To the Beginning of the Christian Era*. New York: Columbia University Press, 1966.

Bar-On, Shani, and David De Vries. "In the Procrustean Bed of Professionalism: Lawyers and the Histadrut Workers' Tribunals in 1920s and 1930s Palestine." *Avoda, Chevra u-Mishpat/Labor, Society and Law* 8, no. 1 (2001): 15–42. [Hebrew]

Beck, Ulrich. *The Brave New World of Work*. Cambridge: Polity Press, 2000.

Belfer, Ella. *A Split Identity: The Conflict between the Sacred and the Secular in the Jewish World*. Ramat-Gan: Bar-Ilan University Press, 2004. [Hebrew]

Ben-Gurion, David. *From Class to Nation*. Tel Aviv: Am Oved Press, 1974. [Hebrew]

"On the Election Regime." In *Vision and Path* 5: 140–146. Tel Aviv: Mapai Press, 1958. [Hebrew]

"Reply to the Disputants (Speech in the Ideologic Conference at Jerusalem, August 12, 1957)." In *Messianism and Mamlachtiut: Ben-Gurion and the Intellectuals between Political Vision and Political Theology*, edited by David Ohana: 144–150. Sde Boker: Ben Gurion Institute Press, 2003. [Hebrew]

"The Spirit Revolution." In *Vision and Path* 1: 29–47. Tel Aviv: Mapai Press, 1951. [Hebrew]

"Zionism's Objectives in this Time." In *In Battle*, 4: 9–29. Tel-Aviv: Am Oved, 1950. [Hebrew]

Ben-Menahem, Hanina. "The Foundations of Law Act – How Much of a Duty?" *Shenaton Ha-Mishpat Ha-Ivri: Annual of the Institute for Research in Jewish Law* 13, no. 1 (1988): 257–264. [Hebrew]

Bialik, Hayim Nahman. "On Hebrew Culture." In *Oral Lectures*, vol. A. Tel Aviv: Dvir, 1935. [Hebrew]

Bialik, Hayim-Nahman, and Yehoshua Hana Ravnitzky. *The Book of Legends (Sefer Ha'agadah)*. Edited with a New Commentary by Avigdor Shinan. Or Yehuda and Jerusalem: Kinneret, Zmora-Bitan, Dvir Press and Avi Chai Press, 2015. [Hebrew]

Biger, Gideon. "The Development of the Built Area of Tel Aviv, 1909–1934." In *The Beginnings of Tel Aviv, 1909–1934*, edited by Mordechai Naor: 42–61. Jerusalem: Yad Ben Zvi Press, 1984. [Hebrew]

Bondy, Ruth. *Feliks: Pinhas Rozen's Biography*. Tel-Aviv: Zemorah-Bitan, 1990. [Hebrew]

Borochov, Ber, "Our Platform." In *Class Struggle and the Jewish Nation: Selected Essays in Marxist Zionism*, translated from Russian and Yiddish, edited by Mitchell Cohen: 75–103. New Brunswick, NJ: Transaction Books, 1984.

Brainin, Reuben. "The Second Zionist Congress." *Hameliz* 38, October 17, 1898. [Hebrew]

Brot, Rivka. "Between State and Community: Trials of Jewish Collaborators with the Nazis." PhD dissertation, Tel Aviv University, 2015. [Hebrew]

Buber, Martin Mordechai. "Judaism and Culture." In *Mission and Purpose: Assays on Judaism* 1, edited by Robert Walsh: 226–234. Jerusalem: Zionist Library Press, 1959. [Hebrew]

Calderon, Nissim. *Multiculturism versus Pluralism in Israel*. Tel Aviv and Haifa: Zmora Bitan Press and Haifa University Press, 2000. [Hebrew]

Cheshin, Mishael. "Jewish Heritage (Moreshet Yisrael) and the Law of the State." In *Civil Rights in Israel: Essays in Honor of Haim H. Cohn*, edited by Ruth Gavison: 47–83. Jerusalem: Association for Civil Rights in Israel Press, 1982. [Hebrew]

Cohen, Asher. *Israeli Assimilation: The Absorption of Non-Jews into Israeli Society and Its Influence on the Collective Identity*. Ramat Gan: Bar Ilan University: The Rappaport Center, 2004. [Hebrew]

"Religion and State: Seculars, Religious and Orthodox." In *The First Decade: 1949–1959*, edited by Zvi Zameret and Hana Yablonka. Jerusalem. Ben Zvi Press, 1997. [Hebrew]

Cohen, Asher, and Baruch Susser. *From Accommodation to Escalation: Secular-Religious Conflict in Israel*. Tel-Aviv: Schocken Press, 2003. [Hebrew]

Cohen, Asher, and Bernard Susser. *Israel and the Politics of Jewish Identity: The Secular-Religious Impasse*. Baltimore: Johns Hopkins University Press, 2000.

Cohen, Uri. *Academia in Tel- Aviv: The Making of a University*. Jerusalem: Hebrew University Magnes Press, 2014. [Hebrew]

"The School of Law and Economics in Tel-Aviv, 1935–1948: The Hopeless Pursuit of Political-Academic Legitimacy." *Bar-Ilan Law Studies* 25, no. 1 (2009): 179–212. [Hebrew]

Cohn, Haim H. *Being Jewish: Culture, Law, Religion, State*. Jerusalem and Or-Yehuda: Kinneret, Zmora, Bitan, and Dvir Press, 2006. [Hebrew]

"The Jewishness of the State of Israel." *Alpayim* 16, no. 1 (1998): 9–35. [Hebrew]

"Looking Ahead." *Hapraklit* 3, no. 2 (February 1946): 38–46. [Hebrew]
Personal Introduction, Autobiography. Jerusalem and Or-Yehuda: Kinneret, Zmora, Bitan, and Dvir Press, 2005. [Hebrew]
Selected Essays 1991–2001. Edited by Aharon Barak and Ruth Gavison. Jerusalem: Nevo Press, 2001. [Hebrew]
"Values of a Jewish and Democratic State: Studies in Basic Law: Human Dignity and Liberty." In *Hapraklit Jubilee Book*, edited by Arnan Gabrieli and Miguel Deutch: 9–52. Tel Aviv: Israeli Bar Press, 1993. [Hebrew]
"Yesterday's Concern." In *Haim H. Cohn: Selected Essays*, edited by Aharon Barak and Ruth Gavison: 25–40. Tel Aviv: Bursi Press, 1991. [Hebrew]
Danziger, Yoram. "A Symbolic Gesture Whose Damage Is Far Greater than Its Benefit." *Hapraklit* 33, no. 4 (1981): 619–623. [Hebrew]
David, Joseph, ed. *The State of Israel: Between Judaism and Democracy*. Jerusalem: Israel Democracy Institute Press, 2003.
Deutch, Sinai. "Jewish Law in Israeli Courts." *Bar-Ilan Law Studies* 6, no. 1 (1988): 7–29. [Hebrew]
Dickstein, Paltiel. "Commercial Deception in the Hebrew Law of Peace." *The Hebrew Law* 1, no. 1 (1925): 150–152. [Hebrew]
"On the Hebrew Law of Peace." *The Hebrew Law* 1, no. 1 (1925): 147–150. [Hebrew]
A History of the Hebrew Courts of Arbitration. Tel Aviv: Yavne Press, 1964. [Hebrew]
"A Jewish State Needs Jewish Law." *Hapraklit* 4, no. 12 (December 1947): 328–330. [Hebrew]
"Proclamation on Jewish Law." *Hapraklit* 5, no. 1 (January 1948): 3–8. [Hebrew]
Don Yehiyeh, Eliezer. "Cooperation and Conflict between Political Sectors: The Religious Sector and the Labor Party and the Ministry of Education in Israel, 1949-1951." PhD Thesis, Hebrew University of Jerusalem, 1977. [Hebrew]
"Ideology and Politics in Religious Zionism: The Zionist Theory of Rabbi Reines and the Politics of the 'Mizrahi' Party under his Leadership." *Hatzionut* 8, no. 1 (1983): 103–146. [Hebrew]
"Judaism and Statism in the Philosophy and Politics of David Ben-Gurion." *Hatzionut* 14, no. 1 (1989): 51–88. [Hebrew]
Dothan, Shmuel. *A Land in the Balance: The Struggle for Palestine, 1918–1948*. Jerusalem: Gefen Books, 1993. [Hebrew]
Dromi, Uri, ed. *Brethren Dwelling Together: Orthodoxy and Non-Orthodoxy in Israel – Positions, Propositions, and Accords*. Jerusalem: Israeli Democracy Institute, 2005. [Hebrew].
Dubnow, Simon. "The Content of Jewish History." In *Nationalism and History: Essays on Old and New Judaism*, edited by Koppel S. Pinson: 260–265. New York: Atheneum Press, 1970.
Dworkin, Ronald. *Law's Empire*. Cambridge, MA: Harvard University Press, 1986.
Edrei, Arie. "Why Teach Jewish Law." *Tel Aviv University Law Review* 25, no. 2 (November 2011): 467–487. [Hebrew]
Eisenstadt, Samuel. "Chronicles of the Jewish Law." In *Zion with Justice: Pamphlets on Jewish and Roman Jurisprudence*, edited by Samuel Eisenstadt: 11–30. Tel Aviv: Hamishpat Press, 1967. [Hebrew]

"The New Codification of Our National Law." In *Zion with Justice: Pamphlets on Jewish and Roman Jurisprudence*, edited by Samuel Eisenstadt: 242–246. Tel Aviv: Hamishpat Press, 1967. [Hebrew]

Zion with Justice: Pamphlets on Jewish and Roman Jurisprudence. Tel Aviv: Hamishpat Press, 1967. [Hebrew]

Eisenstadt, Samuel, and Paltiel Dickstein, "Our Goal" (1918). *Hamishpat Ha'ivri* 1 no. 3 (1925): 6. [Hebrew]

Eliav-Feldon, Miriam. "If You Will It, It Is No Fairy Tale: The First Jewish Utopias." *The Jewish Journal of Sociology* 25, no. 2 (1983): 85–103.

Elon, Menachem. "Constitution by Legislation: The Values of a Jewish and Democratic State in the Light of the Basic Law: Human Dignity and Personal Freedom." *Jewish Law Association Studies* 21, no. 1 (2011): 77–114.

Jewish Law: History, Sources, Principles. Translated by Bernard Auerbach and Melvin J. Sykes. Philadelphia: Jewish Publication Society, 1994.

"Jewish Law and Its Place in Israel Jurisprudence." *Hapraklit* 25, no. 1 (December 1968): 27–53. [Hebrew]

"More about the Foundations of Law Act." *Shenaton Ha-Mishpat Ha-Ivri: Annual of the Institute for Research in Jewish Law* 13, no. 1 (1987): 227–256. [Hebrew]

Religious Legislation in the Laws of the State of Israel and the Decisions of the Courts and the Rabbinic Courts. Tel Aviv: Hakibuts hadati, 1968. [Hebrew]

Elroey, Gur. *Homeland Seekers: The Jewish Territorialism Organization (JTO) and the Zionist Movement, 1905–1925*. Sde Boker: Ben Gurion Research Institute for the Study of Israel and Zionism, 2011. [Hebrew]

Englard, Izhak. "The Integration of Jewish Law in the Israeli Legal System." In *Jewish Law and the State of Israel*, edited by Jacob Bazak: 110–134. Jerusalem: Mossad Harav Kook Press, 1969. [Hebrew]

Religious Law in the Israel Legal System. Jerusalem: Hebrew University of Jerusalem, Faculty of Law, Harry Sacher Institute for Legislative Research and Comparative Law, 1975. [Hebrew]

Even-Zohar, Itamar. "The Emergence of a Native Hebrew Culture in Palestine: 1882–1948." *Poetics Today* 11, no. 1 (Spring 1990): 175–191.

Feiner, Shmuel. "The Struggle over the Pseudo-Enlightenment and the Boundaries of Jewish Modernization." In *Studies in East European Jewish History and Culture in Honor of Professor Shmuel Werses*, edited by David Assaf: 3 25. Jerusalem: Magnes Press, 2002. [Hebrew]

Freiman, Avraham Haim. "Jewish Law in Eretz Yisrael." In *The Jewish Law and the State of Israel*, edited by Jacob Bazak: 110–134. Jerusalem: Mossad Harav Kook Press, 1969. [Hebrew]

Friedman, Menachem. "The Chronicle of the Status-Quo: Religion and State in Israel." In *Transition from "Yishuv" to State – 1947–1949: Continuity and Change*, edited by Varda Pilowsky: 47–80. Haifa: Herzl Institute for Research in Zionism, University of Haifa Press, 1990 [Hebrew]

Friedmann, Daniel. "Another Note on the Provisions Concerning 'the Independence of Law' in the New Israeli Legislation." *Hebrew University Law Review* 5, no. 2 (January 1974): 349–351. [Hebrew]

"Independent Development of Israeli Law." *Israel Law Review* 10, no. 4 (1975): 515–568.

"On the Interpretation of Modern Israeli Legislation." *Tel Aviv University Law Review* 5, no. 3 (June 1977): 463–490. [Hebrew]

"The Provision Concerning 'the Independence of the Law' in the New Israeli Legislation." *Hebrew University Law Review* 5, no. 1 (September 1973): 91–98. [Hebrew]

Frischman, David. "On Judaism." In *The Complete Writings of David Frischman* 8, edited by Fishel Lahover: 7–28. Warsaw: Lili Frischman Press, 1931. [Hebrew]

Frumkin, Gad. *A Judge's Path in Jerusalem*. Tel Aviv: Dvir Press, 1954. [Hebrew]

Gans, Chaim. *From Richard Wagner to the Right of Return: Philosophical Analysis of Israeli Public Affairs*. Tel Aviv: Am Oved Press, 2006. [Hebrew]

Gavison, Ruth. *Can Israel Be Both Jewish and Democratic: Tensions and Prospects*. Jerusalem and Tel Aviv: Van Leer Jerusalem Institute and Hakibbutz Hameuchad Press, 1999. [Hebrew]

"Constitutional Anchoring of Israel's Vision: Recommendations Submitted to the Minister of Justice (November 19, 2014)." In *Defining Israel: The Jewish State, Democracy and the Law*, edited by Simon Rabinovitch: 41–71. Cincinnati: Hebrew Union College Press, 2018.

"Democracy and Judaism – Between Conceptual Analysis and Public Discourse." In *The State of Israel: Between Judaism and Democracy*, edited by Joseph David, 331–359. Jerusalem: Israel Democracy Institute, 2003.

"Reflections on the Meaning and Justification of 'Jewish' in the Expression 'a Jewish and Democratic State.'" In *The Jewishness of Israel*, edited by Aviezer Ravitzky and Yedidia Stern, 107–178. Jerusalem: Israel Democracy Institute, 2007. [Hebrew] A shorter English version was published in *The Israeli Nation State: Political, Constitutional and Cultural Challenges*, edited by Fania Oz-Salzbereger and Yedidia Stern: 135–163 (Boston: Academic Studies Press, 2014).

Gavison, Ruth, and Yaacov Medan. *The Gavison–Medan Covenant: Main Points and Principles*. Jerusalem: Avi Chai Foundation and the Israel Democracy Institute, 2004.

Geertz, Clifford. "Local Knowledge: Fact and Law in Comparative Perspective." In *Local Knowledge: Further Essays in Interpretive Anthropology*, edited by Clifford Geertz, 167–235. New York: Basic Books, 1983.

"Thick Description: Toward an Interpretive Theory of Culture." In *The Interpretation of Cultures*, edited by Clifford Geertz, 3–30. New York: Basic Books, 1973.

Giddens, Anthony. *Modernity and Self-Identity: Self and Society in the Late Modern Age*. Stanford: Stanford University Press, 1991.

Globes, Elazar. "About Hebrew Court." *Hapraklit* 4, no. 1 (1947): 111–114. [Hebrew]

Goldberg, David Theo, and Michael Krausz, eds. *Jewish Identity*. Philadelphia: Temple University Press, 1993.

Goldberg, Giora. "Religious Zionism and the Framing of a Constitution for Israel." *Israel Studies* 3, no. 1 (Spring 1998): 211–229.

"When Planting Trees, You Do Not Need a Constitution: On State-Building and Constitution-Framing." *State, Government and International Relations* 38, no. 1 (1993): 29–48. [Hebrew]

Goldstein, Yossi. *Ahad Ha-Am and Herzl: The Struggle for Zionism's Political and Cultural Profile in the Shadow of the "Altneuland Episode."* Jerusalem: Dinur Center Press and Zalman Shazar Center, 2011. [Hebrew]

Green, Emma. "Israel's New Law Inflames the Core Tension in Its Identity." *The Atlantic*, July 21, 2018.
Gulak, Asher. *The Foundations of Jewish Law*. Berlin: Dwir, 1922. [Hebrew]
Gutwein, Daniel. "The Dialectics of Equality Failure: The Israeli Left-Wing between Neo-Liberalism to Social-Democracy." *Mikarov* 3, no. 1 (2000) 30–57. [Hebrew]
"From a 'Constitutional Revolution' to a 'Counterrevolution': The Legal Logic of the Privatization Regime in Israel." *Tel Aviv University Journal of Law and Social Change* 1, no. 1 (January 2008): 47–62. [Hebrew]
"Identity vs. Class: Multiculturalism as a Neo-Liberal Ideology." *Theory and Criticism* 19, no. 1 (Fall 2001): 241–258. [Hebrew]
Hacohen, Mordechai Ben Hilel. "The Hebrew Law of Peace in Palestine." In *Atchalta*, 111–159. Jerusalem: Ayanot Press, 1942. [Hebrew]
Han, Shiyuan. "A Snapshot of Chinese Contract Law from an Historical and Comparative Perspective." In *Towards a Chinese Civil Code: Comparative and Historical Perspectives*, edited by C. H. van Rhee and Lei Chen: 235–255. Leiden: Martinus Nijhoff, 2012.
Harris, Ron. "Absent Minded Misses and Historical Opportunities: Jewish Law, Israeli Law and the Establishment of the State of Israel." In *On Both Sides of the Bridge: Religion and State in the Early Years of Israel*, edited by Mordechai Bar-On and Zvi Zameret, 21–55. Jerusalem: Yad Ben Zvi Press, 2002. [Hebrew]
"The Spread of Law into the Public Sphere in the Third Decade." In *Israel in the Third Decade*, edited by Zvi Zameret and Chana Yablonka, 251–268. Jerusalem: Yad Ben-Zvi Press, 2007. [Hebrew]
Harshav, Benjamin. "Theses on the Historical Context of the Modern Jewish Revolution." *Jewish Studies Quarterly* 10, no. 4 (2003): 300–319.
Herzl, Theodor. *The Diaries of Theodor Herzl*, vol. 128. Translated by Marvin Lowenthal. New York: Grosset & Dunlap, 1962.
The Jewish State: An Attempt at a Modern Solution of the Jewish Question. Translated by Sylvia D'Avigdor and Israel Cohen. New York: American Zionist Emergency Council, 1946.
Old New Land (Altneuland). Translated by Lotta Levensohn. New York: Bloch Publishers, 1941.
Hirschl, Ran. *Constitutional Theocracy*. Cambridge, MA: Harvard University Press, 2010.
"Negative Rights vs. Positive Entitlements: A Comparative Study of Judicial Interpretations of Rights in an Emerging Neo-Liberal Economic Order." *Human Rights Quarterly* 22, no. 4 (November 2000): 1060–1098.
Towards Juristocracy: The Origins and Consequences of the New Constitutionalism. Cambridge, MA: Harvard University Press, 2009.
Holtzman, Avner. "Born Culture: The Hebrew Literature and the 'Cultural Controversy' in the Zionist Movement, 1897–1902." In *Aesthetics and National Revival: Hebrew Literature against the Visual Arts*, edited by Avner Holtzman: 19–37. Tel Aviv: Zmora-Bitan and Haifa University Press, 1999. [Hebrew]
Jabotinsky, Zeev. *Letters* 5. Edited by Daniel Carpi. Jerusalem: Jabotinsky Institute, 2000. [Hebrew]
Jhering, Rudolf von. *The Struggle for Law*. Translated by John J. Lalor. Chicago: Callaghan and Company, 1915.

Kanamori, Shigenari. "German Influences on Japanese Pre-War Constitution and Civil Code." *European Journal of Law and Economics* 7, no. 1 (January 1999): 93–95.

Karp, Judith. "Basic Law: Human Dignity and Liberty, a Biography of Power Struggle." *Mishpat Umemshal* 1, no. 2 (April 1993): 323–384. [Hebrew]

"The Legal Council: A Legislative Genesis." In *Memoriam Uri Yadin* 2, edited by Aharon Barak and Ṭanah Shpanits: 209–256. Tel Aviv: Bursi Press, 1990. [Hebrew]

Katz, Gideon, and Nir Kedar. "The Jewishness of the Jewish State in the Eydes Jewish Secular Intellectuals." In *When Judaism Meets the State*, edited by Yedidia Stern, Benjamin Brown, Kalman Neuman, Gideon Katz, and Nir Kedar, 423–506. Tel Aviv and Jerusalem: Yedioth Aharonoth Press and Israeli Democracy Institute, 2015. [Hebrew]

"Secular Israeli Intellectuals on Judaism." *Democratic Culture in Israel and the World* 14 (2013): 127–204.

Katz, Gideon, Shalom Ratzabi, and Yaacov Yadgar, eds. *Beyond Halacha: Secularism, Traditionalism and "New Age" Culture in Israel*. Sde Boker: Ben-Gurion Institute and Ben-Gurion University Press, 2014. [Hebrew]

Katz, Shaul, and Michael Heyd. *The History of the Hebrew University of Jerusalem: Origins and Beginnings*. Jerusalem: Hebrew University Magnes Press, 1997. [Hebrew]

Katz, Yossi. "The Role of Hebrew Law in the Legislation Process of the Land Law, 5729-1969." *Karka* 53, no. 1 (2001): 91–134. [Hebrew]

Kedar, Nir. "A Scholar, Teacher, Judge, and Jurist in a Mixed Jurisdiction: The Case of Aharon Barak." *Loyola Law Review* 62, no. 3 (Fall 2016): 659–689.

Ben-Gurion and the Constitution. Ramat-Gan: Bar-Ilan University Press and Dvir Press, 2015. [Hebrew]

"Ben-Gurion's Mamlakhtiyut: Etymological and Theoretical Roots." *Israel Studies* 7, no. 3 (2002): 117–133.

"The Cultural Roots of Civil Codification in Israel." *Law & Business* 7, no. 1 (2007): 169–201. [Hebrew]

"Equality and Partnership in Ben-Gurion's Political Thought in the 1950s and 1960s." In *Society and Economy in Israel*, edited by Tuvia Friling, Daniel Gutwein, and Avi Bareli, 741–777. Sde-Boker and Jerusalem: Ben-Gurion University Press and Yad Ben Zvi Press, 2005. [Hebrew]

"Interpretive Revolution: The Rise of Purposive Interpretation in Israeli Law." *Tel Aviv University Law Review* 26, no. 2 (November 2002): 737–772. [Hebrew]

"The Israeli Early Voting System Battle: A Story of Democracy, Civic Culture and Law," *Tel Aviv University Law Review* 33, no. 3 (2011): 555–592. [Hebrew]

"Law, Culture and Civil Codification in a Mixed Legal System." *Canadian Journal of Law and Society* 22, no. 2 (2007): 177–195.

Mamlakhtiyut: David Ben-Gurion's Civic Thought. Sde Boker and Jerusalem: Ben-Gurion University Press and Yad Ben-Zvi Press, 2009. [Hebrew]

"On the Danger of Enshrining National Character in the Law." In *Defining Israel: The Jewish State, Democracy and the Law*, edited by Simon Rabinovitch: 231–240. Cincinnati: Hebrew Union College Press, 2018.

"The Roots of Ben-Gurion's Opposition to a Written Constitution." *Journal of Modern Jewish Studies* 12, no. 1 (2013): 1–16.

Should Jewish Identity Be Anchored in Israeli Law? Jerusalem: Israel Democracy Institute Press, 2015. [Hebrew]

"'We Need the Messiah So That He May Not Come': On David Ben-Gurion's Use of Messianic Language." *Israel Affairs* 19, no. 3 (2013): 393–409.

Kidron, Anat. *Between Nationality and Location: The Jewish Community in Haifa during the British Mandate*. Jerusalem: Yad Ben-Zvi Press, 2012. [Hebrew]

Kimmerling, Baruch. *The End of Askenazi Hegemony*. Jerusalem: Keter Press, 2001. [Hebrew]

The Invention and Decline of Israeliness: State, Society, and the Military. Berkeley: University of California Press, 2001.

Kirschenbaum, Aharon. "The Foundations of Law, 1980 – Today and Tomorrow." *Tel Aviv University Law Review* 11, no. 1 (1985): 117–126. [Hebrew]

Klausner, Israel. *Opposition to Herzl*. Jerusalem: Ahiever, 1960. [Hebrew]

Kremnitzer, Mordechai. *Disqualification of Lists*. Jerusalem: Israel Democracy Institute Press, 2005. [Hebrew]

Laskov, Shulamit. "Altneuland." *Zionism* 15, no. 1 (1990): 35–53. [Hebrew]

Lau, Martin. *The Role of Islam in the Legal System of Pakistan*. Leiden: Brill, 2005.

Law, David, and Mila Versteeg. "The Evolution and Ideology of Global Constitutionalism." *California Law Review* 99, no. 5 (October 2011): 1163–1257.

Leibowitz, Yeshayahu. "More about Separation of Religion and State." In *Judaism, the People of Israel, and the State of Israel*, edited by Yeshayahu Leibowitz: 177–180. Jerusalem: Schocken Press, 1975. [Hebrew]

Lewinsky, Elḥanan Leib. "A Journey to the Land of Israel in Year 800 of the Sixth Millennium (2040)." In *The Complete Writings of Elhanan Leib Lewinsky*, edited by Joseph Klausner, Haim Nachman Bialik, and Yehoshua Hana Ravnitzky: 4–46. Odessa: Yavne Press, 1911. [Hebrew]

Lifshitz, Berahyahu. "Israeli Law and Hebrew Law – Connection and Independence." *Hebrew University Law Review* 19, no. 4 (May 1990): 859–870. [Hebrew]

"One Derives a Benefit and the Other Sustains No Loss –The Receipt of the Benefit Did Not Involve a Loss to the Benefactor." *Hapraklit* 37, nos. 1–2 (October 1986): 203–218. [Hebrew]

Likhovski, Assaf. "Argonauts of the Eastern Mediterranean: Legal Transplants and Signaling." *Theoretical Inquiries in Law* 10, no. 2 (July 2009): 619–651.

"Czernowitz, Lincoln and Jerusalem and the Comparative History of American Jurisprudence." *Theoretical Inquiries in Law* 4, no. 2 (July 2003): 621–657.

"The Invention of 'Hebrew Law' in Mandatory Palestine." *The American Journal of Comparative Law* 46, no. 2 (1998): 339–373.

Law and Identity in Mandate Palestine. Chapel Hill: University of North Carolina Press, 2006.

"Legal Education in Mandatory Palestine." *Tel Aviv University Law Review* 25, no. 2 (November 2001): 291–342. [Hebrew]

"'The Time Has Not Yet Come to Repair the World in the Kingdom of God': Israeli Lawyers and the Failed Jewish Legal Revolution of 1948." In *Jews and the Law*, edited by Ari Mermelstein, Victoria Saker Woeste, Ethan Zadoff, and Marc Galanter, 359–383. New Orleans: Quid Pro Press, 2014.

Lilienblum, Moshe Leib. "A Temple and a Stumbling Block to the People of Israel." In *The Complete Writings of Moshe Leib Lilienblum* 4, edited by Yosef Zeitlin: 275–282. Odessa: Moria Press, 1913. [Hebrew]

"Between the Imaginary and the Possible." In *The Complete Writings of Moshe Leib Lilienblum* 4, edited by Yosef Zeitlin: 247–255. Odessa: Moria Press, 1913. [Hebrew]

"Guardianship and Supervising in the Yishuv." In *The Complete Writings of Moshe Leib Lilienblum* 4, edited by Yosef Zeitlin: 331–364. Odessa: Moria Press, 1913. [Hebrew]

"If Not Now, When?" In *The Complete Writings of Moshe Leib Lilienblum* 4, edited by Yosef Zeitlin: 411–418. Odessa: Moria Press, 1913. [Hebrew]

Letters of Moshe Leib Lilienblum to Yehuda Leib Gordon. Edited by Shlomo Breiman. Jerusalem: Hebrew University Magnes Press, 1968. [Hebrew]

"On the Vicissitudes." In *The Complete Writings of Moshe Leib Lilienblum* 3, edited by Yosef Zeitlin: 208–231. Odessa: Moria Press, 1913. [Hebrew]

"Peace Thoughts." In *The Complete Writings of Moshe Leib Lilienblum* 4, edited by Yosef Zeitlin: 256–259. Odessa: Moria Press, 1913. [Hebrew]

"The Symbol of Jealousy and Hostility." In *The Complete Writings of Moshe Leib Lilienblum* 4, edited by Yosef Zeitlin: 260–266. Odessa: Moria Press, 1913. [Hebrew]

"To the Keepers of the Wind and Diviners of the Clouds." *Hamelitz*, February 19–23 and March 29–April 3, 1892. [Hebrew]

"We Should Not Confuse One Question with Another." In *The Complete Writings of Moshe Leib Lilienblum* 4, edited by Yosef Zeitlin: 13–16. Odessa: Moria Press, 1913. [Hebrew]

Lilla, Mark. *The Reckless Mind: Intellectuals in Politics*. New York: New York Review of Books, 2001.

Lis, Jonathan. "Israel's Contentious Nation-State Law: Everything You Need to Know." *Haaretz*, July 19, 2018.

"Netanyahu's Cabinet Approves Controversial Bill Enshrining Israel as 'Jewish Nation-State.'" *Haaretz*, November 23, 2014.

Luz, Ehud. *Parallels Meet*. Philadelphia: Jewish Publication Society, 1988.

Maoz, Asher. "The Place of Jewish Law in the State of Israel." *Hapraklit* 40, no. 1 (August 1991): 53–66. [Hebrew]

Margolin, Ron. *The State of Israel as a Jewish Democratic State*. Jerusalem: Hebrew University Magnes Press, 1999. [Hebrew]

Markesinis, Basil, and Jorg Fedtke. "The Judge as Comparatist." *Tulane Law Review* 80, no. 1 (November 2005): 11–168.

Mautner, Menachem, *Law and the Culture of Israel*. Oxford: Oxford University Press, 2011.

Meir, Natan M. *Kiev, Jewish Metropolis: A History, 1859–1914*. Bloomington: Indiana University Press, 2010.

Mintz, Matityahu. "The Jewish Nation – A Zionist Invention? In the Wake of the Historians' Controversy." In *Zionism Controversy*, edited by Avi Bareli and Pinhas Ginossar: 31–51. Sde Boker: Ben Gurion Institute and Ben Gurion University Press, 1996. [Hebrew]

"The Upbuilding of Eretz-Israel and Work in the Present – A Concept of Unity versus the Actuality of Contradiction." *Hatzionut* 9, no. 1 (1984): 147–155. [Hebrew]

Miron, Guy. "Modernization, Assimilation, Cultural Renewal and Public Sphere – New Perspectives in the Research of Eastern and Central European Jews." *Iyunim Bitkumat Israel* 22, no. 1 (2012): 459–488. [Hebrew]

The Waning of the Emancipation: Jewish History, Memory, and the Rise of Fascism in Germany, France, and Hungary. Detroit: Wayne State University Press, 2011.

Moss, Kenneth B. "At Home in Late Imperial Russian Modernity – Except When They Weren't: New Histories of Russian and East European Jews, 1881–1914." *The Journal of Modern History* 84, no. 2 (2012): 401–452.

Motzkin, Leo. "Program and Organization of the Democratic-Zionist Fraction." In *Leo Motzkin: Selected Essays*, edited by Avraham Bein: 55–62. Jerusalem: Zionist Management and the Global Jewish Congress Management Press, 1939. [Hebrew]

Naor, Mordechai. *Tales from My Beloved Country*. Tel Aviv: Ministry of Defense Press, 1979. [Hebrew]

Nathans, Benjamin. *Beyond the Pale: The Jewish Encounter with Late Imperial Russia*. Oakland: University of California Press, 2004.

Nora, Pierre. *Les lieux de mémoire*. Paris: Gallimard, 1997.

Ofer, Tehila. *A Man of Vision and Action: The Life and the Achievements of Prof. Shmuel Eisenstadt*. Herzliya: Milo Press, 1999. [Hebrew]

Ohana, David. *Messianism and Mamlachtiut: Ben-Gurion and the Intellectuals between Political Vision and Political Theology*. Sde Boker: Ben Gurion Institute Press, 2003. [Hebrew]

Örücü, Esin. "The Impact of European Law in the Ottoman Empire and Turkey." In *European Expansion and Law: The Encounter of European and Indigenous Law in 19th- and 20th-Century Africa and Asia*, edited by Wolfgang Mommsen and Jaap Moor: 39–58. New York: St. Martin's Press, 1992.

"Infusion of the Diffusion: Four Circles of Diffusion Infusing the Legal System of Turkey." In *The Diffusion of Law: The Movement of Laws and Norms around the World*, edited by Sue Farran, James Gallen, Jennifer Hendry, and Christa Rautenbach: 7–24. Farnham: Taylor and Francis, 2016.

Oz-Salzberger, Fania. *Israelis in Berlin* (new edition). Tel Aviv: Keter (2014). [Hebrew]

Oz-Salzberger, Fania, and Eli Salzberger. "The Secret German Sources of the Israeli Supreme Court." *Israel Studies* 3, no. 2 (1998): 159–192.

Porat, Benjamin. *Proposal to Amend the Foundations of Law Act, with an Analysis and Critique*. Jerusalem: Israeli Democracy Institute Press, 2016. [Hebrew]

Procaccia, Gualtiero. "The Foundations of Law Act, 1980." *Tel Aviv University Law Review* 10, no. 1 (April 1984): 145–158. [Hebrew]

Rabinovitch, Simon. *Defining Israel: The Jewish State, Democracy and the Law*. Cincinnati: Hebrew Union College Press, 2018.

Jewish Rights, National Rites: Nationalism and Autonomy in Late Imperial and Revolutionary Russia. Stanford: Stanford University Press, 2016.

Radzyner, Amihai. "'A Scholar Who Was Not Properly Eulogized' – J. S. Zuri and His Jewish Law Studies on the Background of Jewish Law Research History."

Shenaton Ha-Mishpat Ha-Ivri: Annual of the Institute for Research in Jewish Law 23, no. 1 (2005): 259–349. [Hebrew]

"Between Scholar and Jurist: The Controversy over the Research of Jewish Law Using Comparative Methods at the Early Time of the Field." *Journal of Law and Religion* 23, no. 1 (2007): 189–248.

"Halakha, Mishpat Ivri and the State of Israel." *Justice* 45, no. 1 (Spring 2008): 8–14.

"Inheritance from Uncle Sam: The American Influence on Israeli Succession Law." *Comparative Legal History* 4, no. 1 (2016): 19–50.

"Jewish Law in London: Between Two Societies." *Jewish Law Annual* 18, no. 1 (2009): 81–136.

"'Jewish Law' between 'National' and 'Religious:' The Dilemma of the Religious-National Movement." *Bar-Ilan Law Studies* 26, no. 1 (2010): 91–178. [Hebrew]

"Mishpat Ivri Is Not Halakhah (but Is Nonetheless of Value)." *Akdamot* 16, no. 1 (2005): 139–167. [Hebrew]

"On the Beginning of Rabbinical Courts' Procedural Regulations: 'Sidrei Ha-Mishpatim,' 1921." *Bar-Ilan Law Studies* 25, no. 1 (2009): 37–75. [Hebrew]

"Rabbi Ouziel, the Tel-Aviv-Jaffa Rabbinate and the Rabbinical Court of Appeal: A Play in Four Acts." *Bar-Ilan Law Studies* 21, no. 1 (2004): 129–243. [Hebrew]

Radzyner, Amihai, and Shuki Friedman. "The Israeli Legislator and Jewish Law: Haim Cohn between Tomorrow and Yesterday." *Tel-Aviv University Law Review* 29, no. 1 (September 2005): 167–244. [Hebrew]

The Religious Community and the Constitution: What Can History Teach Us? Jerusalem: Israel Democracy Institute Press, 2006. [Hebrew]

Rahat, Gideon. "The Israeli Electoral System 1948–1959: From Default to an Entrenched System." *Iyunim Bitkumat Israel* 11, no. 1 (2011): 369–776. [Hebrew]

Rakover, Nahum. *Jewish Law in the Debates of the Knesset*. Jerusalem: Library of Jewish Law, 1988. [Hebrew]

Raniel, Menachem. "Clouds and Winds without Rain – The Law of the Fundamentals of Law – 1980 in Light of Reality." LL.M. thesis, Haifa University, 2005. [Hebrew]

Ratzabi, Shalom. "The Jewish State in Buber's Political Thinking, 1942–1965." In *Independence – Fifty Years*, edited by Anita Shapira: 195–214. Jerusalem: Zalman Shazar Institute, 1998. [Hebrew]

Reitan, Maya. "The Law of Return and the 'Who Is a Jew?' Controversy – The Shalit Case and Its Implication on Israeli Judicial System, Public Discourse and Legislation 1968–1970." MA Thesis, Ben Gurion University of the Negev, December 2013. [Hebrew]

Rettig Gur, Haviv. "In the Jewish Nation-State Kerfuffle, Much Ado over Very Little Substance." *Times of Israel*, November 24, 2014.

Rinawie-Zoabi, Ghaida, ed. *The Future Vision of the Palestinian Arabs in Israel*. Nazareth: National Committee for the Heads of the Arab Local Authorities in Israel, 2006.

Rojanski, Rachel. "Ben-Gurion's Attitude to Yiddish in the 1950s." *Iyunim Bitkumat Israel* 15, no. 1 (2005): 463–482. [Hebrew]

Rosenzweig, Franz. *Briefe*. Berlin: Schocken Press, 1935.

Rovner, Adam L. *In the Shadow of Zion: Promised Lands before Israel*. New York: NYU Press, 2014.

Rozin, Orit. *A Home for All Jews: Citizenship, Rights, and National Identity in the New Israeli State*. Waltham, MA: Brandeis University Press, 2016.

"The Collective Identity in the Proposal Constitution: Historical and Cultural Review." In *The Jewish People Today, Integration and Dispersion: Essays in Honor of Yosef Gorny*, edited by Aliezer Ben-Refael, Avi Bareli, Meir Chazan, and Ofer Shiff, 138–155. Jerusalem: Yad Ben Zvi Press, 2009. [Hebrew]

"Forming a Collective Identity: The Debate over the Proposed Constitution, 1948–1950." *Journal of Israeli History* 26, no. 2 (2007): 251–271.

"From 'We' to 'I': Individualism in Israeli Society in the Early 1950s." PhD diss., Tel Aviv University, 2002. [Hebrew]

The Rise of the Individual in 1950s Israel: A Challenge to Collectivism. Waltham, MA: Brandeis University Press, 2011

Rubinstein, Amnon. "Book Review: 'Law and Culture in Israel on the Eve of the 21st Century' by Menachem Mautner." *Hapraklit* 50, no. 2 (April 2010): 653–658. [Hebrew]

"The Story of the Basic Laws." *Law and Business* 14, no. 1 (2012): 79–109. [Hebrew]

Rubinstein, Amnon, and Alexander Yakobson. *Israel and the Family of Nations: The Jewish Nation-State and Human Rights*. Abingdon: Routledge Press, 2008.

Sagi, Avi. *The Jewish-Israeli Voyage: Culture and Identity*. Jerusalem: Shalom Hartman Institute, 2006. [Hebrew]

Sapir, Gideon. *The Israeli Constitution: From Evolution to Revolution*. Oxford: Oxford University Press, 2018.

Segal, Zeev. "Israel Ushers in a Constitutional Revolution: The Israeli Experience, the Canadian Impact," *Constitutional Forum* 6, no. 2 (Winter 1995): 44–53.

"The Israeli Constitutional Revolution: The Canadian Impact in the Midst of a Formative Period." *Constitutional Forum* 8, no. 3 (Spring 1997): 53–58.

Shachar, Yoram. "The Reference Practices of the Israeli Supreme Court 1950–2004." *Hapraklit* 50, no. 1 (December 2008): 29–69. [Hebrew]

Shachar, Yoram, Ron Harris, and Meron Gross. "Citation Practices of Israel's Supreme Court: Quantitative Analysis." *Hebrew University Law Review* 27, no. 1 (1996): 119–217. [Hebrew]

Shamgar, Meir, and Israel Democracy Institute, eds. *Constitution by Consensus: Proposed by the Israel Democracy Institute*. Jerusalem: Israel Democracy Institute, 2007.

Shamir, Ronen. *The Colonies of Law: Colonialism, Zionism and Law in Early Mandate Palestine*. Cambridge: Cambridge University Press, 2000.

"Lex Moriendi: On the Death of an Israeli Law." In *Multiculturalism in a Democratic and Jewish State*, edited by Menachem Mautner, Avi Sagi, and Ronen Shamir, 589–632. Tel Aviv: Ramot Press, 1998. [Hebrew]

Shapira, Anita. "Ben-Gurion and the Bible: The Forging of an Historical Narrative?" *Middle Eastern Studies* 33, no. 4 (1997): 645–674.

Shashar, Michael, and Haim H. Cohn, *Supreme Court Judge Talks with Michael Shashar*. Jerusalem: Keter Books, 1990. [Hebrew]

Shavit, Ari. "Ex-Chief Justice: Friedmann Reforms Will Make Israel Third World Country." Interview with Aharon Barak. *Haaretz*, April 11, 2008.

Shavit, Yaacov. "Messianism, Utopianism and Pessimism during the 50's." *Iyunim Bitkumat Israel* 2, no. 1 (1992): 56–78. [Hebrew]

Shifman, Pinhas. "Jewish Law in the Civil Courts." *Shenaton Ha-Mishpat Ha-Ivri: Annual of the Institute for Research in Jewish Law* 13, no. 1 (1988): 371–378. [Hebrew]

Shiloh, Shmuel. "Comments and Some New Light on the Foundations of Law Act." *Shenaton Ha-Mishpat Ha-Ivri: Annual of the Institute for Research in Jewish Law* 13, no. 1 (1987): 351–370. [Hebrew]

Shochetman, Eliav. "On Analogy in Decision Making in Jewish Law and the Foundations of Law Act." *Shenaton ha-Mishpat ha-Ivri: Annual of the Institute for Research in Jewish Law* 13, no. 1 (1987): 307–350. [Hebrew]

Silberg (Zilberg), Moshe. *In Inner Harmony: Essays and Articles*. Edited by Zvi Tarlo and Meir Hovav. Jerusalem: Hebrew University Magnes Press, 1985. [Hebrew]

Smith, Anthony D. *The Ethnic Origins of Nations*. Oxford: Basil Blackwell, 1986.

"Zionism and Diaspora Nationalism." *Israel Affairs* 2, no. 2 (1995): 1–19.

Sokolow, Nahum. *To Our Teachers and Rabbis*. Warsaw: Bnei Zion, 1901. [Hebrew]

Stanislawski, Michael. *Zionism and the Fin de Siècle: Cosmopolitanism and Nationalism from Nordau to Jabotinsky*. Berkeley: University of California Press, 2001.

Stern, Anat. "Between Militia to Regular Army: The Standard By-Laws of 'Hagana' Organization." In *Jews and Arabs in a Protracted Struggle*, edited by Assnat Shiran. Tel Aviv: Ministry of Defense Press, 2006. [Hebrew]

Stern, Yedidia. "What Is Jewish in Israeli Law." In *The Jewishness of Israel*, edited by Yedidia Stern. and Aviezer Ravitzky: 13–60. Jerusalem: Israel Democracy Institute Press, 2007. [Hebrew]

Stroumsa, Guy. *The End of Sacrifice: Religious Transformations in Late Antiquity*. Chicago: University of Chicago Press, 2009.

Sussman, Naomi. "Basic Law: Israel – The Nation-State of the Jewish People." Molad (the Center for the Renewal of Israeli Democracy), November 25, 2015. www.molad.org/images/upload/files/StateOfJewishPeople.pdf.

Tedeschi, Guido. "The Abrogation of Article 46, Order in Council, and Its Effect." *Hebrew University Law Review* 8, no. 1 (July 1977): 180–185. [Hebrew]

"Lacunae in the Law and Article 46 of the Palestine Order in Council, 1922." In *Studies in Israeli Law*, edited by Guido Tedeschi: 132–188. Jerusalem: Hebrew University Magnes Press, 1959. [Hebrew]

Tidhar, David. *Encyclopedia of the Pioneers and Builders of the Yishuv*. Tel Aviv: Rishonim Press, 1955. [Hebrew]

Tsurumi, Taro. "'Neither Angels, nor Demons, but Humans': Anti-Essentialism and Its Ideological Moments among the Russian Zionist Intelligentsia." *Nationalities Papers* 38, no. 2 (2010): 531–550.

Unna, Mosheh. *Separate Ways: Religious Parties in Israel*. Alon Shvut: Yad Shapira, 1983. [Hebrew] A shorter English version was published as Mosheh Unna, *Separate Ways: In the Religious Parties' Confrontation of Renascent Israel*, translated by Barry Mindel (Jerusalem: Department of Torah Education and Culture in the Diaspora of the WZO, 1987).

Voltaire (François-Marie Arouet). *Candide and Other Stories*, translated by Roger Pearson. Oxford: Oxford University Press, 2006.

Weinreich, Max. "YIVO and the Problems of Our Time." *YIVO Bletter* 25, no. 1 (1945): 3–18. [Yiddish]

Wieseltier, Leon. "Against Identity." *New Republic* 211, no. 22 (November 28, 1994): 24–28. https://newrepublic.com/article/92857/against-identity.

Yacobi, Haim, and Shelly Cohen. *Separation – The Politics of Israeli Space*. Tel Aviv: Xargol Press and Am Oved Press, 2007. [Hebrew]

Yadin, Uri. "How Will the Custodian Law Be Interpreted." *Hapraklit* 24, no. 4 (September 1968): 493–495. [Hebrew]

Yadin, Uri. "The Succession Law as Part of Israeli Civil Law Legislation." *Tel Aviv University Studies Law Review* 3, no. 1 (1973): 26–33. [Hebrew]

Yanai, Nathan. "Politics and Constitution-Making in Israel: Ben-Gurion's Position in the Constitutional Debate Following the Foundation of the State." In *Constitutionalism: The Israeli and American Experiences*, edited by Daniel J. Elazar: 101–114. Lanham, MD: University Press of America, 1990

Yatziv, Gadi. *The Sectorial Society*. Jerusalem: Bialik Institute, 1999. [Hebrew]

Yavetz, Ze'ev, "Hamizrahi and Its Aspirations." *Hator* 21–22 (1932): 4. [Hebrew]

Yehoshua, Abraham. "Defining Who Is an Israeli." *Haaretz*, September 12, 2013.

Zipperstein, Steven. *The Jews of Odessa: A Cultural History, 1794–1881*. Stanford: Stanford University Press, 1985.

Zweigert, Konrad, and Hein Kötz. *Introduction to Comparative Law*. Oxford: Clarendon Press, 1992.

Index